1921

THE OTTUMWA DAILY NEWS

Leigh Michaels

PBL Limited
Ottumwa Iowa

Copyright 2020 by Leigh Michaels

Cover and design copyright 2020 by PBL Limited

This edition published 2020

10 9 8 7 6 5 4 3 2 1

ISBN 13: 9781892689825

Printed in the United States of America

Illustrations and articles from The Ottumwa Daily News, which started publication in September, 1920.

All rights reserved. Except for brief passages quoted in any review, the reproduction or utilization of this work in whole or in part, in any form or by any electronic, mechanical, or other means, now known or hereinafter invented, including xerography, photocopying and recording, or in any information storage and retrieval system, is forbidden without the express permission of the publisher. For permission contact:
    Rights Editor
    PBL Limited
    P.O. Box 935
    Ottumwa IA 52501-0935
    www.pbllimited.com

Visit our website at www.pbllimited.com for more information about this and other publications. Quantity and wholesale prices are available.

Contents

Why 1921? - 4
January - 7
February - 23
March - 39
April - 55
May - 73
June - 89
July - 105
August - 121
September - 137
October - 153
November - 169
December - 185
Index - 210

Why 1921?

The easy answer is twofold. First, it's a hundred years ago, and looking back exactly a century is always fun and fascinating. Second, it's the year that the bound files of *The Ottumwa Daily News* papers were available to work on in a home setting -- without spending hours with microfilm during a pandemic, when libraries were largely closed and collections were only sporadically available.

But the more deeply I looked into the newspapers, the more interesting the year became. In 1921, the World War -- not yet numbered, with the hope there would never be another one -- was not completely over. Though the fighting had stopped, the various sides involved in the conflict were still arguing about reparations, with France threatening almost monthly to invade Germany again. The Allies demanded that Germany pay all the costs of rebuilding, while Germany argued that the country simply couldn't afford the bill. The punishing and staggering total assessed by the Allies helped to drive Germany into the era of National Socialism, leading in mid-1921 to the election of Adolph Hitler as leader of the National Socialist German Workers Party -- the Nazis -- with absolute powers as party chairman. The events of 1921 led in large part to World War II and the Cold War.

Labor and management were at odds across the country, and a strike at John Morrell and Co. escalated to martial law when Iowa's governor sent in troops. Unemployment was rising, with soldiers coming back from Europe to find jobs scarce and wages falling. As men returned from the war, women who had achieved some measure of independence through war work were being shuffled back to the kitchen. No one quite knew how this new amendment giving them the vote would work out. Were women to be allowed to serve on juries? And if so, would they have to be given extra breaks by the court, so they would have adequate opportunities to powder their noses? (The consensus was that "lady jurors" got no extra privileges -- but only because lighting in courtrooms was generally so poor that powder on noses was unnecessary anyway.)

The nation was well into the Prohibition era, struggling with a crime wave brought about by making alcohol illegal, but starting to tiptoe toward a change of policy by making beer available by prescription.

Coming off a spectacular season in 1920, Babe Ruth announced he would break his own record -- and did, hitting 59 home runs. (He wouldn't achieve his career high -- 60 home runs in a single season -- until 1927.) Bill Tilden followed up his 1920 tennis season as the world's number one player, a title he would hold through 1925. Jack Dempsey defended his heavyweight title against Frenchman Georges Carpentier in what was billed as "the fight of the century." The eight Chicago White Sox players accused of throwing the 1919 World Series went on trial, were acquitted, but were banned from baseball anyway.

Warren G. Harding was inaugurated and promptly turned his administration over to the self-benefiting cronies and crooks who made Teapot Dome the scandal of the 1920s.

Ottumwa Daily News

Congress was frequently at a standstill, debating peace terms and bonus payments for veterans -- but making little progress -- while cutting taxes for the wealthy. Immigration was an issue, with tight limits being set on who could come to the United States, how many, and from where. Nicolo Sacco and Bartolomeo Vanzetti went on trial and were condemned to death more because they were Italian than because they were guilty; they almost certainly did not commit murder during an armed robbery. Much of the planet's gold bullion was locked up in Fort Knox, putting pressure on the money supply world wide. The international economy teetered in a precarious balance that would smash by 1929, with consequences which would last for decades.

There were fears of a national typhus plague, said to be brought to the U.S. by immigrants, and the reality of a local scarlet fever outbreak -- terrifying in a pre-antibiotic era. There are frequent articles about the costs of quarantine and the need for a "pest house" or isolation hospital in the city, unsurprising in the wake of the 1918 flu pandemic. Obituaries for babies, toddlers, children, and young mothers were as frequent as those of the elderly.

And there was rampant racism, unrest, and violence. While the newspaper reported with surface accuracy and seeming objectivity on events like the Tulsa race riots, it also ran an editorial about how northern cities could benefit from the experience of their southern neighbors on how to handle "the Negro problem". There are stories about a most entertaining program about a "darky" family. In fact, 1921's racism is even more disturbing to the modern mind because it was so casual -- and so clearly not an issue to the editor.

In Ottumwa, the school district was absorbed in the task of moving Adams School in order to construct the new Ottumwa High School. Citizens fussed about the lack of street paving, the ruts on rural roads, the need for better housing, what to do about garbage, and how to draw more tourist and convention business to the city.

In short, things were an awfully lot like now. I hope you'll enjoy revisiting Ottumwa in 1921. You may find yourself thinking, as I did, "The more things change, the more they stay the same."

A few words about newspapers of the day. Photographs were rare; any photos which actually made it into the *Daily News* came from subscription services which would have sent out printing plates ready to drop onto the press. Most illustrations, which would also have been prepared by the advertiser or the ad agency, were line cuts -- drawings -- rather than photographs. The paper's pages were set with lead type, with a linotype machine -- an awkward and unforgiving technology in which any error required resetting an entire "line" of type. As a result, typos are everywhere, and spelling is atrocious and inconsistent. Perhaps the lack of quality is in part because *The Ottumwa Daily News* seems to have been very much a one-man operation. A. J. Stump was the owner, publisher, editor, and business manager, and sometimes he was the typesetter as well. There were no bylines (other than occasional credits to other newspapers), so it's hard to tell if he had reporters or if he did all of that work too. Considering the limits of technology and the times, it's a wonder the paper was published at all -- and more of a wonder that so many of the issues survived.

--Leigh Michaels

1921

Every Woman Takes Pride in Her Ironing

How aggravating it is, when your Iron smudges a bit of silken lingerie or soils a carefully washed collar?

If every housewife possessed one of these wonderfully efficient Electric Irons, however, there'd be no more disappointments with the ironing.

And what is more, ironing an entire week's washing can be accomplished with a tremendous saving of time when a really good Electric Iron is used.

PURCHASE FROM ANY DEALER

Ottumwa Railway & Light Co.

Ottumwa Daily News

JANUARY 1921

Jan 2 - First religious service broadcast over radio, by KDKA Pittsburgh

Jan 6 - American pollster Lou Harris born in New Haven, Connecticut

Jan 12 - Kenesaw Mountain Landis becomes first commissioner of major league baseball

Jan 20 - British submarine HMS K5 (equipped with steam turbines) sinks with 57 crew during exercises in the Bay of Biscay

Jan 21 - Barney Clark, first American to recive a permanent artificial heart, born

Jan 27 - American actress Donna Reed born in Denison, Iowa

Jan 31 - American actress Carol Channing born in Seattle, Washington

Jan 31 - Italian-American actor and singer Mario Lanza born in Philadelphia, Pennsylvania

EXTRA!

In the case of Davis Christy versus the C., B. & Q. railroad, in which Christy was suing for approximately $4000 for the death of his two sons, Forrest and Glen, Judge Francis M. Hunter awarded the plaintiff $1600 damages for each boy, a total of $3200.

The two boys, Forrest and Glen, met their death in an accident in which a C., B. & Q. mail train struck the auto in which they were riding and killed them instantly.

PATTERSON-DAVIS, 2 WOMEN JURORS IN HUNTER'S COURT

"I know it's very tiresome but I think it will be interesting and I intend to stick it out until the term expires unless I am taken sick or something else comes up," said Mrs. Minnie Davis, one of the two woman jurors who were drawn for the January term of court under Judge Francis M. Hunter. The court room is not strange to Mrs. Davis as it will be remembered by Ottumwans that her late husband was at one time a lawyer in this city and she was a frequent visitor to the courts.

Mrs. Caroline Patterson, the first woman juror drawn in the county said, gazing around at the roomful of jurors, lawyers and other male courthouse inmates, "No, I'm not the least bit embarrassed. What's the use."

1921

THE OTTUMWA DAILY NEWS

OTTUMWA, IOWA, FRIDAY, JANUARY 7, 1921.

PROHIBITION OFFICE ADMITS FAILURE

MORE ALCOHOL TO BE HAD IN 1921

Washington, Jan. 11.—Alcohol in still larger volume will our out of warehouses during 1921. But not for "beverage purposes." It will be tagged for "industrial uses only." Increased flow of alcohol out of the storage places is made possible by a decision of Secretary of the Treasury Houston, high boss in matters of rum, that many existing barriers be lifted to encourage the commercial use of alcohol, and to promote tre manufacture of that product for industial purposes.

BIGGEST STILL YET TAKEN BY POLICE

Chief Blizzard, Night Captain Lightner and a special state officer last night searched the home of Guy Overturf, 713 East Vine street on a search warrant.

The search developed the discovery of the largest and most complete still for manufacturing "hootch" that has yet been unearthed by local officials. Besides confiscating the plant about 100 gallons of mash and two half-pints of "home brew" were found in his possession.

Overturff has been turned over to federal authorities.

ILLICIT BOOZE TRAFFIC CONTINUES; BUSINESS IS GIGANTIC IN ITS SCOPE

Kramer Says County is Not Dry, Will Take Years to Become So

(International News Service.)
Washington, D. C., Jan. 7—The country is facing a condition in which the illicit whiskey business is shown as one of the largest of the business enterprises, both from the standpoint of capital invested and number of men engaged in it. Prohibition officials frankly admit that the country is not dry and will not be dry for at least a generation. The only hope for making it dry, lies in crystalizing public sentiment behind the existing law. In enforcement, the department has gone as far as possible. Congress is cutting down the dry enforcement appropriation along with the general slashing. Curtailment of the dry forces may be necessary. Meanwhile millions of dollars are being turned over in illicit liquor business and thousands of men continue to be engaged in it. John F. Kramer, prohibition commissioner declared: "The country is not dry. We will be dead and gone before it will be dry."

OLD CUSTOMER BACK

Harry Harper, whose face is a familiar one in the police court, was again sentenced to three days in jail this morning on a charge of intoxication. It has been the occurrence during the past several weeks that Harper has spent three out of every seven days in jail and he has not fallen down on his record this time. Judge Kitto promises to be more severe with him on his next offense.

Ottumwa Daily News

INDICTED MEN MAKE GETAWAY

Jack White and Art Murphy, indicted yesterday afternoon by the grand jury on a charge of maintaining a gambling house left the city last night before the authorities had time to place them under arrest, states one of the officers today.

The other two indictees, Lil Dale and Ida Bryant, were arrested and their bonds fixed at $500 each which they furnished.

Deputy John Bright refused to state whether or not any effort was being made to locate the two men.

15 PCT. CUT COMES TO "Q" EMPLOYES; 30 ARE LAID OFF

And still another cut of fifteen per cent for C., B. & Q. employes.

Word has been received at the local master mechanics' office of the C., B. & Q. that on top of the recent twenty-five per cent cut which was made about a month ago in the mechanical and car departments that another fifteen per cent decrease in force must be made.

Chief Clerk Curtis of the master mechanic's office stated this morning that the order would take effect immediately and that the work of making the reduction had started and would necessitate the discharging of 30 men on the Ottumwa division in the mechanical and car departments.

This cut will be made according to seniority, those youngest in the service being dismissed first.

BURLINGTON GETS NEW EQUIPMENT.

Eight monster new 14-wheel locomotives of special design—"capable of pulling anything the coupling pin will hold," the first of a lot of fifteen, ordered by the C., B. & Q. in April, 1920, have just been shipped from the Baldwin Locomotive Works at Eddystone, Pennsylvania.

Especially designed for hauling heavy tonnage trains, these engines are equipped with five pair of drivers. Each of the ten driving wheels weighs 6,000 pounds. A special feature in their construction is the employment of a special alloy steel in the driving rods and reciprocating parts. The Burlington is the pioneer in the use of special alloy steel in locomotive construction—the practice tending to reduce the hammer-blow effect upon the track.

Mr. and Mrs. Frank L. Daggett

Funeral Directors and Embalmers

Established 18 Years

Chairs and tables for rent for weddings and parties. Complete auto equipment.

126 W. Second—Phone 127

NORMAL TRAINING TEST FOR PUPILS JANUARY 19-21

County Superintendetn of Schools R. L. Gardner announces a number of examinations which are to be held this month and next in Wapello county for both teachers ad pupils.

Next week on Wednesday, Thursday and Friday, January 19, 20 and 21, the normal training examinations for high school students will be held in Ottumwa and Eddyville. The examination in Ottumwa will be held in the county superintendent's office in the court house and in the high school at Eddyville.

On February 3, 4, 5 and 6, the eighth grades will have their examinations in Ottumwa, Eddyville, Blakesburg and Agency. The examination will be held in the Ottumwa commercial college for those who will take their examination in Ottumwa. It is expected there will be between 75 and 100 students in Ottumwa to take the examinations on these days.

HERE'S A PROMISE FOR STREET SIgNS AT INTERSECTIONS

Strangers entering our fair city will no longer wander bewilderingly in Ottumwa's labyrinth of streets. Signs will be placed on every thoroughfare in the city so that anyone looking for an address will not have to wake every family in the block trying to locate the street in question. Not only the residence district but the business district will also be labeled.

This is the decision of Group Six of the Chamber of Commerce which met last night.

Besides marking the streets an attempt will be made to paint the city and improve its appearance by planting trees, shrubbery, etc. The first step

NO PIE ON MENU FOR STUDENTS AT HIGH CAFETERIA

Superintendent Blackmar and Principal Brenneman of the high school conferred this morning on the matter of cafeteria equipment.

Several catalogues and pamphlets were consulted but no definite decision has as yet been reached.

In regard to the matter of charging of the meals, Mr. Blackmar was of the opinion that each pupil patronizing the cafeteria would average twenty cents a meal. This would include meat, vegetables, bread and butter and either milk or chocolate. Pie and coffee are tabooed from the start and neither of the articles will grace the counters.

INJECT ETHER INTO VEINS OF PATIENT

NEW METHOD OF PRODUCING ANAESTHIA IS TRIED WITH COMPLETE SUCCESS IN BOSTON HOSPITAL.

(By International News Service)

Boston, Jan. 13.—Ether administered through a vein in the elbow to induce anaesthia for a major operation was successfully applied for the first time, it is believed, in Boston, in a surgical case at the Elm Hill hospital on Walnut avenue, Roxbury.

The patient, whose name is withheld, went under the knife for cancer of the brain.

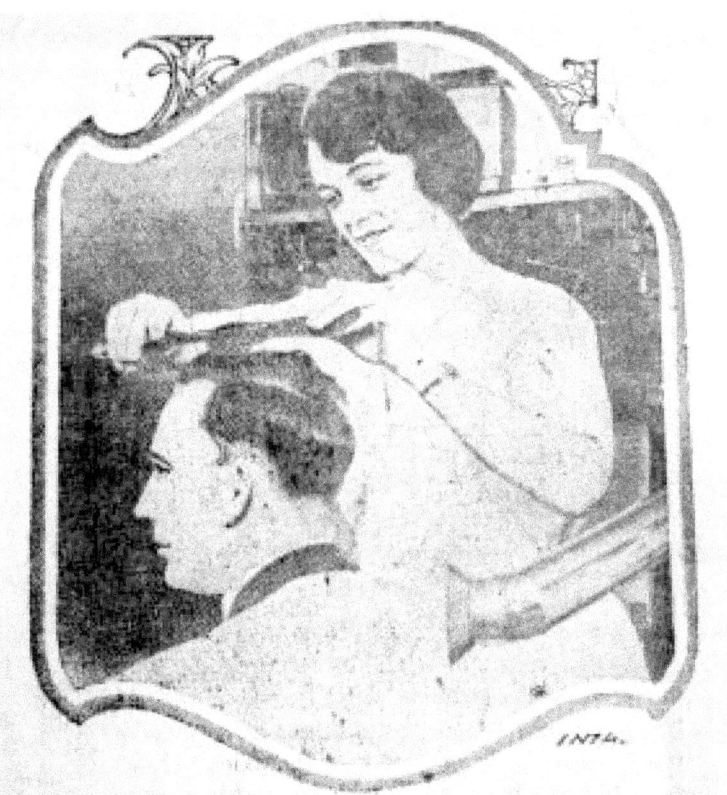

"Do men have their hair marcelled and have their eyebrows plucked?" asked a woman patron in a Chicago beauty shop. "Do they. Well I guess they do," replied the beauty parlor attendant, "and not only that, they go the limit and get a permanent wave. Men are becoming steady patrons in shops of this kind. They buy many cosmetics, including cold cream and perfumes." The photo shows a Chicago business man having his hair marcelled.

LOCAL MERCHANTS DENY REPORTS OF REDUCING FORCES

The employmetn situation in Ottumwa is becoming one of the most discussed subjects of the day. With the entire country in the throes of industrial depression, it is small wonder that Ottumwa should feel the pinch somewhat.

The latest report being widely circulated throughout the city is that many of Ottumwa's largest merchants are being compelled to lay off many many of their old employes to cut down overhead expense.

A representative of the NEWS visited several of the most prominent establishments on Main street and inquired regarding this rumor.

"This store has not dismissed a single employee who has been with us any length of time. Naturally we were compelled to do away with the holiday extra help but that is the entire extent of our cutting down the force," said one manager.

PULLMAN MEN IN PROTEST OVER EXTRA HOUR; 1,500 RESUME TIN PLATE WORK

GEDDES RECALLED BY GEORGE

Chicago, Jan. 17.—The Pullman company has resumed the nine-hour day schedule and ordered 20,000 employes to accept this ruling and work nine hours hereafter instead of eight. The employes agree to work the extra hour under protest and until they have received a ruling from the labor board on the matter.

1921

Autopoint Pencils 50c

You cannot afford to be without one.

They are being adopted by large offices everywhere as standard equipment.

Extra Leads, 10c a Package.

R. B. Swenson
Jeweler

PARIS TO BUY TWO GRAMME OF RADIUM

Paris, Jan. 13.—The Paris municipal authorities have voted a credit of two and a half million francs with which they want to purchase two grammes of radium. While the money is forthcoming, even the small quantity of the precious mineral needed cannot be found in France. There exists in the whole country but one gramme of radium and this is in the care of Madame Curie, widow of the celebrated French savant.

Madame Curie, who proposed to the authorities that they should purchase some radium in order to supply Paris and French hospitals with its eagerly sought "emanations," said that failure to supply such gases meant the death of some 3,500 people annually from cancer in Paris alone. She has received beseeching letters from all parts of the country asking for her help, but in many cases she had to refuse be-

Immediate Improvements Planned In Park System

City officials felt a blow yesterday morning when Councilman Weidenfeller submitted his resignation.

Charles P. Parker, former building inspector, has been appointed to fill the vacancy created by Weidenfeller's departure.

Mr. Weidenfeller has been an office holder in the city hall since April, 1919, and will still remain one although in a different capacity. He resigned only to accept the position of superintendent of parks of the city, succeeding Pierce E. Cain, who has been ill for several months.

The park board felt that with the many plans in store for Ottumwa's park system that someone capable of handling a job such as this will be must be placed in this position as superintendent and Weidenfeller was selected.

The city at present has approximately 130 acres of park land which is in nine distinct parks, there being a park in every section of the city. The parks owned by the city at present are Caldwell, Wildwood, Riverside, Central, Ballingall, Foster, Jefferson, and Memorial. Extensive plans have been drawn up for the improvement of these parks and work will proceed as far as funds permit. It is expected by the council that Ottumwa's parks will not be actually completed until at least five years as the plans call for a large amount of money and many days of work.

One feature of Ottumwa's park system and which will be started very soon is the comfort station which will be fitted out under the new bandstand located in Central park. Superintendent Weidenfeller stated that this would be the first step taken toward improving the parks of Ottumwa.

The parks owned by the city at present range all the way from one and a half acres to thirty acres and are the most beautiful spots of land in the district.

Mr. Weidenfeller will work with Edwin Manning, Frank Gibbons and Ben Grotz, the present park commissioners.

Ottumwa is getting in line for a real park system, blue prints prepared some time ago by a visiting expert who spent several weeks in the work, indicating the pride and interest taken in this department of our civic life.

The park board will spend $75,000 the next five years, providing the council permit the millage levy to be as generous as at present which for 1920 yielded between ten and twelve thousand.

Ottumwa has eight of the more important spaces where recreation will be modernly afforded for the public. It is going to take a lot of money to maintain and beautify that the purchase investments return a fair dividend, on health and enjoyment that may be had in parks properly dedicated to the people.

Owing to the larger responsibilities, the more complex because of increasing improvements and betterments for our parks, as the years go by, this selection of Mr. Weidenfeller who is to take major charge of the parks, gives his undivided attention to the work, also assume other duties now delegated to the city auditor and it is claimed that while the position carries a salary of $1,800 per annum no actual additional expense will be added to the park fund.

Ottumwa Daily News

CITY PHYSICIAN HAS CONTAGIOUS WELL IN CONTROL

The monthly report of City Physician Anthony for the month of December was submitted to the city council yesterday morning.

The report showed a big decrease in the number of smallpox cases over the previous month, the number for December being 69 and for November, 123.

Scarlet fever cases show a large decrease for December over November, there being only 17 houses quarantined for December and 97 in November.

Diphtheria cases were also smaller in number, the report showing 11 for December and November's report showed 18 cases.

City physician Anthony stated he had vaccinated 25 persons in December and 94 in November.

Miller's Antiseptic Oil, Known as

Snake Oil

Will Positively Relieve Pain in a Few Minutes

Try it right now for Rheumatism, Neuralgia, Lumbago, sore, stiff and swollen joints, pain in the head, back and limbs, corns, bunions, etc. After one application pain usually disappears as if by magic.

A new remedy used externally for Coughs, Colds, Croup, Influenza, Sore Throat, Diphtheria and Tonsilitis.

This oil is conceded to be the most penetrating remedy known. Its prompt and immediate effect in relieving pain is due to the fact that it penetrates to the affected parts at once. As an illustration, pour ten drops on the thickest piece of sole leather and it will penetrate this substance through and through in three minutes.

Accept no substitute. This great oil is golden red color only. Manufactured by Herb Juice Medicine Co. only. Get it at F. Z. Kidd & Co.'s West End Drug Store and Central Drug company, corner Main and Green streets.

Are you reading the O. HENRY stories?

They appear daily in this paper.

VOCATIONAL FUNDS FOR SUNNYSLOPE WORLD WAR VETS

The musicale benefit for Sunnyslope hospital held at the First Congregational church Sunday evening was most gratifying for the cause, although not a considerable amount of cash was realized, $46.50. The helpfulness will come later as the public must realize what a good work is being done, especially for the soldier patients for whom the above proceeds will be invested, for vocational training.

These veterans are finding time heavy upon them and are interested in having something to do. There is a demand and urgent need for tools to aid the men in their habits of industry, samples of which were shown at the church last evening, including some very pretty bird houses, singles, doubles and apartment designings, selling at from $3 to $5 and the men who make them say half the purchase price will be turned into vocational fund. Secretary Mrs. W. C. Newell announced orders would be gladly received and turned over for these desirable little houses.

Have Your Home Modernized

Install Electric Service

Have your home wired for modern Electric Service this Spring.

Know the matchless convenience of "push-button" light—its unequalled economy, safety and cleanliness.

Enjoy the blessings of Electric labor-saving appliances—every one a servant of usefulness that helps to banish household drudgery.

Electrical contractors will gladly submit a free estimate of the cost of this twentieth century improvement.

Telephone Them.

BUT ONE PAVE JOB IN SIGHT FOR 1921 NEED AUTO MONEY

The city commissioners have not as yet conferred on the matter of paving for 1921 and according to one, Commissioner Chilton, the outlook for a discussion of this subject is not as bright as it might be.

At the present time the only paving job that is in sight for this year is the contract for the stretch around the cemetery on Court street which was contracted for last year but failed to be executed due to the lack of material throughout the country at that time.

Very little improvement was made along this line last year, the only two jobs which were completed being the sections around the city park and the lower end of Cass street.

"Unless something is done on the question of the city obtaining part of the money turned in to the state on automobile licenses at the coming legislature, paving for this year is practically out of the question. I think it probable that something will be done on this question and if not I feel the highway commission will make some arrangements whereby they will pay a certain per cent on all paving which leads into main highways in and out of the city," said Commissioner Chilton.

ABOUT $11,000,000 RAISED

It is reported that thus far about $11,000,000 has been raised for the relief of the children of Central and Eastern Europe until the next harvest. For food and medical supplies and care $33,000,000 is required to keep alive and well about 3,500,000 children. The $22,000,000 still needed should be raised by February 1st. Mr. Hoover, who is at the head of the great work seems confident that America will not fail in this emergency.

The children dependent upon American aid are distributed about as follows: Germany 1,250,000, Poland 1,250,000, Austria 300,000, Czecho-Slovakia 100,000, Baltic States 200,000.

The United States is said to have food enough on hand for eighteen months, and another crop will be harvested within eight. This country will not miss the food required to save these children. The results will be a better coming generation for Europe and a greater friendship in Europe for this country.

FORD TRACTORS IN $165 REDUCTION

Detroit, Jan. 26.—The price of Fordson tractors has been reduced from $790 to $625.

This reduction was due to the price in materials which has decreased considerably and the operation of the Ford plants at maximum production. The announcement also stated the price of Ford cars would be restored to as high a level as that reached during the war period unless there is an increased demand for automobiles which would enable the Ford plants to operate at maximum production and minimum cost.

1921

Rockford Sox

Former price was 30c, out they go at 12½C

MARTIN'S

JANUARY 8, 1921.

O. H. S. LOSES IN BASKETBALL GAME TO MT. PLEASANT

The O. H. S. basketball five lost to Mt. Pleasant 19-12 in the first game of the season last night at Mt. Pleasant.

Manager McKown was of the opinion that the game was lost through the inaccuracy of the team in throwing fouls the locals missing 10 straight free throws out of 12 decisions. Many a substitutions were made during the game as Coach Yount was making an effort to pick out a suitable team from the many candidates who turned out this year.

Fisher playing at guard for Ottumwa starred throughout the game with the able assistance of Stirneman, the only two veteran players on the team. The other three players and all the substitutes were playing practically their first real game, not only of the season but of their basketball career.

CITY HAS INCREASE IN 1920 BUILDING AROUND 100 PCT.

Building in Ottumwa for the year 1920 showed a remarkable increase in the report submitted today to the city council by the city building inspector.

The total amount of building during 1920 was $723,920. $690,614 of this sum was contracted due to the erection of buildings, of which 1$209 fees was paid to the city. $3,306 was spent on the installation of furnaces of which $194 went into the city treasury as fees. The building and installation of furnaces both amounted to $723,920 the above mentioned amount.

There were 441 building permits issued and 112 furnace permits.

In the year of 1919 there was approximately $394,000 spent in building and is a small figure comparatively with the $723,920 spent during 1920.

The 1920 report shows that the building last year was nearly double that completed in 1919.

Kill That Cold With

HILL'S CASCARA BROMIDE QUININE

FOR Colds, Coughs AND La Grippe

Neglected Colds are Dangerous

Take no chances. Keep this standard remedy handy for the first sneeze.

Breaks up a cold in 24 hours — Relieves Grippe in 3 days — Excellent for Headache

Quinine in this form does not affect the head — Cascara is best Tonic Laxative — No Opiate in Hill's.

ALL DRUGGISTS SELL IT

Ottumwa Daily News

THE OTTUMWA DAILY NEWS

NO-PASSPORT ALIENS TO BE DEPORTED

DAVIS CONSIDERS 2 CASES, MAY ACT ON OTHERS; IS FIRM FOR RESTRICTIONS

(International News Service.)

WASHINGTON, JAN 22.—THE STATE DEPARTMENT IS NOW CONSIDERING THE QUESTION OF DEPORTING ALL ALIENS IN THIS COUNTRY WHO DO NOT HAVE PASSPORTS. ASSISTANT SECRETARY OF STATE DAVIS SAID NO POLICY HAD YET BEEN DECIDED UPON BUT ADMITTED THE CASE OF HARRY BOLAND AND SECRETARY EAMON DE VALERA, WHO ARE UNDERSTOOD TO HAVE ENTERED THE UNITED STATES WITHOUT PASSPORTS, WERE BEING CONSIDERED.

T. R. CRANDALL, Gen'l Mgr.

Wholesale—Retail.

Wapello Battery and Electric Company., Inc.

101-103-105 W. Main St. Phone, 673
Ottumwa, Ia.

Full stock of genuine parts for Connecticut, Atwater-Kent, Remy, Delco and Klaxon.

DISTRIBUTORS FOR

United States Light and Heat Corporation, American Bosch Magneto Corporation; Also Gray and Davis equipment.

Distributors—Factory Service.

---

* * * * * * * * * *
WHY?

The Daily News will print each day a "why." Send in a "why" and it will be printed with your name and address if desired.

Why is it most of our girlies wore longer skirts to church Sunday? Wouldn't it be a good thing to have all seven days given to same observance. Might be restful for the eyes of the weaker sex. "One of the weakest."

WHY?
* * * * * * * * * *

1921

CLOSE SCORE IN BOTH GAMES AT "Y" LAST NIGHT

The O. H. S. won a doubleheader over Albia last night, the boys winning by a small margin of 2 points, the final score being 15-13 and the girls' game was won on even a smaller margin and had it not been for Pogue who scored a free throw in the last 60 seconds of play the score would have been a tie. The additional point made by Pogue made the final score 14-13.

The boys' contest was a fast, snappy affair throughout the game and although both teams were playing something of a five-man defense the locals romped around the floor and broke up their defense without much exertion.

Your Home Band

"THE FIRST CAVALRY"

With Cleveland Dayton, Leader, Presents the First Concert of Mid-Winter

---AT THE---

GRAND OPERA HOUSE
Monday Eve., January 24

All may anticipate this appearance with a program of many specials as the most elaborate and delightful for many seasons.

Admission Only 50 Cents

Seats Reserved at Sargents

EXONERATION FOR ELLIOT IS SOUGHT IN TRIAL, JAN. 22

January 22 the police and fire commissioner board of the city of Ottumwa, Chairman J. P. Swanson, John Boler and R. E. Ruckman, will hear arguments and consider testimony involved in the information that led to the dismissal of Charles A. Elliott, for several years member of the Ottumwa police department, and since April, 1919, until his recent resignation, under the supervision of Commissioner Weidenfeller.

The deposed patrolman, who had a beat on East Main street, was charged with having accepted money from divers persons, including it is said, Forrest Canfield, Lily Dale and others, presumably for protection. Elliott's attorney, L. L. Duke stated today in his mention of the case that each and all persons who are named as having paid money to his client while a policeman, deny having done so.

"We are going to make it clear to the commission board representing the fire and police departments, that Elliott is not guilty of having taken bribes, and doing so completely exonerate the accused. We will have no difficulty in clearing the case of these ugly charges because they are not true. There is nothing to the case. The accusation of bribery guilt is the most important charge and it will not amount to anything when the trial comes up."

Ottumwa Daily News

"Y" WILL OPEN MARCH 1-BEST IN EVERY WAY

The new Y. M. C. A. building will be ready for occupancy by March 1st, according to Physical Director Eigenmann.

"The building is to have the most complete and up-to-date ventilating and lighting system of any similar building in the country, I was told this by the national secretary of the Y. M. C. A., who was here a short time ago and looked over the building," said Mr. Eigenmann.

BONUS FOR IOWA SOLDIERS DOUBTED AT THIS TIME

An item that will undoubtedly be of much interest to ex-service men especially, has been received at the local Red Cross headquarters listing the states that have passed laws regarding bonus for soldiers, sailors and marines.

From the following it will be noticed several states have been very liberal with their war veterans and Iowa is among the missing.

The state of Maine has granted $100 flat to all ex-service men.

Massachusetts has donated the sum of $100 and $10 per month from the time of enrollment to January 15, 1918.

LOCAL HIGH SPLIT A DOUBLE HEADER WITH EDDYVILLE

The O. H. S. split with Eddyville in a doubleheader last night at Eddyville when the locals were victors 18-12 and the girls' team lost 25-17.

Coach Yount was exceedingly well pleased with the manner in which the team played and was of the opinion that he will have a fast set within a few weeks from the showing made last night. The game was "fast" in its utmost meaning and with the able supervision of Referee Jennings of Iowa the game was a splendid exhibition of real basketball.

Neither game was scheduled but were more or less of practice games but the O. H. S. five played a game that would fill the hearts of our veteran players with gladness.

The girls' team has not yet become duly organized and therefore the rather one-sided score. Eddyville has for many years had an extraordinary good girls team but in the last three or four years Ottumwa has been slightly lax in this feature of athletics but the candidates who played last night are determined and confident of ending their season in a different manner.

The line up follows:

Stirneman, center; Thompson and Von Schrader, forwards; Fisher and Matheney, guards Substitutions: Funk for Stirnaman; Ferguson for Dookin, Sponsler for Thompson, Dookin for Sponsler, Ferguson for Dookin and Sullivan for Matheney.

JUDGE HUNTER DECLARES CHURCH SHOULD HANDLE DIVORCE PROBLEM MORE

Says Catholicism Has One of Best Solutions For Prevalent Evil

(The alarming number of divorces being granted in Wapello county and throughout the entire country is an indication that something is wrong either in our laws or home life. This is the first of several articles by Judge Francis M. Hunter dealing with this situation, the causes and remedies.)

"I think the law is exceedingly lax on the matter of divorces and something ought to be done whereby these cases could be investigated as the public and the children are undoubtedly the ones who suffer. The children are left without the care and influence of one of their parents which is vitally necessary in the rearing of children. Without the father, the children lack discipline and very soon develop many weaknesses along that line and without a mother they become morally deficient," said Judge Francis M. Hunter in an interview with a News reporter last night on the subject of divorces.

"I look upon divorces as a necessity, as a matter of fact, and they are so recognized in all civilized countries among civilized people to a large extent, but in many countries there are so many restraints against it as to make them much fewer than the number we have in this country.

"In England, the most frequent grounds on which divorces are based is that of infidelity, unlike America which has many charges on which one may secure a divorce with very little effort.

"In this country as in all countries where there is a large Catholic population, among that church there are very few divorces granted. In fact, in my ten years experience as a judge I have had only four cases where both the plaintiff and defendant were of the Catholic religion... This experience has only proven beyond a doubt in my mind that education such as is practiced in the homes of those of this religion is the only solution to the matter. The education along religious lines in this country is sadly neglected...

"Up until the last two or three years the most reliable and frequently practiced method of securing a divorce was on the grounds of habitual intoxication. While that charge was brought in, in nine cases out of ten it was not justifiable. There have been many things said in a case based on these charges that were not true and did not belong there but in practically every case then and now, the defendant ... is not present to dispute or argue the case and what is there left for a judge to do but grant a divorce. This is why I think there should be some means of investigating all divorce cases before a decree is granted.

"The favorite charge of a plaintiff at present is that of cruel and inhuman treatment and has proven as successful as the former charge of intoxication. Usually no one, not even a lawyer, is present to defend.

"In my estimation the most legitimate grounds for divorce is that of infidelity and desertion. "Speaking of infidelity, it recalls to mind the statute of England several years ago on the infidelity charge. At that time, a woman could not secure a divorce from a man guilty of this offense, only a man could secure a divorce from the woman, but this has recently been changed and both sexes are liable for divorce on these grounds...."

THE OTTUMWA DAILY NEWS

GERMANY IS TAXED FIFTY BILLIONS

ALLIES SIGN AN INDEMNITY AGREEMENT; WILL ALLOW 42 YEARS TO MAKE GOOD

PARIS, JAN. 29.—THE ALLIED PREMIERS HAVE SIGNED AN INDEMNITY AGREEMENT DRAWN UP BY A SPECIAL COMMITTEE LAST NIGHT BY WHICH GERMANY MUST PAY THE ALLIES BETWEEN FIFTY AND SIXTY BILLION DOLLARS WITHIN THE NEXT 42 YEARS. SIGNING OF THE AGREEMENT ENDS THE POSSIBILITY OF THE THREATENED SPLIT MATERIALIZING BETWEEN GREAT BRITAIN AND FRANCE.

THE PREMIERS ALSO SIGNED A DISARMAMENT AGREEMENT AND PROVIDING THAT GERMANY MUST DISARM IN ACCORDANCE WITH THE SPA PROCTOCAL BY THE END OF JUNE. THIS AGREEMENT ALSO SANCTIONS A PROLONGED OCCUPATION OF RHINELAND AND OCCUPATION OF THE RUHR DISTRICT TO ENFORCE THE ALLIES' DEMANDS.

In addition to these annual payments, the allies will exact 12 1-2 per cent of the total value of German exports annually, which will bring the total indemnities up to the amazing sum of $60,000,000,000.

The decision was arrived at late yesterday by the committee of experts and was at once communicated to the allied premiers. They will take up the subject and conference circles are expecting a tentative approval of the plan at a conference which will be held with the Germans probably in March.

The Jefferson Hotel is Now Ready

Take Care of Fifty Guests

with a capacity that will

in rooms that have been thoroughly re-equipped and given every renovated benefit by an experienced Manager-Owner recently taking charge.

STEAM HEAT IN EVERY ROOM

Modernized to be most inviting and at the

Very Reasonable Rates of 75c to $1.50

"THE JEFFERSON," (formerly The La Clede) is at the corner of Main and Jefferson, 1 1-2 blocks from the Milwaukee-Wabash Union station. Out-of-town guests will be agreeably surprised, we feel sure, when registering at

THE HOTEL JEFFERSON

K. KENT, Prop.   (With Personal Supervision of the Owner)   Phone 1097

THE HOTEL JEFFERSON

Mr. Kent says:

"Yes, we are now ready for guests, after several weeks putting the Jefferson in order. It is the policy to have patrons get clean rooms and enjoy the best of service, which is charged at rates much less has ordinarily, from 75 cents to $1.50.

"You will see," he said to the advertising man, "that these rooms have been carefully gone over and with the idea that those who come here may find conditions entirely acceptable. Every room is steam heated, the furnishings are very good, I would say, and the location is of the best, less than two blocks from the Milwaukee Wabash union depot."

Mr. Kent is recently from Des Moines and is experienced in the hotel line. His efforts to make THE JEFFERSON a homey and attractive place have been quite extended, his personal investment to this end most generous. This fact is impressed upon those who register there for a room, under the new management.

1921 CHAUTAUQUA PLANNED FOR JULY, TWO NEW DIRECTORS

At a meeting of the Ottumwa Chautauqua committee at the Chamber of Commerce last night two changes made in the officers and directors. Secretary Bond of the Chamber of Commerce was elected secretary to succeed M. L. Toulme and Charles Hallberg was elected to the directors as an additional member.

There was nothing definitely decided at the meeting other than that an attempt would be made to secure the Chautauqua for the same dates this year as last, July 16, 17, 18, 19 and 20 and at the same location.

A system of disposing of tickets has been arranged for and in fact a large number are already sold.

CECIL DIXON WILL MANAGE NEW CAFE FOR HIGH SCHOOL

Cecil Dixon, former manager of the Frasier Cafe, has been selected as manager of the new high school cafeteria which is rapidly nearing completion and will in all probability be ready in operation by next Monday, according to Secretary Wagner.

Carpenters are installing the tables and equipment that have arrived. A special heating plant has been installed as heretofore the attic of the building was not equipped in such a man to receive heat from the furnace in the basement.

The school board is confident the cafeteria will be a success and according to Secretary Wagner cannot be otherwise after the new period system is arranged.

Ottumwa Daily News

FEBRUARY 1921

Feb 4 - American author and feminist Betty Friedan (*The Feminine Mystique*) born in Peoria, Illinois

Feb 5 - New York Yankees purchase 20 acres in the Bronx to build Yankee Stadium

Feb 8 - American actress Lana Turner born in Wallace, Idaho

Feb 12 - Democratic Republic of Georgia is invaded by forces of Bolshevist Russia

Feb 21 - Coup d'etat installs Reza Khan (Reza Shah) as ruler of Iran.

Feb 25 - Red Army enters the Georgian capital, Tbilisi, and installs a Moscow-directed communist government

BLAKESBURGER PARKS HIS FORD NEAR BUSY CORNER AND IT'S SNEAKED AWAY

A Ford touring car belonging to Alex Robertson, which was stolen several days ago, has been reported found at the police station about at a point four miles west of town and in a very bad condition.

Two new inner tubes were missing, all light bulbs, both rear and front cushions, four coils, cylinder head and bolts, cylinder head gasket, radiator connection and all the tools had been recovered.

Another case of a stolen car was reported this morning to Chief Blizzard. Ronald Robinson of Blakesburg parked his Ford touring car on Market street next to the Iowa National bank yesterday and the car was missing when he returned for it.

Tom Orman also reported to the chief this morning that a car driven by an unidentified man struck his wagon coming into town on the east road. He claimed he had injured his back and that his wagon had been badly damaged.

Orman had secured the number of the car before the driver could get away and identified it as having been registered in Sigourney.

1921

SAWS STEEL BAR INTO SAX STORE, STEAL CLOTHES

What is thought by the police to be a lone robber entered the J. B. Sax clothing store either Saturday night, Sunday or Sunday night and carried away a quantity of clothing such as suits, overcoats, underwear, etc.

The burglar entered by sawing off a steel bar some three-quarters of an inch in thickness from a window located on the top floor in the back of the building.

The Sax company has been entered a number of times. A. E. Gustivison, vice-president of the company, said: "We must handle a splendid line of goods as they always pick on us. We thought everything was secure as all the windows and doors were barricaded with steel bars."

After the thief had cut away the bar an entrance had been made about eight inches wide, hardly wide enough for the average man to enter.

ASSESSORS' SALARY CUT 8 CTS AN HOUR BY SUPERVISORS

Again commotion in the office of City Assessor Alderdice. The board of supervisors have been trimming on the salaries' end of it, reducing the pay of the deputy assessors, six in Ottumwa, 53 cents an ohur to 45 cents and that of the office help to what is practically $2.50 a day, according to a statement of Alderdice this morning.

That is not all the board did to the tax bureau. The pay of Mr. Alderdice was fixed at $5.25 a day and to be in effect for only eight months of the year.

CARS IN SCRAMBLE DUE TO ICE—SHEATH ON LOCAL PAVES

Early birds this morning witnessed the results of many accidents last night with automobiles and wagons huddled up against telephone poles as a result of the glass-like ice coating taken on by the sidewalks and pavement during the night.

Many cars this morning were vainly trying to move but all efforts were futile. The slippery pavement was a source of trouble, not only for automobiles but pedestrians who also skidded. More than one person "hit" this morning and so if your friends have bruised faces and other portions of their anatomy discolored believe their story and don't suspect them of a wild week end.

In several cases automobiles were piled up against each other and unable to move, with other cars sent to their aid also rendeerd helpless. In one instance on East Second street three cars were all jammed up together and none of them able to move.

After hours of futile attempt to remove the cars one of the unfortunates said, "What shall we do now?"

"I know what I'm going to do. I'm going home and wait ofr it to thaw out," was the reply.

BLACKSBURG MAN IS SECOND VICTIM OF CAR STRIPPING

The Ford touring car stolen several days ago from the corner of Main and Market street belonging to R. E. Robinson of Blakesburg was found yesterday in Harrow's Branch stripped of the following equipment:

Two Fisk tires, one Federal non-skid tire, two sets of chains, one headlight, all tools and other equipment.

Ottumwa Daily News

BACK OF THE GARDNER COMPANY STANDS OVER A THIRD OF A CENTURY OF SUCCESSFUL BUSINESS EXPERIENCE.

THE LAST WORD IN MOTORDOM

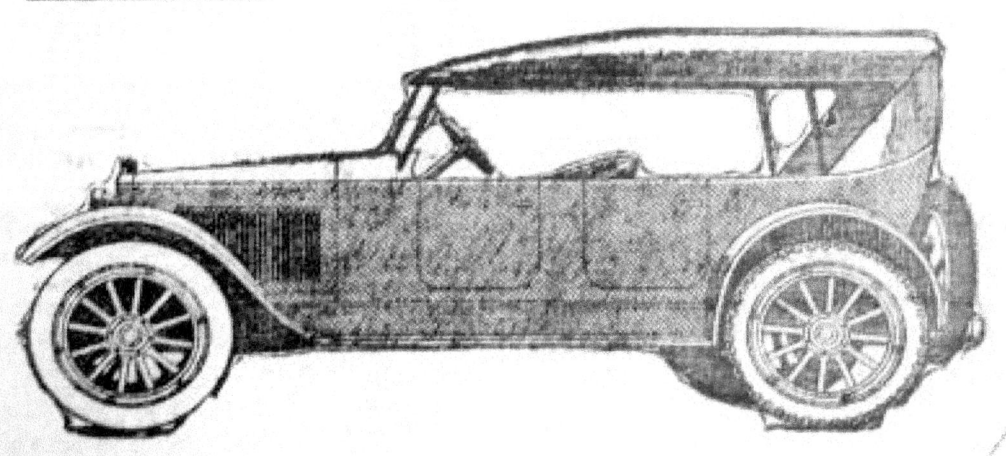

This car is now being shown upside down and every part of it that's vital, the adjusted motive parts, can be seen and explained to an understanding of the superi-orities. The body of the car is enameled, a complete competition in this respect with cars costing double asked for this one.

Parr's Auto Exchange

Phone 761   413-15 Church St.

1921

THE OTTUMWA DAILY NEWS

TYPHUS PLAGUE FEAR: WILSON ACTS

HOUSTON'S INSTRUCTIONS TO PROVIDE SAFEGUARDS AGAINST ALL IMMIGRANTS

MAINTAINS ZONE QUARANTINE

WASHINGTON, FEB. 11.—PRESIDENT WILSON REFERRED TO SECRETARY HOUSTON TODAY A TELEGRAM FROM DR. ROYAL COPELAND, HEALTH COMMISSIONER FOR NEW YORK, REQUESTING THAT QUARANTINE ACTION BE TAKEN TO PREVENT TYPHUS FROM BEING BROUGHT TO THIS COUNTRY: THE PRESIDENT ASKED HOUSTON TO ADVISE HIM ON THE MATTER.

Assistant Secretary of the Treasury LaPorte and Surgeon General Blue Began are conferring on the matter and considering some means of protecting the United States from an epidemic. Immigration commissioner Caminetti declared that typhus carriers were entering the country despite the most drastic protective measures. He also expressed confidence however that a plague could never get beyond the quarantine zone.

CLOSE FOR CASH CITY'S DILIMMA

On a statement from City Solicitor Hunt while discussing the payment of bills for quarantine, totaling $1,500, there is no certainty that the customary monthly payrolls will get by, for February. Mr. Hunt admitted to his audience that unless the county comes across with a share of the quarantine expenses "we will be in a tight fix" this with relation to salaries.

It is understood the county will stand only that part of this expense, which will run up to $2,000, as charged to indigent poor of the city and county.

NEW YORK, FEB. 16.—PHYSICIANS ANNOUNCED AT 9:30 THIS MORNING THAT ENRICO CARUSO, THE FAMOUS TENOR, WAS RALLYING AFTER A SHARP RELAPSE IN THE EARLY MORNING AND THAT HE IS CRITICALLY ILL WITH A COMPLICATION OF DISEASES. TWO PRIESTS WERE CALLED DURING THE NIGHT AND ADMINISTERED THE LAST RITES OF THE CATHOLIC CHURCH. ALTHOUGH VITALITY WAS FAST EBBING AWAY CARUSO WAS CONSCIOUS DURING MOST OF THE NIGHT AND NOT SUFFERING ACUTE PAIN, HIS SECRETARY STATED.

Physicians administered oxygen during the morning hours.

Ottumwa Daily News

OBITUARY

INFANTS PENNISTOR

The infant twin sons of Mr. and Mrs. L. H. Pennistor died this morning at 3 o'clock at the home of their parents, 545 West Main street.

Private funeral was held this afternoon from the residence. Burial in Ottumwa cemetery.

SOUTH OTTUMWA IS GIVEN NIGHT PATROLMAN OFFICER

Superintendent Parker of the police department announces that South Ottumwa will now have the protection of a night patrolman, also afternoon, only from 6 a. m. to noon with no officer on a regular beat. "We have only one patrolman for the entire city from breakfast time to 12 o'clock noon," said Mr. Parker, "but Ottumwa is getting along very nicely." The head of the department does not think there is any chance at present to augment the present force with a few extra men.

Officer McDonald has the night work for South Ottumwa.

ROOMER IS LOSER OF $130; ENTERED THRU A WINDOW

Albert Hoffstatter was the victim of a new method of banditry when an unidentified man entered his room and stole his trousers containing $130 in cash.

Hoffstatter, who rooms at South Ash street at the home of Mrs. Egilabeth Snyder, had retired for the evening when someone entered the window and removed his trousers which contained his bank book, a pearl-handled knife ad the pocketbook which contained two $20 gold pieces and the balance of the $130 in currency.

Some Daughter, Weighs 14½ lbs. Yes, Ottumwa

Is Ottumwa some live city? Listen to this birth report from Dr. W. B. Stoker: Born this morning, Wednesday, February 23, a daughter, to Mr. and Mrs. Earl Sylvester McCalester, 808 Lee avenue. The little miss, christened Eula May, weighed 14½ pounds at birth, which is believed to be a local if not an Iowa record.

Boys' Knee Pants One-Half Price
NEW SPRING SHIRTS
Fancy Pin Stripes and Checks with collars to match
at $1.15
New Spring Patterns, $1.50 Values 95c

J. B. Sax Co.

1921

BANISH THE ENEMY OF MANKIND
When your body is racked with RHEUMATISM, poison is gradually destroying the life-giving forces within. Neutralize the toxins and destroy the poisons by using

ALBERT'S RHEUMATIC REMEDY

It rapidly and surely eliminates the poisons, and relieves all rheumatic symptoms. Don't overload your system with harmful drugs. Half a teaspoonful taken once or twice daily banishes rheumatism and makes good health your companion.
PRICE $1.00
THE KELLS COMPANY, NEWBURGH, N. Y.

SEIZE 3 STILLS AND GALLONS OF CORN WHISKEY

Anyone happening in the Federal Clerk of Court's office in the Federal building today would witness a scene that will undoubtedly be classed in about 1940 as priceless historical relics.

Following a series of raids carried out by local and Federal authorities last night, three modern and complete stills are in the clerk's office this morning along with many gallons of corn whiskey and mash.

The raiding party, consisting of Chief Blizzard, Captain Lightner, Deputy Sheriffs Bright and Smith and Federal Agent Webb first visited the residence of Buriel Finley, 410 North Adella street, where a large copper still capable of handling 25 or 30 gallons was seized in action, with five gallons and a half of corn whiskey and 100 gallons of mash. Finley and Jimmy Travis were at work with the still at the time of the raid.

Finley's hearing was held this morning before Commissioner Mitchell, who bound him over to the grand jury under $500 bonds.

$700,000 IN BOND BIDS CONSIDERED; ACTION NEXT WEEK

It developed last night that the Board of Education must take more time in consideration of contingent and involved bids for the $700,000 in school bonds which Ottumwa is desirous of putting on the market within the near future, the coming week if possible.

Clarence Harper, speaking of the session last night, said it was utterly impossible within a few hours and in first sitting to determine which of the bids was most acceptable. He expressed the opinion that another meeting would be held soon.

The three bids accepted Wednesday night for the removal of the Adams school and for the excavation and foundation to be laid in the new location, also for the excavation for the new high school building, as previously announced, are held up until disposition of the bonds.

EDISON BELIEVES DEVICE TO TALK WITH DEPARTED POSSIBLE IF UNIT SYSTEM

(Copyright, International News Service.)
WEST ORANGE, New Jersey, Feb. 8.—Thomas A. Edison has expressed the belief that it may be possible to device appratus by which the dead can communicate with the living. In answering a query he stated that "if my theory is correct that the machine called men is only the dead matter and real life is in millions of individual units, which navigate this machine, and if on destruction of the machine these units keep together and including those in charge of memory, then I think it possible to devise apparatus to receive communications if they desire to make them. All this will be very difficult."

194 ARRESTS FOR JANUARY REPORT; FINES NET $364.20

The reports of Chief Blizzard and Judge Kitto showed a startling increase for the month of January over December.

Judge Kitto's report shows that out of 37 cases brought before him he collected $364.20 in fines. An increase over the month of December of $247.90. Of the $364.20 taken in during the month of January, 19 cases were $10 fines, 15 were $5 fines, two were $20 fines and one was a fine of $7.50.

Chief Blizzard's report showed a total of 194 arrests an increase of 127 arrests over the month of December.

Following are the individual charges:
Assault 2
Beating board bill 1
Disturbing the peace 10
Fugitives from justice 3
Intoxication 37
Running a disorderly house 1
Lewdness 4
Lodgers 111
Search warrants for liquor 4
Street walking 1
Violating traffic ordinance 5
Vagrancy 2
Allowing minors in pool halls .. 1
Insane 2

One rather noticeable item about the above report is the number of lodgers which totaled 111. This means furnished a place to sleep and breakfast for men who drift into Ottumwa without money and asked for lodging at the jail.

The Daily News, 60 Days, $1.00

PHONE 2400

CONSENT AGE MAY BE RAISED TO 18 FOR IOWA GIRLS

Des Moines, Feb. 18.—Leaders of the W. C. T. U. of Iowa are lobbying diligently in behalf of a measure that will tend to improve the morality laws of Iowa. The house judiciary committee received the plea presented through Judge Utterback and H. W. Byers.

The Mayne bill, to raise the age of consent at which a girl may become a willing victim to immorality is raised from 15 to 18 years.

"Our daughters' virtue should be protected as long as their property is safeguarded," declared Mrs. Ida B. Wise Smith of Cedar Rapids, president of the state W. C. T. U. "If a woman isn't wise enough to make a deed or contract before she is 18 years old, she isn't competent to give away her virtue before that time, either."

BUILDING INSPECTOR MAKES IN A LIGHT REPORT

The monthly report of the building inspector, G. W. Ferguson, shows that during January he collected $64 on building permits and $1.50 on furnace permits, totalling $65.50 for the month.

During the month of December the total amount of fees collected was $55.

1921

BIDS WANTED

Notice is hereby given that the Board of Education of the Independent School District of Ottumwa, Iowa, will receive sealed proposals up to the hour of 7:30 p. m., on Wednesday, February 23rd, 1921, at the office of the Secretary, for the excavation of basement and the construction of foundations for the new location of the Adams School, in accordance with specifications prepared and furnished by Croft & Boerner, Architects and Engineers.

Bids will be received on the form of the bid supplied by the Architects and Engineers, and no other form will be considered. Bids must be accompanied with a certified check for the amount of 5 per cent of the bid, made payable to the Secretary of the above School District.

COUNTY PAYS $1400 QUARANTINE CLAIMS

President Knox of the board of supervisors stated today that the county will pay all quarantine bills passed upon recently and for the months of November, December and January with the exception of those collectible by the city when the quarantine service is rendered by the sanitary officer and bill presented therefor. The board, according to Knox, does not intend to O. K. bills other than those which have been incurred by families too poor to meet the expense. From the list now filed a number of names will be used in a statement form with a request to settle.

The entire county quarantine season will total an estimated expense of $3,000. The county pays these bills, but officers in all communities are required, and more so than in the past, to make an attempt to collect and then no charges will be entered for consideration of the supervisors.

COOKING FIRST-CLASS

None better, perhaps none quite so good, in Ottumwa. We take pride in serving those wonderful pies—and other good pastry.

SPECIAL SUNDAY DINNERS, 50 CENTS, REGULAR MEALS, 40 CENTS.

You'll praise our cooking and all attentions to guests afforded, under the new management.

- FRASIER CAFE -

Ottumwa Daily News

JOHN KELLY SUFFERS PECULIAR ACCIDENT

John Kelly, residing at 106 South Vine street, was the victim of an unfortunate accident at his home Wednesday evening which rendered him unconscious for several hours.

Kelly's back yard ends at the edge of a deep gully or ditch some 45 or 50 feet in depth and on this edge of this ditch, Kelly was just at the verge when the ground gave way, letting him roll down the steep incline turning over and over. He was taken out of the wreckage unconscious and Dr. Rambo called.

His condition is greatly improved.

WOMAN CANDIDATE FOR SCHOOL B'RD. MRS. BROCKMAN

Governor Kendall and his assistants in the legislature failed to secure legislation making it compulsory that at least one woman be named member of the board of control, but in Ottumwa there is a chance, it is believed by friends, that the new school board will have at least one woman in its personnel, if not the announced candidate Mrs. D. C. Brockman, then another, or could be two for that matter.

Mrs. Brockman stated to The News at noon today that she was a candidate and Mrs. Dr. Mills and Bailiff Lucy C. Dysart both prominent citizens, the latter chairman of the women's republican county committee, have the petitions filled and ready for filing that qualifies for the candidacy.

Princess

Now Playing

Elliott Dexter

—and—

Gloria Swanson

in another Great De Mille Picture

"Something to Think About"

Creating more discussion and praise than did "The Miracle Man" and "Humoresque."

MOSCOW TO MAKE MOVIES, PRAISE SOVIET REGIME

Smolensk, Feb. 11.—The Moscow "Narkompress" (People's Press Commission) has assigned a very large sum of money for the organization in Moscow of a big motion picture studio. Experts from Germany have been invited.

A special committee presided over by Lunacharski announced a competition for ten scenarios. The "winners" will have to answer the following requirements: they must be entertaining, with many thrills, but above all they paint in black colors "all the horrors of the bourgeois system in Europe." The first prize is as high as two million roubles.

In the words of Lunacharski, "while all the world continues to foolishly amuse itself by melodramas or detective pictures, we shall use the Russian cinematograph for greater purposes, and by its means will make another attack on bourgeois psychology."

One of the themes announced for competition is "Woman's Role and Participation in the Building of a New Social System."

1921

Freshly-Ironed Frocks and Rompers Each Day

Let the kiddies enjoy clean, crisp frocks and rompers daily. Keep your favorite blouses always fresh. This is easy with a handy Electric Iron. No trouble—no waiting for irons to heat. The Electric Iron is ready instantly—and as quickly put away when you are finished.

ON SALE AT ALL DEALERS

THE OTTUMWA DAILY NEWS

OTTUMWA, IOWA, MONDAY, FEBRUARY 14, 1921

DES MOINES BAD MEN IN OTTUMWA

ROB McGARRITY'S CAFE IN BANDIT STYLE, SPEED ON, CAUGHT AT LIBERTYVILLE

"It's an ill wind that blows nobody good," so the little saying goeth and Iowa's road facilities for once proved of value when the two youthful bandits, Fremont Staples and Albert W. Greenleaf of Des Moines were found stuck in the mud a few miles from Libertyville after holding up the restaurant belonging to Dennis McGarrity, 835 E. Main street, Ottumwa, where $108 in cash was taken from the cash register.

At 4:55 o'clock Sunday morning Staples and Greenleaf entered McGarrity's restaurant, lined up with four or five other customers and ordered breakfast. After finishing the meal they arose apparently to pay their bill and flashed two guns on the occupants. One of the men covered the cashier Mrs. Keller while the other emptied the cash register of its contents which amounted to $108. McGarrity had taken $60 out of the register before going home Saturday night.

The men then jumped in a car, a small Buick roadster and headed for town, where they circled about and went back east toward Agency. They stopped at the A. W. Cowgers' home in Agency and procured water and from there departed for Eldon, arriving there about 7:30. Staples left the car and purchased a lunch and they left for Libertyville.

In the meantime Chief Blizzard informed neighboring towns of the holdup including Libertyville. A man named Roberts residing in Libertyville saw the men pass through the town and with a companion followed them on a railway motor car. When a few miles out of Libertyville the men were sighted struggling along in the mud and Roberts commanded them to halt. When they refused Roberts' companion opened up on them with a small rifle he had in his possession. The bullet passed between the two men, breaking the windshield of the car.

Staples and Greenleaf then abandoned the car and concealed themselves in a small ditch, about two miles west of the car. Here they were surrounded by nearly 150 farmers and residents of Libertyville when Chief Blizzard and deputy sheriff Bright arrived on the scene.

Sheriff Walter Harris of Fairfield brought the two men into Fairfield where they were placed in handcuffs and brought to Ottumwa.

A search of their persons resulted in the recovery of $72.

GREENLEAF STILL IN DUNGEON CELL; MAY TALK TONIGHT

Greenleaf, self-confessed holder-up of the McGarrity restaurant and who has been in a dungeon cell for 48 hours at the county jail in the expectation that a statement would be forced to link him with the murder of the Des Moines grocer, Fosdick, shot to death February 5, is still holding out at 2 this afternoon. Sheriff Giltner is confident there will be some developments tonight, but why he entertains this opinion is not expressed.

STRAND THEATRE
THREE DAYS STARTING SUNDAY
WILLIAM RUSSELL
in
"The Cheater Reformed"
And one of those famous two-reel Sunshine Comedies
HIS NOISY STILL
A Real Program—Don't Miss It.

SERIOUS SHORTAGE OF STUDENTS IN MEDICAL SCIENCES IN COLLEGE

Cambridge, Mass., Feb. 23.—There is a serious shortage of young men in the medical sciences today in the United States, and the laboratory branches of medicine will suffer unless a change takes place in the current of young men taking up medical careers, according to Dean David L. Edsall, of the Harvard Medical School.

1921

Appetite of This Giant of Swatters Only Whetted By Record of Last Season

Big Bambino Is Confident He Can Shatter His Mark of Fifty-four Home Runs, and Impatiently Awaits Call to Play Ball to Begin Supreme Effort of Career Which Has Thrilled the World of Baseball.

Long before Springtime's balmy breezes fan the Northern States Babe Ruth, balldom's most sensational star, will trek southward to prepare for another big season.

The Home Run King has a grand ambition. He also boasts a generous waistline. For these two reasons he is going to Hot Springs, Ark., with the batterymen of the New York Yankees. He will reduce his girth that it may not interfere with his grand ambition—to hit SEVENTY-FIVE home runs during the 1921 campaign!

Here is a champion who stands in a class by himself. In 1919 he shattered all previous home records by hitting out a grand total of twenty-nine. His achievement caused the fans to marvel.

"He has made a record that will stand for a long, long time," they said.

And then, in 1920, the Colossus of Swat came back in all his glory, adding twenty-five homers to his 1919 performance for a season total of FIFTY-FOUR, a mark no player of past days had ever dreamed of.

Ruth is now in his prime. He reached his twenty-seventh birthday February 7. As star players go he has many a year in baseball to look forward to and if he takes the proper care of himself and Dame Fortune does not interfere to dim the light of his batting eye he may hold his ground as world's champion hitter of home runs for some seasons to come.

With the optimism of a man who believes in himself, though with never a sign of self-consciousness, Ruth recently said that he has every reason to believe he can beat his 1920 record of fifty-four home runs, and added that he would like to reach the seventy-fifth mark.

Meryl Marie Eakins, aged two months, daughter of Mr. and Mrs. Hyter Eakins, died this morning at the home of her aunt, Mrs. Campbell, 123 South Moore street. The body was taken overland to the home of the parents, three miles south of Blakesburg. Funeral Thursday afternoon at Union chapel, conducted by Rev. F. A. Heilman. Burial at Bailey cemetery.

WILSONS ARE ALL MOVED EXCEPT 'PRIVATE STOCK'

Washington, Feb 25.—The last two vanloads of heavy household furniture owned by President and Mrs. Wilson were moved from the White House to S street. The president's private stock of liquors, held chiefly for medicinal purposes, it is explained, is all that remains to go.

Careless movers were about to place several innocent boxes aboard a van when it was discovered that a legal permit to move liquor had not been obtained. It was said at the White House:

"The shipment would probably never have been questioned, but it will be delayed until the permit is issued."

RELOCATED HIGHWAY REQUIRES A BRIDGE AT COST OF $5,700.

Seven miles out on the Bloomfield road, at a point where the re-located primary road has been designated, is the crossing over the Wabash tracks, said railway 25 feet below the established grade. Thursday the railroad commissioners of the state have been here in conference with the supervisors and on leaving for home they said the overhead bridge at this crossing must be built.

It now comes to the matter of expense, or rather as to whether the county or state or both, pay the bill which President Knox says is around $5,780. "We expect to hear from the commissioners soon in this detail, but the bridge will be constructed under order of these officials, said this supervisor.

FOUR BIDS SIGHTED TO MOVE BUILDING

Superintendent Blackmar stated this afternoon that at least four bids will be submitted for the removal of the Adams school building, bids opened February 23. Work will start at once, if one of the bids is acceptable. Five hundred pupils at Adams must be cared for and this is the next problem. If the Froebel building is purchased and removed to a nearby lot and the use of it allowed that would be the happiest arrangement, according to Mr. Blackmar's statement today.

Firms reporting to date include those from Cedar Rapids, Chicago, Kansas City and Pittsburgh.

1921

"MELTING POT" FAILS TO MELT
SAYS DR. JACOB GOULD SCHURMAN
(By International News Service.)

NEW YORK, Feb. 19.—The "melting pot" fails to melt, according to Dr. Jacob Gould Schurman, former president of Cornell University. Speaking at Columbia University under the auspices of the Society of Arts and Sciences, he warned the American people that they must protect themselves from the perils of denationalization by hordes of foreigners difficult to assimilate. He proposed a limit on immigrants to the number and kind who could be absorbed into American social and economic life.

Discussing the peril of denationalization, Dr. Schurman added:

"The conclusion is obvious. Either we can never become a homogeneous American people, either unassimilated masses of European nationalities must share our domain with us, or we must set limits to the tide of immigration so that a unified national life and consciousness may remain possible for us."

Dr. Schurman said that he favored the Welty bill, permitting immigration of a maximum of 10 per cent now domiciled here who have become naturalized and their native-born children. He thought it necessary to modify the bill, particularly with respect to unskilled labor.

He gave these figures on the present foreign population:

"We now have in the United States all the Jews in the world 24 per cent; of all the Scandinavians, 17 per cent; of all the Germans, 13 per cent; of all the Slovaks, of all the Poles and of all the Finns, 8 per cent each; of all the Italians, 7 per cent; of all the Dutch and of all the Lithuanians, 5 per cent each; of all the Greeks and of all the French, 3 per cent each."

LEGAL

NOTICE OF BOND SALE

The Independent School District of Ottumwa, Iowa, offers for sale $700,000.00 of 5 per cent School Building Bonds dated May 1, 1920, in denominations of $1000.00 each; $15,000.00 of these bonds due May 1st each year from 1930 to 1939 inclusive and $550,000.00 due May 1, 1940.

Sealed proposals accompanied by certified check for 1 per cent of the amount of bid will be received by C. D. Evans, President of the Board of Education, Ottumwa, Iowa, up to February 25th, 1921, at ten o'clock A. M.

J. A. WAGNER,
Secretary.

Feb. 11-18.

ORPHEUM

4 Acts Vaudeville and Pictures

Tonight 7 and 8:30
Stevens & Stevens, Claire Bethway, Hunter & Ross, Cleveland & Fay.

Sunday and Monday
FUGI,
The Nipponese Wonder

SUE STEAD & SIS
Singing Novelty

FRANK NORTON
Dancing Imitations

FITZGERALD DUO
Barrel Jumping

Sunday Matinee 2:30 & 4—Daily at 2:30—Nights 7 & 8:30

Ottumwa Daily News

OTTUMWA DAILY NEWS, MONDAY, JANUARY 24, 1921.

FORESEE GERMAN TRADE WAR IN 1921; WORLD INVASION, TO SELL GOODS AT EXTREMELY LOW PRICES

By W. H. ATKINS,
International News Service Staff Correspondent

WASHINGTON, Jan. 24.—Look out for Germany in the trade war in 1921. The hand of the German trader is beginning to show renewed cunning in world marts. The bold plan of German trade kings is to dump goods at lower prices than domestic makers can sell them. Cheap labor makes it possible for Germany to do this, and her purpose to direct a price-cutting campaign of unprecedented scope in all parts of the world is plainly revealed by latest advices to Government officials from trade and fiscal agents abroad.

England is now feeding the force of this German effort to crowd British goods out of British markets. German commodities in many lines are being delivered in London and other English centers at prices considerably lower htan the cost of British manufacture. Secretary of Commerce Alexander was informed by Consul Clairborne that rare laces of German origin are being offered for sale in Nottingham at prices lower than the cost of manufacture in that great centre of the Briish lace industry. German products over a wide range are being sold on British markets at equally low figures.

GET THIS RIGHT

Ottumwa steam users are called upon to pay an advance of 25 per cent in the price of steam for heating purposes.

Manager Fahrney says notices will be sent out March 15, six months prior to September 15, current year, that service will be discontinued unless the raise is granted by an adopted resolution by the city council.

There is a claim that the Ottumwa Railway and Light Company experienced a deficit of $2,000 in last year's receipts as compared with operating expenses.

Mr. Fahnrey says 75 per cent of the reason which is offered why the rates should go up is due to the tripling of coal prices since the days when theplant might have been considered capable of meeting its expense account.

"CANNED MUSIC" IS SENT TO NEIGHBORS WIRELESS METHOD

(By International News Service)
Akron, O., Feb. 28.—Success in sending music by wireless has been won by Donald A. Hoffman, twenty-one, of this city.

Within a radius of forty miles of Akron operators of wireless outfits are picking up daily the music from phonograph records sent out on air waves by young Hoffman.

"With the attachment of certain coils to magnify the sound at the receiving end and the addition of a horn similar to that on an ordinary talking machine, the wireless concerts can be received in any part of the city with the same volume of sound as when records are played on the machine," Hoffman said.

"There would be no more difference in the sound coming from the horn at the receiving end than if the horn was part of an ordinary phonograph," he continued.

Hoffman said that the musical sounds are picked up at a South Akron station with such strength as to be heard all over the room from the ordinary wireless head receivers. He stated that when the wireless receiver was placed against the transmitter of a telephone the music could be heard plainly in the receiver at the other end of the line.

According to Hogman, the operator of the wireless outfit can send his voice on the air waves and can be heard at all the wireless stations in the vicinity.

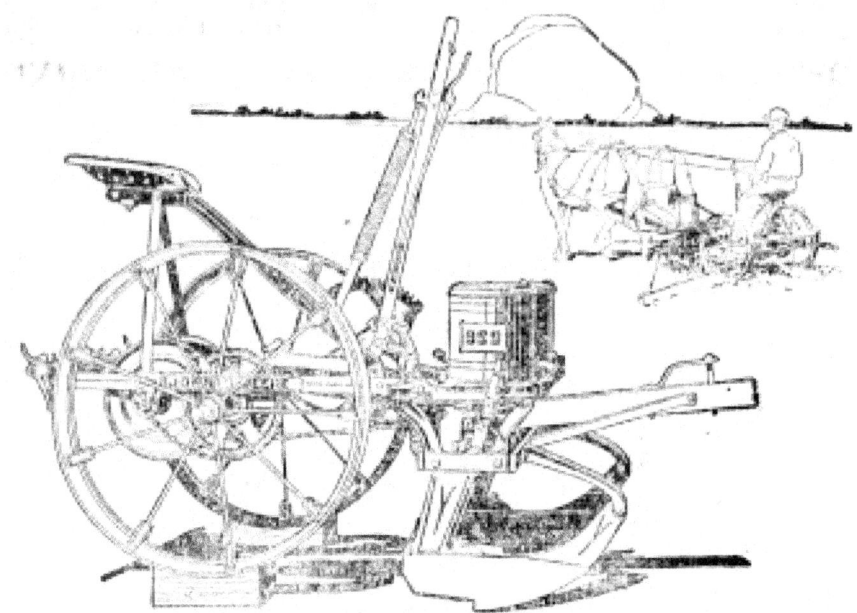

MARCH 1921

Mar 4 - Warren G. Harding sworn in as 29th president of the United States

Mar 4 - Hot Springs National Park created in Arkansas

Mar 8 - Alan Hale (the skipper on Gilligan's Island) born in Los Angeles, California

Mar 13 - Russian White Army captures Mongolia from China

Mar 17 - Dr. Marie Stopes opens the first birth control clinic in London, England

Mar 24 - 1921 Women's Olympiad (first international women's sports event) begins in Monte Carlo

Spring - Russian famine of 1921-22 begins; death toll is roughly 5 million

G.O.P. SPENDS $8,100,739.21 DEMOS. USE $2,237,770.70 WOOD WAS HIGH MAN

Lowden Near Half-Million

WASHINGTON, March 1.—Senator W. S. Kenyon, chairman of the senate committee which investigated last year's campaign expenditures, submitted to the senate a report stating the democrats and republicans spent in excess of ten and a quarter million dollars in the presidential campaign of 1920. The republicans $8,100,739.21, democrats $2,237,770.70. He declared these figures did not by any means represent the entire amount expended on campaign funds but included these funds spent in congressional, senatorial and state campaigns.

The fifteen men in the pre-convention campaign for presidential nominations had a total of $2,980,033.00 expended in their behalf, as follows: Wood, $1,773,303.00; Lowden, $414,982.00; Hiram Johnson, $194,393.00; Herbert Hoover, $173,542.00; W. G. Harding, $113,109.00 for the republican nomination.

For the Democratic nomination Palmer, $59,610.00; Cox, $22,000; Gerard, $14,040; Edwards, $12,900.

The report recommended legislation to prevent excessive campaign expenditures.

1921

THE OTTUMWA DAILY NEWS

GERMANS BALK ON ALLIES' DEMAND

ASK 226 BILLION, OFFER 30 BILLION MARKS; IS CRISIS STAGE FOR TODAY

Military Chiefs Talk War

LONDON, March 2.—It is reported that the Allied Supreme Council has agreed to the occupation of the Rhine bridgeheads as the first step to new military and economic pressure to compel Germany to meet the allies' demands of 226 billion gold marks indemnity.

PARIS, March 2.—There are no plans for the participation of United States troops to act should the allies take steps to force on the indemnity terms. It was stated by the state department that American forces in Germany, under terms of the armistice, would have no further use for troops by allies and is a matter in which the United States is not concerned.

LONDON, MARCH 2.—THE ALLIED MILITARY CHIEFS HAVE SUBMITTED TO THE PREMIERS A REPORT ON THE MILITARY OPERATIONS NECESSARY TO COMPEL GERMANY TO MEET THE DEMANDS FOR 226 BILLION GOLD MARKS, OR 56 BILLION 500 MILLION DOLLARS. GERMANY IS CONFRONTED WITH THE POSSIBILITY OF AN INDEMNITY ULTIMATUM THIS AFTERNOON WHEN THE ALLIES MAKE THEIR REPLY TO THE GERMANY COUNTER PROPOSALS OF YESTERDAY.

THE SITUATION MAY BE HANDLED BY THE GERMAN DELEGATE INDEMNITY CONFERENCE. DR. SIMONS, GERMAN FOREIGN MINISTER, ANNOUNCED THAT THE GERMAN GOVERNMENT HAD INSTRUCTED THE GERMAN DELEGATION TO STAND PAT THE COUNTER PROPOSAL OF 30 BILLION GOLD MARKS. THE CONFERENCE WHICH WAS SUDDENLY INTERRUPTED YESTERDAY NOW REACHES THE CRITICAL STAGE.

Dr. Walter Simons, speaking for the German government at the opening session of the indemnity conference offered the allies 30,000,000,000 gold marks ($7,500,000,00) to be paid within the next thirty years. But at the same time Dr. Simons contended Germany already has paid the allies 20,000,000,000 gold marks in reparations, making the total amount offered by Germany, 50,000,000,000 gold marks ($12,500,000,000).

(Germany's indemnity offered today is less than one-fourth of that the allies demanded. The allies demanded 226,000,000,000 gold marks ($56,500,000,000) and a 12 per cent tax on German exports. The Germans today offered to pay 30,000,000,000 gold marks ($7,500,000,000). However, the Germans claim already to have paid 20,000,000,000 gold marks ($5,000,000,000).

Make Many Demands.

The Germans renewed their previous suggestion that German labor be utilized for the reconstruction of the devastated districts of northern France, the work being credited against Germany's indemnity bill. Furthermore, they held that payments through cessions and deliveries by Germany of such goods as ships and war materials and floating docks already equal the amount called for by the Versailles treaty, and that henceforth they shall cease.

The Germans demanded that upper Silesia remain German instead of being subject to a plebiscite to determine if it shall continue German soil or go to Poland. Additional German demands were that the commerce of the world be freed from existing impediments, that economic freedom of established, and that "equality of rights" be put into effect throughout the world.

In the brief session of the indemnity conference at Lancaster House today the Germans were flatly informed that no quibbling would be allowed and that they must accept the allied decision.

German Cabinet Defiant

BERLIN, March 5.—The German Cabinet is still defying the Allies on indemnity, according to the best information obtainable today. It is reported that the opinion expressed at a long session of the ministry yesterday was that it would be more preferable for the French to carry out their threats than for the Germans to grant demands.

Some members of the cabinet expressed hope that negotiations will not be broken off entirely.

Ottumwa Daily News

BEAN HAS NO FEAR OF THE JIU JITSU

It will be a rare treat for the sport fans Monday night. Alex Bean will meet Matty Matsuda and everything the Japanese has in his repertoire of tricks, including the jiu jitsu stuff, in a catch-as-catch-can match.

"I don't care what he's got, I'll be ready for him," was the comment of Alex this morning. And before the visitor from Nippon left Wednesday night for his Chicago match he was in a state of pleased expectancy on what he was going to do to Mr. Bean the next time.

Promoter Flannigan report an extraordinary demand for ringside seats, nearly a hundred reservations made two days in advance, which is taken to mean that a good-sized crowd will be present. The notime limit event will be staged at the Armory and every arrangement made to give the regulation accommodation to the principals.

As a semi-windup Tony Naraccio will meet Bill Greeling, the Sigourney athlete who says his brother defeated Tony and at once issued a challenge in his own behalf. In the preliminary Farmer Kelse and Farmer Grable will stage a good show.

The unique features that go with the Bean-Matsuda match will be a special attraction that's new to Ottumwa.

The Campaign Issue

City campaign issues suggested by the present trend of public sentiment:

Better paves and permanent roadways and wider or more city bridges.

Question of indorsement for the management of our waterworks plant and with particular stress upon the five years lighting contract, together with the sale of electrical energy at 1.6 cents per kwh.

Question whether Ottumwa is representative of the better types of American cities as to its moral conditions and with special reference to the startling charge that Ottumwa has 600 immoral women and "three prominent business men" supplying the information.

Question whether or not the higher assessments for tax income is warranted and if so what is going to be done with the money.

Question whether the reordered system with relation to parks and the creation of a special superintendent's office is to meet with the approval of the public.

Question whether or not Ottumwa is entitled to more police protection.

Question as to public utility service rates.

Question involving a program for larger municipal jurisdiction and for the discontinuance of the commission form of government for the city of Ottumwa.

Question as to what shall be done about the introduction of a garbage collection plan and the disposition of all refuse and whether or not the disposal plant is a profitable investment, or could be made so with the fertilizer sales idea netting income to offset some of the attendant expense.

THE NEWS HAS THIS PROPHECY: WE ARE ABOUT TO ENTERTAIN A CALAMITY THAT IS NATION-WIDE IN THE EXTREMIST SENTIMENT THAT IS SWEEPING OVER THE LAND IN THE NAME OF GOOD CITIZENSHIP AND CHRISTIANITY.

1921

THE OTTUMWA DAILY NEWS

1200 QUIT AT MORRELL CO. PLANT

MASS MEETING CALLED; SENIORITY AND OVERTIME PARAMOUNT QUESTIONS

Company Sets Time Limit for Workmen to Return

Chicago, March 8 -- Swift and Company and Armour and Company, two of the largest packing establishments in the United States, announced wage reductions effective March 14. Eight cents an hour for time workers and twelve and one-half per cent for piece workers. Labor leaders predict strike. Reductions effect (sic) emoloyes all over the country. The order also abolishes the 8-hour day.

T. Henry Foster of the Morrell company stated this afternoon that the Chicago order will not affect employes at Ottumwa, at least not at the present time. "We have no intention of acting along the above order outline," said Mr. Foster.

The gates of our plant are open; we invite and urge each and every employee to return to his post at once.

ALL EMPLOYEES WHO ARE BACK at work by Tuesday, March the 8th, will be reinstated in full standing and at the old war time wage and no discrimination will be made on account of affiliation with any organization.

All employees who do not report for work by Tuesday, March the 8th, will be considered off our pay roll and will have to take their chances of being hired as we require men thereafter, and on the same basis and terms as apply to new help.

Conditions in the Packing Industry are anything but satisfactory. For a year or more business has been operated generally at a loss and, unfortunately, our company has been no exception. Some plants have been forced to cut down their working forces; others have reduced wages, abolished overtime and returned to the 10 hour day; still others have gone out of business entirely.

In view of conditions sustained at our plants these facts are worthy of your careful consideration.

Respectfully submitted,
JOHN MORRELL & CO.
By T Henry Foster
Vice-President

March 3rd 1921

EVERYBODY TALKS

The annual report of the Bell phone company shows there are 12,601,935 phones connected with this particular system in the United States. This, is claimed, represents two-thirds the number of the entire world.

That's an enormous business enterprise, and growing, at the rate of 70,000 a month during the past year.

Talk should be cheap, and the charges uniform. One of our legislators at Des Moines is striving after such a law as will place the phone system on a basis where service may be had with a fair distribution, equalization, of the toll, also holding, as it might well be argued, that no charge should be made unless the party called is connected.

Motion picture films are to be fewer and better in the future, according to an announcement from a group of the big producers. The announcement is in line with the natural development of the industry, which has steadily been offering better and better films, working toward a higher standard which is heralded by many of the pictures unreeled at the present time in cities of any size.

NEWS, FRIDAY, MARCH 4, 1921.

Booze Ruling are Farcical Making Laws Impotent

By W. H. ATKINS,
International News Service Staff Correspondent

WASHINGTON, March 4.—What about "booze" under the new administration? Both "drys" and "wets" are anxious for an answer to that question. President Harding is expected to fulfill his promise to give the country "real enforcement." The "booze" laws are to be enforced in a different fashion, unless all signs fail. What seems probable is that new dry law chiefs, pursuant to the new administration policy, will begin by slashing "red tape" eliminating stage plug and get down to an application of the Volstead act as it was framed.

President Harding comes into power to find that "dry law administration is enveloped in utter confusion. Allowing for all of the logical mistakes that were to be expected in the first year of experiment under the dry law, officials will find in force a maze of rules and regulations, in the hands of dry law branches that are not co-ordinated, and which fail in their purpose. Many of these rules, found to be impractical, and some of them ridiculous, will be rescinded and workable rules substituted.

Higher officials having supervision of "dry" laws now frankly admit that prohibition enforcement would have proved less farcical had no attempt been made to impose restrictions of doubtful legality.

It is a grand farce to see smuggling and bootlegging operations upon a gigantic scale, and even illicit whiskey manufacturing to an extent that baffles enforcement directors, and to note the apparently helpless attitude of the Government's prohibition bureau.

Whiskey operations of an illicit character will be dealt with in a firm manner by the new administration, it is expected, by a closer co-ordination of the Government's agencies.

During the last few weeks of the Wilson term dry law enforcers have been stopping all of the possible holes through which whiskey and other liquors have been leaking out to the bootleg trade. With the backing of the Department of Justice many new and severe regulations have been imposed. Among these was a rule putting the wholesale liquor dealers out of business and limiting legal sale of whiskey through whiskey manufacturers and wholesale druggists.

But in these recent steps taken by dry chiefs there is much to indicate that the Volstead "exemptions" were virtually scrapped, and there is serious doubt whether or not they will be allowed to remain in effect. If not overturned in the courts, where many of the rules are now being contested it is thought many of them will be cancelled.

1921

President Harding Takes Oath of Office at Shortest Inauguration in History and is Already at Work This Afternoon

President Warren G. Harding Takes Office Today

1921 – President Harding rides to inauguration in a motor car.

Far More Elaborate Inaugurals Have Been Celebrated Than This Today and Some Have Been More Simple, but President Harding Reaches Happy Medium—Solemn, Impressive and Interesting.

March 4 -- Until 1937, Inauguration Day was in March, because the Founding Fathers wanted to leave plenty of time for a newly-elected president to make his way to the capitol city. After eight years under Democratic President Woodrow Wilson, including World War I and the 1918 flu, the Republicans were back in charge. "The great iron gates of the White House stood open unguarded today for the first time in four years and visitors are roaming the White House grounds at will," the Daily News announced.

Ottumwa Daily News

1921

Held for Trial in Famous White Sox Case

REFUSE TO TAKE WHITE SOX TRIAL OFF COURT CALL; CASE UP SOON

CHICAGO, March 15.—Judge William E. Dever today refuse to comply with a motion by the state that the trial of Chicago White Sox players and others indicted for the alleged throwing of the 1919 world series be taken off the court call. He ordered another hearing for next Thursday when it is believed a date for trial will be set.

Attorneys for the defense moved that an immediate trial be held Thursday and Judge Dever said that he would announce his decision on this matter later. Claude Williams, Buck Weaver, Oscar Felsch and Swede Risberg were in court. Eddie Cicotte, Bill Burns, Joseph J. Sullivan, Rachel Brown, Chick Gandil and Abe Attel were represented by counsel. Hal Chase was the only defendant not present or represented by counsel.

SERMONS BY WIRELESS

Pittsburgh, Pa., March 1.—Sermons by wireless are being heard in this district by amateur operators on Sunday evenings. By means of a sound board above the pulpit in Calvary Episcopal church at East Pittsburgh the sermon and even the singing of the choir is flashed over a wide radius. The sermon and hymns are sent on a wave of 880 meters.

HUMAN INTELLIGENCE IS ABOUT THE SAME AS 2,000 YEARS AGO

(By International News Service)
Worcester, Mass., March 5.—Human intelligence has increased little during the past two thousand years according to Dr. William H. Burnham, professor of Pedogogy and School of Hygiene at Clark University.

Ability to do things, the psychologist acknowledges, has advanced over the hours of labor though he worked many improvements.

But fundamentally he believes we are no further along than the people were in ancient Athens.

Correction of this stagnation, Professor Burnham believes, lies with the proper training of children.

"Many children are hopeless morons from birth," he said, "but a much larger number have their mental development retaded because of misunderstanding by parents or teachers. If we should change that conition the improvement of the child's intellect would be easy."

He advocates more rigid mental tests for immigrants.

ONE "DATE" A WEEK FOR CO-ED STUDENTS

(By International News Service)
Chicago, March 5.—Co-eds at the University of Chicago, aroused by reports that "blue law" restrictions are to be placed upon them, are protesting to Marian Talbot, dean of women.

The rumors have it that the university authorities are considering a regulation which would limit each girl to a mere one "date" a week—on either Friday or Saturday night—and then she would have to be in the dormitory by midnight.

Tiresome Sewing Machine Methods Ended

The Portable Electric Sewing Machine Brings New Pleasure to Home Sewing

Most women enjoy making smart little frocks at home; yet the wearisome grind of the foot-treadle machine deters many of them from home sewing.

Electric Sewing Machines require none of the laborious effort necessary to run the foot-driven models. Just imagine what this means to your sewing comfort! And of equal importance—these machines are PORTABLE. All you need is a convenient Electric Light socket—a flat surface—and you're ready to sew wherever the light is best. A slight pressure of your foot regulates the speed.

See them at any Electrical Dealers.

Ottumwa Railway & Light Co.
Second and Market Street.

$100 REWARD, $100

The readers of this paper will be pleased to learn that there is at least one dreaded disease that science has been able to cure in all its stages and that is catarrh. Catarrh being greatly influenced by constitutional conditions requires constitutional treatment. Hall's Catarrh Medicine is taken internally and acts thru the Blood on the Mucous Surfaces of the System thereby destroying the foundation of the disease, giving the patient strength by building up the constitution and assisting nature in doing its work. The proprietors have so much faith in the curative powers of Hall's Catarrh Medicine that they offer One Hundred Dollars for any case that it fails to cure. Send for list of testimonials.

Address F. J. CHENEY & CO., Toledo, Ohio. Sold by all druggists, 75c.

WHAT NEW YORK SCIENTISTS SAY

Scientists in this city scoff at the idea of any one proving parentage by blood tests. The laboratory of New York hospital has issued a statement that such tests would be futile.

"We know of no possible means to determine parentage in such fashion. We do not know the details of Dr. Abram's tests and therefore, cannot comment upon them.

"Tests of this character show the difference between animals and human beings. They do not show nationality or individual traits or 'vibrations' insofar as we know."

DIES AT IOWA CITY.

M. I. Hodges, 61, died Monday at the Iowa City hospital. The remains arrived on the Milwaukee last midnight and were taken to the home, 804 West Mill street. The funeral will be held Thursday afternoon at 2 o'clock at the Sullivan and Jay chapel. Rev. McClure officiating. Burial in the Agency cemetery.

THE OTTUMWA DAILY NEWS

GERMANY UNABLE TO MEET TERMS

ALLIES EPPECTED TO ACT AT ONCE; PARIS DEMAND IS READY FOR EXECUTION

Dr. Simons is Standing Pat

LONDON, MARCH 7.—THE INDEMNITY CONFERENCE CONVENED THIS AFTERNOON FOLLOWING A RECESS. LLOYD GEORGE ANNOUNCED THAT THE ALLIES BEING DISSATISFIED WITH THE COUNTER PROPOSAL THAT THE GERMANS SO FAR HAVE MADE, HAVE DECIDED TO PUT INTO EFFECT IMMEDIATELY THE PENALTIES TO ENFORCE GERMANS TO OBEDIENCE TO THE ALLIES REPARATIONS DEMANDS. LLOYD GEORGE STATED THAT THE ALLIES DEEPLY DEPLORED THE SITUATION IN INTEREST OF THE WORLD'S PEACE. THE CONFERENCE BROKE SHORTLY AFTER SIX P. M. IT IS OFFICIALLY ANNOUNCED THAT THE TROOPS WILL BE ORDERED TO MOVE INTO GERMANY TOMORROW.

NEW JOURNALISM COURSE FOR WOMEN

Madison, Wis., March 8.—Newspaper and magazine departments of interest to women, the first course of the kind to be given in any school of journalism, has been introduced at the University of Wisconsin by Mrs. Genevieve Jackson Bonghner, an experienced newspaper woman.

FAIRFIELD IS VICTOR. GIVES TO IOWA CITY

Ottumwa eliminated. Coach Yount's five won handily over Hiteman, 15 to 3, and then lost to Keokuk, which defeat eliminated the locals from state tournament entry honors at Iowa City two weeks later. Fairfield won from Burlington in the finals score 16 to 14 and thereby becomes the representative of the Southeastern Iowa Basketball association in a state contest.

Fairfield will have expenses paid to the state meet.

RADIATOR BURSTS SOUNDS LIKE BOMB CLERKS SCARED

Public Safety Commissioner Parker of the city hall department had his attention focused this morning on an unusual incident. It might have been a tragical story. In the front window near the northeast radiator with which the office was heated. At nine o'clock and shortly after the clerks had taken their desks at the Iowa Steam Laundry a terrific detonation and clouds of hot steam enveloped the front of the building, corner Third and Market streets. No one was hurt.

The radiator bottom blew out, a 3-4th inch cast bottom and the concussion blew the panels below the window outward and well into the street 20 feet distance. The explosion had an outward direction and thus the office was very slightly damaged. One of the clerks had a desk not more than four feet from the radiator that gave way, but was on the safe side of it.

LEGAL

NOTICE TO ABSENT VOTERS

Any voter who expects to be absent from the city on Monday, March 14, 1921, may by making application to the City Clerk of the City of Ottumwa, Iowa, vote an absent voters ballot.

All applications for an absent voters ballot should be made not later than Friday, March 11th.

The city Clerk's office will be open Friday, March 11th, until 10 o'clock p. m. that all absent voters may have an opportunity to vote.

If you wish to cast an absent voters ballot call at the City Clerk's office where you will receive the proper instructions.

M. A. SHEEHAN,
City Clerk.

Publish in the Ottumwa Daily News

NOTICE OF CANCELLATION

Mr. J. M. O'Halleran:

You are hereby notified that you are 21 weeks delinquent in your weekly payments upon the purchase of Tract 151 in Wildwood Countryside being a sub-division of Sections 26 and 27, Township 72, Range 14, West, in Wapello County, Iowa and that unless you call at the office of the Phoenix Trust Company, 111 South Market street in Ottumwa, Iowa, and pay up your delinquency amounting to $81.00 within thirty days of this notice your contract will be forfeited and the Tract will be offered for re-sale.

PHOENIX TRUST COMPANY,
By Geo. F. Heindel
Vice-President.

Ottumwa, Iowa, March 4, 1921.

"AIR LORRY" WILL LIFT FOUR TONS

(By International News Service)

London, March 11.—The commercial world is promised an air lorry in the near future. It will be capable of carrying four tons of goods at an average speed of about seventy-five miles an hour.

The machine is the result of experiments with a new type of wing, known as the "Alula," which is a faithful copy of the wing of a gull and capable of remarkable "lift."

It will have an unusual wing spread span and both wings and body reproduce the form of a bird.

1921

SEVEN TO FORT LEAVENWORTH

Tonight, as planned, six drug addicts and dispensers of contraband drugs will leave Ottumwa for Fort Leavenworth, in charge of United States Marshal Reed, two deputy marshals, three guards. Numbeerd in the six is Michael Meany, former police chief of Ottumwa and well known. His wife, also convicted, each receiving one year and one day, goes to Rockwell City reformatory. A seventh prisoner is a man from Centerville who had been raising dollar bills to the ten denomination.

$147,000 IN CASH FOR FAIR PREMIUMS, AUG. 24, SEPT. 2.

More than $147,000 in cash premiums will be offered to exhibitors at the 1921 Iowa State Fair, August 24-Sept. 2, according to announcement just sent out by the fair management.

This is the largest amount ever offered in premiums by any state fair in the country. It is expected to make Iowa's state fair exhibits this year supreme among the big American expositions.

Special increases have been made in the Junior Fair offerings, for boys and girls, where approximately $7,000 is offered to boy and girl winners in judging, demonstration and exhibit work.

Premium lists in almost all departments of the fair are now being completed by Secretary A. R. Corey and full details about entering in the various departments may be obtained by writing to him at Des Moines.

Officials, in issuing the premium offerings, stated that the 1921 fair will be the greatest in the entire country. The Iowa exposition has already been conceded supremacy as a live stock and agricultural fair.

OTTUMWA SAVINGS BANK

It the only Saving Bank in Southern Iowa that has been admitted to the customers of the bank, as it Membership in this Government system enables the bank to take their securities to the Federal Reserve Bank at any time and exhange them for money.

This privilege is of great value to the Federal Reserve system. is an additional assurance that they can get their money at any time and also enables the bank to loan more freely on approved security.

OTTUMWA SAVINGS BANK

Capital, Surplus and Profits,
$190,000.00

OLDEST SAVINGS BANK IN OTTUMWA

AIRPLANE WITH "AUTOMATIC" PILOT

(By International News Service)

London, March 1.—The aeroplane of the future may require no pilot. A life-saving device for flying men in the shape of an "automatic pilot," which does everything but steer the machine, has been invented by a former pilot in the French army.

A Handley Page plane flew for two hours on a trip to Paris under the control of the new invention while the pilot steered the course.

Small air pumps, fitted beneath a part of the fuselage and worked by propellers, compress the air, which is conveyed into a reservoir. A gauge informs the pilot that the necessary pressure is maintained.

This pressure keeps steady a quantity of mercury in a circular container while the airplane is level. The mercury moves as soon as there is a tilt to either side or a dive downwards and causes an electrical contact, and valves, acted upon by the current, set in action the with the pilot's controlling mechanism.

The British government has adopted the invention and fourteen Handley Page bombers have been equipped with the "automatic pilot."

1921

JIU JITSU LOSES BUT GOOD MATCH AND BIG CROWD

With the matmen in first-class physical condition, a n immense attendance inspiration of the sportive character uscharging the Armory hall atmosphere until the psychology of it all provided the way for a big night of glee, Alex Bean and Matty Matsuda presented a contest of thrills, the honors, two in three falls, going to the local athlete, but not until he had suffered agonies in certain holds the jiu jitsu artist applied.

The first round went to Bean in 24 minutes the second to Matty, the third to Bean with his body scissors and strangle hold, his victim turning divid white and tongue protruding, another 30 seconds looking like his finish and here the referee awarded the decision and prevented any serious consequences to the Nipponese.

Alex did not come through without extraordinary punishment, his left arm ligaments in the bicep section having been cruelly crushed by the adept pressure of the visitor, as privileged under the catch-as-catch-can and no holds barred.

This morning the little brown man left Ottumwa, but his neck was still swollen and altogether feeling uncomfortable. "He's the best little man I ever met," said Bean.

It was a profitable night for the promoters and more than made up for the less interesting bout a week ago.

Y. M. TO NEW QUARTERS

The Young Men's Christian Association will remove headquarters from the location at Second and Washington streets to the quatrer million dollar edifice at Green and Second three blocks east Monday, March 14th.

STILL HAS EARNED OWNER $144,000

(By International News Service)
Chicago, March 14.—Gaston Rogers, chemist, rented the entire second floor of a South Side building eight months ago rigged up a fifty gallon still and made moonshine. It was good stuff.

He refined it through charcoal to give it the proper color and his agent sold it for $12 a gallon. Prohibition agents arrested Gaston recently. His profits for the eight months had been $144,000, he declared.

BOLSHEVIK RULE LOSING ITS GRIP WRITES EDITOR

Columbus, O., March 9.—"The apparent facts are conclusive, I think, that the Bolshevik government is weakening," said Dr. Gregory Zilboorg, Russian author and newspaper editor of Petrograd and Keiv, who addressed the Columbus Art Club here.

"The Bolsheviki are not fighting. They are ruling by force—many are being executed, many are being imprisoned—and when a government rules by force it is not popular" he continued.

"There are two Russias, one inside and one outside. Generally speaking, most of the intellectuals are outside—2,000,000 of them."

Dr. Zilboorg expressed belief that in a short time the Constitutional Assembly organized under the temporary government of Premier Kerensky, which met at Paris recently, will meet within the borders of its native land to lay the foundation for a permanent democratic government.

Ottumwa Daily News

THE OTTUMWA DAILY NEWS

4 PER CENT BEER FOR DRUGGISTS

NEW REGIME MAKES RULING IN RESPONSE TO DOCTORS, BREWERS MAY GET BUSY

Shortage Will Cause Worry

BEER ALLOWED AS MEDICINE.

WASHINGTON, March 8.—The prohibition lid is removed on beer with the kick for medical purposes. The Department of Justice physicians authorized the ruling under the Volstead law, beer may be prescribed when in their judgment it will be beneficial to the patients which places beer on the same status with wine as a curative agent legally listed by the government.

Physicians will be allowed a wide latitude in its use. Officials are now considering amendments to the existing rules to allow brewers to sell beer at about four per cent alcoholic content and order an ample supply that would be available to meet the expected demands of druggists.

DECREASE WAGE TO FARM HANDS

Farm hands who a year ago and for several years in the past were receiving from $85 to $100 in addition to board and room and laundry are feeling the general wage reduction along with other laborers throughout the country, and wage reductions, while not startling, have nevertheless been made.

According to local farmers, conditions now do not justify paying more than $35 per month for hired help, although the most of them at the present time are paying an average of $50.

Statistics show that at present there is a dearth in farm jobs as many of the former hired men, unable to obtain work in the cities, have returned to their former occupations, thus throwing on the market a surplus supply of farm help. General conditions with the majority of the farmers make it impossible to pay higher wages.

OBITUARY

Juanita Edna, year-old daughter of Mr. and Mrs. Clarence Palmer, Cedar Rapids, died Sunday and the body was brought to Ottumwa this morning and taken to the home of the grandparents, Mr. and Mrs. A. J. Palmer, 825 Clinton avenue. The funeral services will be conducted at the address given at 2 p. m. Tuesday by Rev. Isaac Bussing. Interment at the Shaul cemetery.

1921

BACK TO NORMALCY IN MORALS IS SLOGAN IN MISSOURI NOW

(By Internaitonal News Service.)

KANSAS CITY, Mo., March 10.—"Back to normalcy in morals."

This is the 1921 slogan of the Women's Christian Temperance Union, according to Mrs. Nellie G. Burger, Missouri State president. The W. C. T. U., while watching hip flasks, parlor stills and "blind tigers," will turn its attention to a crusade for social morality, says Mrs. Burger.

"The pendulum already is swinging back to temperance in morals—even in saneness of woman's dress," Mrs. Burger added. "We had about reached the climax of nakedness in the latter. Recently in Chicago I actually saw a woman with a dress above her kees—above, mind you, and her stockings were rolled down below the knee, leaving her knees bare to the winds.

"It is bad enough when young girls dress this way, but when their mothers and grandmothers, even, do so, it is unspeakable."

Mrs. Burger denied that the W. C. T. U. backed "blue law" legislation or anti-cigarette crusades.

"We will not and have not backed such legislation," she added. "We are not out to take away all the rights and pleasures which men possess."

BASEBALL FOR OTTUMWA NOW EXPECTED WITH PLANS NOW UNDER CONSIDERATION

The legionaires of our local Post through their chairman at last night's meeting have named a committee to materialize a local baseball association, with special appeal to the legion, the commercial travelers and the Burlington contingent that is inclined to the game.

Following up the work of the committee will be a strong effort to negotiate a deal that will secure the west Ottumwa grounds south of Second street and opposite the old Caldwell park, a splendid stretch of ground with natural amphitheatre incline and then plenty of space adaptable to a diamond layout.

This afternoon it was stated progress of the most encouraging character had been made and that Ottumwa surely will have baseball this season.

NEW AIRPLANE MUFFLER INVENTED BY SWISS

(By International News Service)

Washington, March 2—An airplane muffler has been invented in Switzerland whic hhas considerable practical value, according to a report received by the Army Air Service from Major H. S. Burwell, commanding officer of the air station at Weissenthurm in the Coblenz area. It does not overheat, and reduces the motor noise to the extent that conversation can easily be carried on between pilot and passengers in the plane. By use of a suction fan the efficiency of the motor is not impaired through back pressure of exhaust gases. Major Burwell recommends that the air service purchaser construct several types of this muffler for experimental purposes.

OXYGEN RUSHED TO CARUSO

New York, March 2—Three tanks of oxygen were taken last night to the apartments of Enrico Caruso, world famous tenor, ill with pleurisy, who had been operated on earlier in the day to relieve him of a collection of pus on one side of the pleural cavity. It was stated that he was resting easily, but that the oxygen would be necessary to relieve him of unnecessary suffering.

OPENWORK PANELS IN LADIES' HOSIERY

(By International News Service)

London, March 14.—Silk stockings with openwork panels are the newest fashion in ladies' hose.

The panels are about three inches high and one inch broad and are arched at the top, looking like Gothic windows set in groups of two. The flimsiest of silk is used and the stocking look stout enough to last about two days.

APRIL 1921

Apr - US Figure Skating Association is formed

Apr 10 - American actor, author, and professional athlete Chuck Connors is born in Brooklyn

Apr 10 - American vocalist Sheb Wooley, best known for "Purple People Eater", born in Erick, Oklahoma

Apr 16 - British actor, author, and comedian Peter Ustinov born in London, England

Apr 27 - Allied reparations commission announces that Germany has to pay 132 billion gold marks ($33 trillion) in annual installments of 2.5 billion marks, as repayment to the Allies because of the World War

1921

THE OTTUMWA DAILY NEWS

BEAT NEGRO; BRAND HIM WITH "K.K.K."

HAD WHITE WOMAN FRIEND AT HOTEL; IN CONFESSION GUILT WAS ESTABLISHED

Quiet Follows Riot Night

DALLAS, Texas, April 2.—Quiet followed a riotious night during which the KuKlux Klan seized Alexander Johnson, a negro, and carried him to a segregated spot in the suburbs where Johnson confessed to having improper relations with a white woman in one of the leading hotels.

After stripping the negro and beating him until he was unable to stand, the Klan branded his forehead with "K K K."

PLEASANT TWP. FARMERS IN PROTEST OVER HIGH TAXES

City folk are not the only ones who groan under the excessive, extortionate tax being levied. Ottumwa is going pretty strong and there is higher assessments in sight, but the farmer with his fifty-cent-dollar product marching up to pay 100-cent-dollar taxes is adopting a course that will be felt like an earthquake in Wapello county within the near future.

One of the leading farmers of northeast Wapello county handed us the following today. It is a serious document as it reads and the import of it should not be underestimated:

DEMAND FOR RELIEF.
Bladensburg, Iowa,
April 1, 1921.

The problem of increased taxes was up before a determined mass meeting of the taxpayers of Pleasant township, held here today in the township house. The rise in assessments to unprecedented heights, coupled with the fall in prices of farm products, to below pre-war levels, is causing much bitterness among the farmers, who are disposed to hold their servants in public office to strict accountability. Charley Morrison was chairman of the meeting and Madison Warder secretary. The following resolution was unanimously adopted, and signed by 75 per cent of the taxpayers of the township:

"Be it resolved: by the taxpayers of Pleasant township, in convention assembled, that it is our earnest desire that the assessment for the current year be reduced to the 1919 basis; and we demand that our township board make said reduction."

ADAMS SCHOOL WILL MOVE SOON CHICAGOAN'S HERE

The massive, powerful equipment that arrived today from Chicago and is being taken to the Adams school site, will soon be in operation. Laborers under skilful direction are setting up plans for the removal work, which is practically begun with today's progress made to that end.

CIGARET SMOKING O K AFTER JULY 4, KENDALL SIGNS

Governor Kendall today signed the Dodd bill legalizing the sale of cigarets to adults.

On July 4 the measure will become law, and all dealers must take out licenses, which cost from $50 to $100 annually, and affix state revenue stamps to all cigarets sold.

Sale of cigarets to minors is strictly forbidden. Dealers' permits, which are revokable, are to be issued by city councils and county boards of supervisors.

After signing the bill Kendall issued a statement explaining his action which stated that a majority of the people were opposed to the existing law absolutely forbidding the sale of cigarets and that a "legislative enactment is effective only so far as it is supported by an aggressive public opinion."

"We are confronted, not by an attractive theory but by a practical condition," his statement continues, and he declares that the Dodd measure provides means for checking the sale of cigarets to minors.

The sale or nonsale of cigarets depends upon the discretion of the citizens in any community, acting through their elected representatives, the city council or county board of supervisors and that several hundred thousand dollars will annually accrue to the state through the tax on cigarets.

IOWA IS VOTED NEW FLAG DESIGNED BY STATE D. A. R.

The beautiful state flag for Iowa designed by the D. A. R., the original to be seen at the local Chamber of Commerce where displayed, has been voted the official flag for Iowa by both houses of the state legislature. Up until this year the D. A. R. had sponsored the idea, after submitting the design, and experienced one defeat in attempt to have it legalized, but this year the Women's Federation of the state joined in and the bill has passed.

In a letter to Mrs. F. B. Thrall, the state chairman of the 5,000 D. A. R.'s of Iowa congratulates the local citizen, ardently patriotic member, on the victory and stated that "You may be interested to know that the senator from Wapello not only voted against the measure but opposed it in an impassioned address, which carried little weight however, there being only three dissenting votes in the senate against it and one of those from Whitmore"

BEAUTIFUL IN DESIGN

Mrs. Thrall briefly described the Iowa flag by saying it was in blue, white and red, the French arrangement, and that the white carried the picture of the eagle with pennant in his claws reading after the state seal, Our liberties we prize and our rights we will maintain. Beneath the pennant is the word, IOWA, in red.

Local D. A. R. members are amazed at the very active opposition launched by Senator Whitmore and comment that all soldiers in the legislatures were for the bill.

"We had a flag before there were any soldiers, for that matter," stated one D. A. R. member.

That the local women should have had such a large part in getting the flag legalized, meeting with success for their endeavors, is of more than passing concern.

The flag is not a D. A. R. flag, the design being significantly a design to fittingly symbolize Iowa.

BRIDE AT FOURTEEN IS LATEST RECORD FOR LOCAL COUPLE

Not often they request a marriage license for such youthful couples as this one. District Court Clerk Dungan today issued a permit to wed to Roy Lathrop (17), Ottumwa, and Miss Mary 14-year-old daughter of Mrs. Ira Walker, who signed consent to the nuptials.

The bride-elect was slightly past the fourteenth birthday and with parental sanction was eligible for the altar under the Iowa laws which fixed the minimum at fourteen.

The ceremony was performed by Justice H. J. Cremer.

MR. HARDING'S TROUBLES
(New York World.)

"Government is a very simple thing, after all," remarked Mr. Harding during the campaign, but Mr. Harding as president of the United States is not finding government a very simple thing after all.

For campaign purposes all that was necessary to put the country on its feet after the most devastating war known to human history was to elect a Republican President and a Republican Congress. Then everything would automatically be for the best in the best possible of worlds. It is quite a different story, however, when campaign rhetoric is subjected to the acid test of responsible administration.

Although the Harding Administration is not yet three weeks old, Mr. Seibold, The World's political correspondent, reports from Washington that "a pronounced note of pessimism" regarding the outlook for economic and industrial relief is always prevalent in the discussions between high officials of the Administration and the newspaper representatives. There is plenty of ground for pessimism, but the Republican Party, or to put it more precisely, the Republican Party in Congress, is the architect of its own blocked peace and reconstruction for two years, it is now confronted with all the consequences of its folly and mendacity.

The Harding Administration is on its way, but it does not know where it is going. It has no foreign policy that it can define, and it has no domestic policy that is worthy of the name.

MINISTER DISGRACED; SUICIDES

MARIETTA, Ohio, April 6.—Rev. J. H. Mindling, Methodist minister, committed suicide in the court house at noon today. He had just stepped from the courtroom where an inquest was being held on the death of his 19-year-old daughter, Elizabeth, upon whom, he confessed, he had performed a criminal operation which resulted in her death last Thursday.

ELECTRICITY WILL DETERMINE THE KIND OF VOCATION

(By Intrnational News Service)

Denver, April 9.—Dr. H. P. von David, noted psychologist, who made known in 1915 that he was developing a system for the "mechanicalization of the mind," has established a laboratory in this city and will continue experiments in an effort to perfect the mechanism, that will read the human mind.

Dr. von David's theory is based on the fact that the emotions experienced in the human mind give varying reactions when an electrical current is passed through the body, and the expects to construct a machine that will read the mind of a child, determine its latent possibilities, and establish a vocation more favorable to the individual's capacity.

MORE JOBLESS THAN AT ANY PERIOD SINCE 1915, SAYS RESERVE BOARD

WASHINGTON, April 1.—The federal reserve board has announced that unemployment is due to reduced volume of trade and continues one of the most unfavorable factors in the general economic situation. Employment is still lower, with the exception of a few special industries due to seasonable orders. The only bright spot in the labor situation is noted in sections where the demands of the country and districts has absorbed much unemployed labor. Relief agencies have reported more unemployed in the middle west than any time since 1915. The increase of the jobless is from 10 to 15 per cent as shown in Kentucky, Missouri, Arkansas and Indiana. The conditions in Illinois district are slightly less favorable.

GENERAL CONSTRUCTION OF HIGH SCHOOL BUILDING, OTTUMWA, IOWA.

Notice is hereby given that the Board of Education of the Independent School District of Ottumwa, Iowa, will receive sealed proposals up to the hour of 7:30 p. m. on Tuesday, April 26, 1921, at the office of the Secretary, for the erection of the new Ottumwa High School, in accordance with the plans and specifications prepared by Croft & Boerner, Architects and Engineers. Separate bids will be received on the following:

(a) General Construction, (b) Reinforcing Steel, (c) Structural Steel and Erection, (d) Power House Stack, (e) Tests and Inspection of Materials.

Bids will be received only on the form of the proposal supplied by the Architects and Engineers and no other form will be considered. Bids must be accompanied with a certified check for the amount of 5% of the bid, made payable to the Secretary of the above School District.

The successful bidders will be required to furnish the above board with an approved surety bond in the amounts called for in the specifications for the above items.

Copies of the plans and specifications may be seen at the Offices of the Architects and Engineers, Secretary of the Board of Education and also at the Builders' Exchanges of Minneapolis, Des Moines, St. Paul, Chicago, and Omaha. Bidders desiring blue prints for their own exclusive use may obtain same from the office of the Architects and Engineers, and such bidders will be required to pay the net cost of blue printing. A deposit of $50.00 will be required for all copies of plans and specifications, which amount, minus blue print cost, will be refunded upon the return of plans and in case a bona fide bid is submitted.

The Board reserves the right to reject any or all bids.

J. A. WAGNER, Secretary.
C. D. EVANS, President,
Board of Education, Independent School District, Ottumwa, Iowa.
CROFT & BOERNER, Architects and Engineers, 1006 Marquette Ave., Minneapolis.

1921

New Tuberculosis Vaccine is Discovered by British Surgeon

Ravages of the Great White Scourge May Be Checked if New Serum Proves Curative—Tested with Success in Cattle—Result of Eighteen Years of Research.

The following table shows the death rate from tuberculosis in the United States in 1918, as compiled by the United States Bureau of Census.

Total deaths in U. S. in 1918 1,471,367
From tuberculosis 114,275
(5,910 of these died from tuberculosis meningitis, the rest from tuberculosis of lungs)
Tuberculosis of lungs 108,365
Rates per 100,000 population 132.4
Per cent of total deaths .. 0.4
Tuberculosis meningitis.. 5,910
Rate per 100,000 population 7.2
Per cent of total deaths 0.4

Tuberculosis ranked fourth in the death toll of disease in 1918. Influenza was first pneumonia second, organic diseases of the heart third, tuberculosis fourth, cerebral hemorrhage or softening fifth and cancer sixth.

Tuberculosis in 1918 took 15,007 lives in New York; Pennsylvania, 11,401; Illinois, 7,691; Ohio, 6557; California, 5,429; Massachusetts, 5,184; Mississippi, 4,477; Tennessee, 4,303; New Jersey, 4,295; Kentucky, 4,234; Indiana 3,470.

Utah suffered least with 178 deaths; Vermont, 312; Montana, 442; Oregon, 561.

(By International News Service)
London, April 30.—Has science discovered a vaccine which will effectually prevent tuberculosis, the Great White Scourge? After eighteen years of research, Dr. Nathan Raw, president of the Tuberculosis Society of Great Britain has announced to the Royal Society of Medicine that he believes he has been successful in this quest.

"We have reluctantly to admit," said Dr. Nathan Raw, that we have not got a specific remedy which will effectively destroy in the body the tubercle bacilli which are the cause of the disease. But immunity to resist attack by virulent bacilli can be secured by producing an artificial active immunity in the tissues to the bacillus itself."

There are two distinct types of tuberculosis, states Dr. Raw, one human and one bovine, and the bacilli that cause them are antagonistic to one another. Bovine bacilli render human beings immune and vice versa.

From this discovery Dr. Raw started

HOLDS AIR FORCE WINS NEXT WAR; GIVES A REASON

British General Says Lessons of Last War Proved Necessity for Penetrating Heart of Enemy's Country.

By EARL C. REEVES,
International News Service Staff Correspondent.

London, April 4.—The great war proved that warfare must, in these days of modern invention, be carried into the heart and centre of civilian populations and that offensives must be instantaneous and launched first from the air.

Major General Sir F. H Sykes, controller-general of civil aviation, lays down these new principles of modern warfare and outlines others so graphic as to overshadow the products of the imagination of H. G. Wells.

He is conducting an fight for the development of civil aviation in order that Britain may build, in peace time, the framework of a great war machine. For he sees the days of Britain's supremacy through her felet near an end, and the possibilities of strangling an enemy by blockade waning.

"In 1914," General Sykes declares, "it was some twenty days between the declaration of war and the exchange of the exchange of shots. In the next war, between great powers a mobile force of aircraft will be ready for action before the signature of the declaration is dry and the air battle will be joined in as many hours."

WILL LAND VALUES DROP?
(Dubuque Times-Journal.)

You who own land or are thinking of buying, lately have wondered: "Are land values going to depreciate along with the general deflation of prices?

The value of farm land during the past year decreased seven per cent, says the Department of Agriculture. Here is its estimate of the average value of an acre of plow land in the United States.

March 1, 1914	$52.94
March 1, 1916	$58.00
March 1, 1917	$62.17
March 1, 1918	$68.38
March 1, 1919	$74.31
March 1, 1920	$90.01
March 1, 1921	$83.78

The drop in farm land values has been greatest in southern states—22 per cent in Georgia and 24 per cent in Kentucky. That's due to the cotton and tobacco situation.

Iowa has the highest-priced farm land —averaging $200 an acre, compared with $219 a year ago.

Nepotism At White House

WASHINGTON, April 2.—The Department of Justice has announced the appointment of Rev. Heber Votaw of Tokoma Park, Maryland, Superintendent of the Federal Prisons. Votaw is a brother-in-law of President Harding and will take office April 6.

The Daily News, 60 Days, $1.00

PHONE 2400

AUTO IN PLUNGE, ONE BADLY HURT TWO INJURED

One seriously hurt and at the St. Joseph hospital, two others injured and the fourth shaken up, totals the casualty list of an automobile nose-dive off the Vine street embankment at the south end of the Vine street bridge about 3:40 Sunday afternoon.

I. O. Brink, Davenport, here in charge of a crew that is engaged in replacing telephone poles on the Bloomfield road for convenience of the graders, is badly hurt and at the hospital found to be crushed about the chest where the car rested upon him after the 20 feet plunge. Report was first that Brink had suffered a broken back but Manager England of the phone company who is looking after the injured men and in behalf of the company, said an X-ray taken of Brink's injuries did not reveal a serious back injury but physicians declare he is badly hurt. He's now under influence of anaesthetics and only semi-conscious today, hence cannot tell much about how it happened. His wife and daughter arrived last night from Davenport.

Next apparently in the list as most damaged by the accident is Frank Brady, 2006 Bertha street, a phone call at 2 o'clock this afternoon stating that he is in considerable pain.

Ray Morrison, also of Ottumwa, is a sufferer and only one of the four escaped with only bruises and a shake-up.

NO BLAME IS FIXED.

From the Brady home comes a statement that it is apparently nobody's fault through carelessness that the accident occurred. Brady was driving, as the story is related, the machine headed south. A short distance from the bridge it was the purpose of Brady to pass an automobile just ahead and he started to execute the turn and just then some people started to leave the side of the road and approach the car ahead, which would bring the pedestrians right in the path of the Brady car. Seeing a collision was threatened Brady slowed and veered when behind the advanced car again he is thought to have lost control and the crash against the embankment railing followed, all four men and machine plunging down to the bottom of the bank, a distance of about twenty feet.

The city ambulance was called at once, and Brink, seen to be the most serious case, was taken to the hospital arriving at 4:20 with Driver Ryttenberg making a record drive, forty miles an hour, and taking desperate chances in the midst of the Sunday afternoon traffic.

Late today it was yet a question whether Brink would survive, but chances were reported in his favor.

ISSAAC O. BRINK DIES OF INJURY IN AUTO UPSET

Isaac O. Brink, injured in the auto wreck Sunday afternoon, passed away at 9 o'clock late evening at the St. Joseph hospital at the age of 43 years. He is survived by his wife, Mary, one daughter, Pearle, his parents, Mr. and Mrs. P. H. Brink of Dubuque, one sister, Mrs. Ida Delbridge of Cedar Rapids, one brother, John, also of Dubuque. The body was taken to the Moroney Funeral Home. The body left the home at 1 o'clock this afternoon and sent to Dubuque, at 1:53. Funeral announcement later.

KRAMER'S SUGGESTIONS HELD NOT ACCEPTABLE; NEW COM. NAMED SOON

WASHINGTON, April 8.—Tentative regulations for prescribing beer and wines by physicians as drawn by prohibition Commissioner Kramer's legal staff, is not to be approved by the Revenue Commissioner Williams, he announced today. Williams said that he would consider regulations which he understands would limit beer prescriptions to two bottles per day. The approval will be left to the new commissioner who is soon to be named.

Responsibility for the issuance of permits to manufacture real beer under the ruling of Former Attorney General Palmer will fall upon new commissioner of internal revenue, it was learned today. A hundred applications for permits to breweries are on file. No permits can be issued until regulations are promulgated.

TWO WEEKS FOR CLEAN UP WITH DRIVE ON ALL DIRT

Secretary Bond of the Chamber of Commerce says everything is ready for Monday when the start will be made to clean up Ottumwa and the first attack in cooperation with Lincoln school, thence to another school and on and on for the entire week in North Ottumwa, the second week in South Ottumwa.

"The city will furnish four teams and men and all organizations will be with us and Ottumwa is going to have the biggest drive of its kind in history," according to Mr. Bond.

The group committee will be leading the army of gleaners and cleaners and stick through to the finish.

"SPOONING PARK" FOR KANSAS TOWN

(By International News Service).

Kansas City, Kan., April 8.—Boy, page Mr. Cupid."

Louis H. Chapman, water commissioner, has officially decreed that Kansas City shall have a "Cupid's" park. Because "spooning" is condemned in other city parks, his department will set aside eleven acres of land to be converted into a park. In Chapman's park there will be "nooks", benches and swings, just comfortable for two. Chapman says so himself.

"There is no place where young couples can go for spooning purposes," Chapman declared. "So my department is going to give them a park. We were all young ourselves."

1921

LONG PHONE TALK BY 2 PRESIDENTS

President Harding at 5:30 last evening, New York time, talked over the new U. S.-Cuba telephone wires and chatted pleasantly with the new president of that republic, President Menocal.

Across the United States, in many of the more important cities, and extending even to the Catalina Islands of the Pacific, the wire was left "open" and Harding called the towns in order and responses were made, the novelty for the elight of Menocal.

As a compliment to the two presidents, and incidentally the Bell System, will stage the longest telephone conversation in number of miles ever known. This will consist of a roll-call of cities from Havana, Cuba, all the way across the United States to Catalina Island in the Pacific ocean on the coast of California.

This talk, a combination of deep sea cable, land lines and wireless telephone, will be heard not only by President Harding and President Menocal, but several thousands gathered in the Pan-American Union building in Washington and in the presidential palace at Havana.

The cross-continent Atlantic to Pacific talk was made permissable by the deep sea cable from Key West to Havana, the longest deep sea telephone cable in the world, an instrumentality in which many serious engineering and electrical problems have been solved.

The line used today is 5,762 miles in length, and the roll-call will be heard in Havana, Richmond, Philadelphia, Harrisburg, New York, Pittsburg, Chicago, Omaha, Denver, Sacramento, San Francisco, Los Angeles and other points

FRANCE PLANS NEW WAR SHOULD GERMANY FAIL

Paris, April 16.—France today put the finishing touches on the preparations for the new war against Germany if necessary, in case Germany fails to meet the reparations and demanys by May first. France will strike hard even if the Allies fail to co-operate with the occupation of the Ruhr district, which is Germany's richest reservoir of natural resources, is where the first blow will be delivered.

Premier Briand today advises the French cabinet that it might also prove to be advisable to occupy the district adjoining Ruhr, including portions of Westphalia. Possibility of blockading Hamburg was also discussed. The cabinet approved of Marshal Foch's plans for occupation and suggested that classes of 1918 and 1919 be mobilized for any eventuality.

5 YEARS FOR BROWN, HE STOLE CLOTHES AND PLEADS GUILTY

Glenn Brown pleaded guilty to the stealing of clothes from one of the business firms of Ottumwa and this afternoon at 2 o'clock he stood up before Judge Cornell and received a five years' sentence to the state reformatory prison at Anamosa. Brown is about 20 and an Ottumwan. It is reported that he had been a close friend of the woman who was apprehended in the theft case as having received stolen goods, and for which act she is serving 30 days in jail under sentence from Judge Kitoo.

Brown will probably leave for his new address Monday, along with four other similarly tagged. On the same day a sixth criminal is expected to leave Ottumwa for a considerable stay, five years at Fort Madison, which makes a halfdozen and the seventh may be coming up, as they say at the ball game.

Ottumwa Daily News

RUTH OUT TO MAKE NEW RECORD

(International News Service.)

NEW YORK, April 13.—Seventy-five homers in 1921! Babe Ruth started his quest for the new record here today when the Yankees and Philadelphia Athletics opened the local baseball season at the Polo Grounds.

Thousands of New Yorkers vied with each other to get into the big stadium to see the Yanks and the "Big Bambino" swing into action. Ruth is the greatest card in baseball, and though he found it difficult to take off poundage accumulated during the Winter and entered today's game still a trifle over weight, his attack on his own record of fifty-four home runs made last year will be watched with the keenest interest.

MAN HAS COLLISION WITH STREET CAR; MAY NOT RECOVER

While attempting to cross the street opposite the Wapello Restaurant about 6:30 last evening, James Telfer, one-time business man of this city, in conduct of the Longfellow Book Store at one time, stepped in front of an oncoming street car which struck him down. The skull of the unfotrunate man was fractured and his unconscious condition this afternoon at 2:30 indicated small chance for recovery. He is at the Ottumwa hospital and this morning his sister, Miss E. A. Telfer, arrived from Chicago. Mr. Telfer is well advanced in years and not robust in health. There is no blame attached to the car operator in the story told by those who witnessed the accident.

OFFERS TO SELL WIFE FOR $5; SHE SUES HIM

Chicago, April 15.—Frank Byrns, a tailor, offered his wief for sale for $5 and now it looks as though he will have to pay fifty times that much defending the divorce suit filed yesterday by Elsy Byrns, 6358 Melrose street. One sentence in the bill reads:

"In August, 1920, the edefendant offered me for sale to any friend for $5."

They were married in 1911 and have two children.

1921

OBITUARY

Joseph Oliver, infant son of Mr. and Mrs. C. B. Wilson, died this morning. Besides the parents surviving are two brothers and two sisters. The funeral service will be held from the residence, 719 Gladstone street, Tuesday morning at 10 o'clock with Rev. Burroughs officiating. Interment in the Brooks cemetery.

OBITUARY

Melvin Leo, 6-year-old son of Mr. and Mrs. Vern Wilson, died last night at the home of his parents, 719 Gladstone street, at 10:30 o'clock. Besides his parents, he is survived by two sisters and one brother. The funeral will be held Sunday at 2 p. m. with Rev. Burroughs officiating. Interment at the Burch cemetery.

Three Are Called From One Home In 21 Days

Three children taken from the home of Mr. and Mrs. Verne Wilson, 719 Gladstone street, is the sorrow of loss sustained within three weeks, two of the children victims of scarlet fever.

The latest and third death was that of Violet Fayette, aged 8, which occurred at nine o'clock last evening. The funeral will be held at 2 o'clock tomorrow afternoon, interment at the Brooks cemetery.

The first death occurred when an infant son of six weeks was found dead in bed Easter morning. Next came the scarlet fever death of Melvin, aged 6, and now the loss of the daughter from the disease, and still another baby child, Donald, not expected to live.

Scarlet fever is a bacterial infection that can occur after strep throat. Even in 2020, there is no vaccine; treatment is typically with antibiotics --which were not available in 1921. Though scarlet fever has never truly been gone, it made a resurgance in 2017 in England, leading to as many as 15,000 cases per year in the country.

Symptoms include a telltale red rash that covers most of the body, very red and sore throat, high fever, headache, body aches, a red and bumpy tongue ("strawberry tongue"), and bright red skin in the creases of the underarm, elbow, and groin. Individuals who are infected can spread the disease

FOURTH CHILD DIES AT WILSON HOME

Mary Maxine Wilson, 4, died at the home of her parents, Mr. and Mrs. Verne Wilson, 719 Gladstone street at 2 a. m. Sunday. She is survived by the parents and one brother, Donald. A private funeral was held this afternoon at 2 o'clock with Rev. Burroughs officiating. Interment at the Brooks cemetery.

Little Mary Maxine is the fourth child that has been taken from this home within thirty days. Donald, 2, is not expected to live. He is the surviving child of the little family. Three of the four deaths were caused from scarlet fever.

FIFTH DIES TODAY IN WILSON HOME, SOUTH OTTUMWA

The fifth child died this morning at 10:30.

Here is the mortuary record in the now childless home of Mr. and Mrs. Verne Wilson, 719 Gladstone avenue, Ottumwa.

In order of the deaths, all within 30 days, is recorded:

Joseph Oliver Wilson, aged 6 weeks, died March 28, 1921, of inanition

Melvin Leo, aged 6 years, 10 mos. 7 days, died April 15, 1921, of scarelt fever.

Violet Fayette, aged 8 years, 8 mos., died April 20, 1921, of scarlet fever.

Mary Maxine, aged 4 years, 8 mos., died April 24, 1921.

Donald, aged two years died at 10:30 a. m., April 27, 1921, of 'flu' following scarlet fever, whose funeral services will be conducted from the home at 2 o'clock tomorrow afternoon. Interment at the Brooks cemetery in the new family lot, which for the first time is to be visited by the mother as Donald is tenderly laid away.

Rev. U. Earl Burroughs officiates for the fifth call to his services and is to use the same text Thursday for the last child of the household as for the other four preceding in death within four weeks, his sermons from the text: "The Lord is my Shepherd, I shall not want."—23rd Psalm. Also "Let not your heart be troubled, ye believe in God, believe also in Mee."—St. John 14th chapter first verse.

through coughs and sneezes or by sharing drinking glasses and eating utensils. The disease is also contagious through contact with skin sores and rashes. Most common in children from 5 to 15 years of age, if left untreated it can result in damage to heart, kidneys lungs, and other organs. Rarely, it can lead to rheumatic fever, pneumonia, or meningitis.

The first death in the Wilson family, that of infant Joseph, was reported as caused by inanition -- medically defined as "severe weakness and wasting as occurs from lack of food, defect in assimilation, or neoplastic disease" -- but it seems more likely that this, too, was connected with the scarlet fever which took his brothers and sisters. Scarlet fever sufferers are infectious for up to seven days before symptoms start, and without antibiotics can remain infectious for two to three weeks after the start of symptoms.

1921

WIRELSS GRAND OPERA HAS BEEN ACHIEVED; HEAR SONG FROM FRISCO TO HONOLULU

San Francisco, April 22.—The first attempt to stage a grand opera by wireless was successful when Frieda Hempel singing into a wireless telephone, was heard at Honolulu, southern Alaska, Salt Lake and Point Loma on the Mexican border. Ships 1,500 miles in the Pacific heard the concert.

CITIZENS WAR ON AUTO THIEVES

Des Moines, April 20.—A vigorous drive against automobile thieves in the city, county and state as the next step in the campaign of the citizens' league to rid the city of vice and crime was decided upon Monday at a conference between agents of the attorney general's office and J. B. Weede, president of the league.

Issuance of special cards to automobile owners, bearing all information on their particular car, will be the first step in the drive. The cards will be distributed through the league, according to present plans.

If such a thing is practical the overlay of brick paves in our downtown district with some sort of composition, inches thick, would be a fine setting for the new lighting system that comes into keen discussion and strong probabilities tomorrow evening. All the council has to do is order a certain prescribed area be supplied with "white way" illumination and the thing is done, as a new law requires. Chairman Madden is chief engineer for "W-W" benefits and he is expected to prevail.

Supervisor Knox pleased the city mightily when he declared that at least $15,000 would be available for next year's help-out on paving, and this sum with as much more as the abutting properties will reasonably stand will be applied to paving the thoroughfare known as East Main street, from Iowa avenue to the city limits.

HARDING-MADER CASE TO JURORS THIS AFTERNOON

The Harding-Mader jury retired at 2:15 this afternoon after hours of arguments offered following the close of a salacious case in which the defendants were charged with an immoral crime.

Motion made for a directed verdict in the case of "Ralph Harding" on the grounds that he was a married man failed and the case was fought to the finish in one of the bitterest character attacks in recent years.

Harding, whose real namee is said to be Jones which he admits is the case, registered at the Hotel Ottumwa and that later he and Bernice Mader, wife of Worth Mader, were arrested in his room. Evidence showed that they had been in the room not to exceed 20 minutes, stated by some of the witnesses to be less, when the door was ordered opened by an officer accompanied by the husband's assistants.

County Attorney Roberts in his plea appealed to the jury to consider the situation and the reasonableness of guilt, but followed by White for the defense, later by Duke, it was argued that not one specific thing had developed in the testimony, or could be shown in numerous letters that passed between "Bernice and Joe" to show improper relations.

All yesterday afternoon until court adjourned at five o'clock, and again for the three hours this morning and back again in numbers for to hear the final plea and the instructions of Judge Cornell, men and women, even girls in their teens, were rapt listeners to the risque word portrayals of the attorneys.

It is not generally believed the jurors will be long in reaching a verdict.

Ottumwa Daily News

"The car that takes you there and brings you back"

STAR BALL PLAYERS ASK TRIAL
Chicago, April 29.—Five of the former members of the Chicago White Sox, Buck Weaver, Swede Ruberg, Happy Felsch, Claude Williams and Joe Jackson are under indictment for conspiracy to throw the world series of 1919. They formally demanded immediate trials before Chief Justice McDonald today.

500 KILLED IN THREE MONTHS
DUBLIN, April 1.—Nearly 500 persons were killed in the Irish disorders during January, February and March according to the casualty list which has been compiled today. It shows that 179 crown forces have been killed, 266 wounded; 319 civilians killed and 285 wounded.

1921

DESPONDENT; TAKES OWN LIFE, LEAVES FAMILY

Between the hours of 1:30 and 3:30 Friday afternoon Charles Eakins, 44, 961 West Sherman street, which is in the vicinity of the Milwaukee Junction, took a fatal draught of carbolic acid and died shortly after physicians, Dr. Barton and Dr. Stoker were summoned to attend the case.

Mrs. Eakins had taken one of the younger children to a doctor and leaving home about 1:30, returning at 3:30 an dfinding the blinds drawn and door locked. Calling to her neighbor, Mrs. Joe Best, entrance was forced into the small room where at once the odor of carbolic acid was detected. Eakins was unconscious and lying acorss the bed. He survived only a few minutes after being found. A bottle emptied of the poison was found nearby, every evidencepointing to a suicidal intent. It is believed that despondency was the cause of the act, the man having been out of work for some time.

The body was taken by request of Mrs. Eakins to the Moroney Funeral Home from which funeral services will be held Monday at one p. m. and at two p. m. from the Ormanville church. Interment at Ormanville cemetery.

Mr. Eakins was born in Kansas April 25, 1887. He is survived by the wife, Hattie and sons Ernest, Everett, Robert and daughters Mabel and Virginia, also one brother Albert Eakins of Fremont, Iowa, and one sister, Mrs. Emma Gibson, Seattle.

Unusual community sympathy obtains in this pathetic case because of the destitution apparent, the frail health of the bereaved wife, and her heart's desire to keep the children in one family circle, which is to prove a great trial even if possible to accomplish.

MRS. EAKINS FUND GROWING; THOSE WHO WILL, MAY

Mrs. Eakins and her five fatherless, at 517 Church street, will receive a heartfelt, substantial aid in the fund that is accumulating through the Daily News this week, six full days, ending at this office at 6 p. m. next Saturday night.

Those who contributed today, as follows:

James Naylor	$ 1.00
Mrs. Crabb	1.00
John Crawford	1.00
Florence Richards	2.00
S. C. Snow	1.00
O. B. Feidler	1.00
F. H Finley	1.00
R. Mair	5.00
Rotary Club	30.50

The list will be extended tomorrow with other names and with $43.50 to start the receipts will be of no small help to this worthy family by the close of the week.

Ottumwa Daily News

Better Ice Cream

To The Responsible Dealer in and Around Ottumwa

—Our sign in your Store will be a "Beacon Light" to the ice cream buying public.

We have the goods, plenty of it, and can give you real service.

That's Good News
For the Season of 1921

No war restriction or shortage of materials. Every batch tested and is graded to a positive standard.

You can get it at the busy stores or order it direct when delivery is desired.

Ours is Two-Way Value in Ice Cream

—worth its price in food value and twice that in the fun of eating it.

Graham Ice Cream Co.
PHONE 1960   OPP. POSTOFFICE

THREE PER CENT FOR IMMIGRATION

WASHINGTON, April 20.—The Johnson Immigration bill which is in the same form as it was when it passed both houses last Congress and was vetoed by Wilson, was taken up by the house this afternoon under the agreement allowing for four hours of general debate. Under this bill, immigration will be restricted to three per cent of the respective nationalities residing in the United States as based on the 1910 census.

Those 30c Dinners
and SHORT ORDERS

327 East Main—A Good Place to Eat

HARRY HERMAN
Third Door West Grand Opera House

The Hot Summer Days
Will Soon Be With Us

Will Your Electric Fan Be Ready When These Hot Days Arrive?

We would suggest that you phone us now to look over your fans, clean up and oil. There may be new parts needed which takes several days to get from the factory. Don't delay, do it now; then you will not have to wait when the fan season arrives.

Our Shipment of Westinghouse Fans Will Be Here in About Six Weeks

If you are in the market for a new fan, look first at our stock before you purchase. Westing-house fans deliver more air and give years of service.

Poling Electric Co.

Phone 202   202 E. Second Street

MAY 1921

May 3 - West Virginia imposes first state sales tax

May 3 - The province of Northern Ireland is created within the United Kingdom.

May 14-15 - Major geomagnetic storm – most intense geomagnetic storm of the 20th century. Northern lights were visible throughout the eastern US. Telegraph service slowed and then stopped due to blown fuses and damaged equipment, but damage was limited because the storm occurred before the general dependence on electricity in the developed world.

May 19 - The Emergency Quota Act is passed by Congress, establishing national quotas on immigration and drastically limiting immigration from Eastern Europe.

May 25 - In the Irish War of Independence, the Irish Republican Army occupies and burns the Custom House in Dublin, the center of local government in Ireland.

May 31 - Tulsa race riot begins

LABOR IS DEMORALIZED WITH THOUSANDS DAILY ADDED TO IDLE RANKS

New York, May 3.—The situation on the world's labor front is grave today.

There are 20,000 marine workers idle here, 10,000 printers out at Indianapolis, 12,000 print paper makers out at Albany, 25,000 building tradesmen out at Cleveland, and 1,500,000 of the coal miners are out in England.

Other places that are affected are St. Louis, 3,000; Denver, 2,000; Pittsburgh, 10,000; Youngstown, Ohio, 4,000 and Wheeling, W. Va., 4,000. Both morning and evening newspapers at Glen Falls have been suspended because of the printers' strike.

1921

$412,888 CONTRACT GETS O.K.

Contracts for the construction work in the erection of Ottumwa's $700,000 high school building have been negotiated. An agreement was reached this morning following a conference between the architects and the board.

The general construction contract goes to a national construction company of Minneapolis. The figure is $412,888. This was the bid submitted yesterday and rejected but finally accepted when concessions were made by the bidder which represents the valuation of several thousand dollars. Members of the board expressed themselves as highly pleased with this contract. There were six bidders and the range was from $412,888 to $539,000.

The contract for reinforcing steel construction was in a range from $21,569 to $26,000 with five bidders.

Structural Steel and erection bids range from $15,328 to $20,070, with seven bidders.

The general construction cost, $412,888, does not include what is designated as the mechanical costs which has reference to such items as heating, plumbing, lighting or plastering and is exclusive of the excavation work.

60 TO 80 CENTS, HR. "HI" WAGE

FIRM GETTING SCHOOL CONTRACT WILL PAY MINNESOTA SCALE FOR CARPENTERS

The News carried a front page story announcing the new High school contract to be let at $412,888 to National Construction company, Minneapolis. This particular contract for general construction and not including the steel work nor the heating and lighting and plumbing.

Today it is reported that the scale of wage to be paid carpenters will be 65 cents an hour for the rough and 80 cents an hour for the finished carpentry, which is the Minnesota scale. What effect this wage, 65 and 80 cents an hour, will have on the local union scale is not understood at this particular time. Ottumwa's union carpenters are standing firmly for the continuance of the dollar an hour schedule.

Ottumwa Daily News

ONE RECAPTURED, TWO ARE MISSING; OFFICERS BUSY

Andrew Schwendeman, one of the three men who broke jail here at 2:30 Tuesday afternoon was recaptured at 10 o'clock last night. He was discovered in hiding in the brush north of the city and was soon back in his accustomed place and ready to appear for that sentence which is due him today, on a charge of forgery of which he was convicted a few days ago.

Both Isaacson and Able are still at large. They are described as follows:

HILMER ISAACSON: Six feet, slender, blue eyes, shocky black hair combed straight back, with suit of blue, pin stripes, brown oxfords. Weighs 150; age 24.

CLARENCE ABLE: 5 feet 11 inches, light brown hair, blue eyes, wearing nearly blue overalls and dark cap. No coat. Weighs 165; age 18.

"UNLOADED" GUN TAKES ITS TOLL.

Fairfield, Ia., May 3.—Paul Martin, aged 8, son of Swan Martin, residing four and a half miles northwest of here, was shot and killed while playing with his 11-year-old brother in their home today.

The Martin brothers, in company with four neighbor children, were playing on an upper floor of their home. Two guns were found and were being used in their play.

With the words, "I'll shoot you!" shouted in childish play, a 22-calibre rifle, believed by the children to be unloaded, was discharged in the hands of the dead child's brother.

The gun's charge struck Paul in the forehead. Death was instantaneous.

ALLIES' ULTMATE DEMAND SIGNED; INVASION ORDER IS DUE MIDNIGHT, 11TH

Stresman Succeeds Ebert

ALLIES DEMAND FULL PAYMENT

London, May 5.—The Allies today formally called upon Germany to pay the war indemnity in full and to meet all other demands of the treaty on the penalty of invasion. The Allied ultimatum was signed by the statesmen attending the Supreme Council at 10 o'clock and an hour later was delivered to the German ambassador.

The ultimatum expires at midnight, May 11. The ultimatum demands that Germany pay within 25 days, 1,000,000,000 gold marks which is one half of the initial indemnity.

It is announced that within 25 days the Allies will establish a committee on guarantees and will include a report to the United States in event the American government desires to accept the formal invitation or to participate.

1921

THE OTTUMWA DAILY NEWS

OTTUMWA, IOWA, FRIDAY, MAY 6, 1921

3 LIVES TAKEN AT VINE ST. CROSSING

Number of Tragedies Annually on Railroad Tracks is Crime of State

MAN, WOMAN, GIRL DIE UNDER WHEELS, BODIES DECAPITATED, MANGLED

Four Others in Hospital

The dead are:

Ed. E. Kelly, 42, C. B. & Q. track fore-driver of the car, 234 Freitag avenue.

Mrs. Elina Williams, 60, mother-in-law of Mr. Kelly, also of 234 Freitag avenue.

Pauline Frazier, 12, granddaughter of Mrs. Williams, of Brush, Colo.

The injured:

Miss Roxey Downing, 16, Albia road, sustained compound fracture of right leg, below knee, and several deep puncture wounds on body, will recover.

Mrs. Ed. Kelly, 40, wife of Mr. Kelly, very seriously injured about hips, back and head, pelvic bone broken.

Miss Stella Shelton, 25, 2014 Roemer, painful contusions and bruises. Condition not serious.

Floyd Shelton, 18, 2014 Roemer, brother of Miss Shelton, painful but not serious contusions and bruises.

A fatal and horrible accident occurred at the Vine street crossing, last night, at about 9:30 o'clock, when the Ford touring car of Edward E. Kelly, track foreman for the C., B. & Q., was struck by a cut of freight cars. Seven persons were in the car, three of whom were killed instantly and the other four injured.

CAUSE OF ACCIDENT.

The cause of the accident does not seem to be very clear, but it is supposed Mr. Kelly, who purchased the car, new, only some three weeks previously, and was learning to drive, became confused when arriving at the crossing, and seeing the approaching train.

According to the best information obtainable, he apparently halted the car at the crossing, but suddenly slipped his gear into the low, and the car is said to have fairly leaped onto the track in front of the cars.

HAVOC FRIGHTFUL.

The havoc wrought was frightful. The occupants were dumped upon the track and the car carried a distance of some sixty or seventy feet on west, and completely demolished. The bodies of the dead victims were horribly mangled from being ground under the wheels of the cars.

VICTIMS BEHEADED

Mrs. Williams and Mr. Kelly were completely beheaded, their heads being ground off their bodies. Nearly every bone in little Pauline Frazier's body was broken and a great, gaping wound made in the back, which all but severed the trunk. The skull was also crushed.

Of the injured, Mrs. Kelly was the worst. Her back, head and hips were badly injured, from being dragged along the ties before the train could be stopped.

Miss Downing suffered a compound fracture of the right leg below the knee and several deep wounds. Miss Shelton and her brother, Floyd, were the more fortunate of the occupants of the car. They sustained no serious injuries, being badly shaken up and sustaining only skin bruises and contu-

(Continued on Page Four)

FOURTH DEATH IS IN RECORD TODAY, MRS. KELLY DIES

Mrs. Edward E. Kelly, 234 Freitag avenue died at the Ottumwa hospital at 1 o'clock this afternoon, as a result of injuries sustained in the Vine street crossing accident Thursday night, May 5. Mrs. Kelly was known to be the most seriously hurt of the four survivors of the accident. Her husband, Edward E. Kelly, her mother, Mrs. X. A. Williams, and her niece, Pauline Jones, were killed instantly.

Mrs. Kelly's remains were removed to the Roscoe Funeral Parlors. Funeral announcements will be made later.

Of the remaining three survivors, Floyd Shelton, 2014 Roemer, who sustained only contusions and bruises, left the hospital Sunday. The other injured, Miss Stella Shelton, sister of Floyd, and Miss Roxey Downing, remain at the hospital. Miss Shelton sustained painful bruises and contusions. Miss Downing sustained a compound fracture of the right leg and deep puncture wounds on the body.

Three Lives Taken At Vine Street Crossing

(Continued from Page One)

Ottumwa hospital in passing autos.

RETURNING FROM VISIT.

It seems that the party had spent the evening visiting at the home of the sister of the Sheltons, on the South Side, and were returning home. The accident occurred at the first track on the south approach to the crossing.

SWITCH TENDER THERE

M. S. Ballagh, switch tender at the crossing, it is said, was at his post of duty, and was a witness to the accident. C. A. Barber, 212 Sheridan avenue, night switch foreman, was riding the car, at the head of the cut, which struck the machine. There were eighteen cars in the cut. Engineer Mike Canny, 920 North Cooper, was piloting the engine, while F. W. Wallace, 138 South Willard, was his fireman.

A call was put in for the ambulance from the Ottumwa hospital, but for some cause was unable to get to the scene, which was the reason the injured were taken to the hospital in passing autos. Walter A. Rowen was the first of the undertakers on the scene and the bodies were taken to his morgue on Second street.

IS FIVE-TRACK CROSSING

The tracks of the Burlington, numbering five a few feet east of the crossing merge into three as the switch tender sets the rails, both for the through trains and the switch engine with its cars attached. His business is to take care of the switches. He has a little shanty house at the southwest corner of the crossing and the levers are near. He steps out as occasion requires and handles these levers. He is the man who looks strictly after the company's traffic not that of the public. He is not a flagman. There is no flagman at this crossing, never was, as bystanders explained. And trains at 25 to 40 miles an hour thunder over this crossing without signals displayed to protect the public, except probably in case of mail and passenger trains.

KEEP SPEED GOING ON

The company did not order any change in the rate of speed. As soon as a clear track was gained the thousands of tons of iron was projected with usual velocity at this death spot. No flagman was on duty at 9 o'clock this morning when the scores of people visited the scene, as the railroad track workers moved the demolished automobile to the freight house and housed it. City Solicitor Hunt and a News representative asked questions and answers that trains "went through here at high rates of speed and there was no regular flagman."

ROCK ISLAND INTERESTED

The Rock Island company has two tracks over Vine but some distance to the north of the Burlington tracks. The Rock Island keeps a man guarding from six in the morning until four in the afternoon. And two trains only after four o'clock, and the company has enforced the order rigorously. It is declared that no trains run faster than five miles an hour after leaving May street, East Ottumwa.

REJECT VIADUCT PLAN

Ottumwans will recall that the railroad commissioners decided in favor of the Burlington last year when the city tried to secure a viaduct structure over the tracks, which would mean an expenditure of probably $200,000. Today three victims are sacrifices to this decision for delay.

Then there is a decision of the supreme court handed down less than five weeks ago in which it is held that the public must "stop, look and listen" as practically an exclusive obligation for its safety. In this decision, as remarked by an Ottumwa attorney today, there is slight chance in any circumstances for damage recovery where an accident occurs on an Iowa highway railroad crossing.

ARRANGEMENTS FOR INQUEST.

Owing to some difficulty in getting witnesses together and arranging other details, the coroner, Dr. Hammer, could not give the exact time for the holding of the inquest, but it will probably be held some time this evening.

The funeral of Mr. Kelly will probably be held Sunday, the Rev. Fisher of the East End Presbyterian church, officiating. The arrangements for the funerals of Mrs. Williams and her granddaughter have not been made.

It is understood little Pauline Frazier, who is from Brush, Colo., was here at the home of the Kellys on account of better school facilities. She had been attending the Garfield school, it is said.

MRS. KELLY CRITICAL

Mr. Kelly is said to have been an employe of the Burlington at this point during the past twentyfive years.

The condition of Mrs. Kelly, according to reports from the hospital at a late hour this afternoon, was said to be unchanged. Although her condition is very serious, she never lost consciousness.

1921

DRAIN ALL GARBAGE WRAP IT. LEAVE IT FOR COLLECTION MAN

The Clean-Up and Paint-Up campaign is progressing very satisfactorily. The effects of the aint-up end are noticeable even in the downtown district. This is also true of the residential district, and in probably more pronounced proportion. But there is yet considerable to be accomplished.

All garbage should be drained and wrapped in paper and placed at the edge of the alley, where it will be collected by the city teams. In all cases where it is not collected after a reasonable time, property owners are requested to report to the mayor or the Chamber of Commerce.

FLOUR GOLD MEDAL and POCONO
- 49-lb. Sack, each ... $2.50
- 24 1-2 lb. Sack, each $1.25
- 12-lb. Sack, each ... 63c

Shredded Wheat, 13c	Campbell's Soup ... 10c
Quaker Oats, pkg.. 12c	Corn, can 10c
Puffed Wheat, pkg. 12c	No. 3 Can Tomatoes 15c
Kellogg's Corn Flkes 10c	No. 2 Can Tomatoes 10c
Krumbles, pkg. ... 13c	Telephone Peas, can 18c

FRESH GINGER SNAPPS 15c lb.

Jo-Bro-Coffee ... 35c per lb., or 3 lbs. for ... $1

Uneeda Biscuit package ... 7c	Saratoga Flakes, package ... 19c
Graham Crackers, package ... 15c	Potatoes, peck ... 24c

Specials for Friday and Saturday

10-lb. PAIL SORGHUM 85c | Grand Union Tea Co. 222 East Main St. Ottumwa's Leading Tea and Coffee House | 10-lb. PAIL PURE LARD $1.75

There are 22 banking firms, so titled in Wapello county. You might care to look over the list of banks, in Wapello county, where they serve as reservoirs to receive the inflow of money from so many sources, so here they are:

Citizens Savings Bank, Ottumwa.
Farmers and Merchants Savings Bank, Ottumwa.
First National Bank, Ottumwa.
First Trust and Savings Bank, Ottumwa.
Iowa National Bank, Ottumwa.
Iowa Savings Bank, Ottumwa.
South Ottumwa Savings Bank, Ottumwa.
Phoenix Trust Company, Ottumwa.
Wapello County Savings Bank, Ottumwa.
Agency Savings Bank, Agency.
Blakesburg Savings Bank, Blakesburg.
People's Savings Bank, Blakesburg.
Chillicothe Savings Bank, Chillicothe.
Eddyville Savings Bank, Eddyville.
Manning & Epperson State Bank, Eddyville.
Eldon Savings Bank, Eldon.
Farmers and Merchants Savings Bank, Eldon.
First National Bank, Eldon.
Farson Savings Bank, Farson.
Kirkville Savings Bank, Kirkville.

YEAR AGO AND NOW

One year ago today corn was selling at $1.70 to $1.90, oats at $1, hay $32 to $37. These products are delivered in the local market on the corresponding date in 1921 as follows: Corn, 45c to 50c; oats 32c to 35c, hay $12 to $15. And there is such sharp fluctuations in wheat that the newspaper can not reach the public fast nor frequent enough to gauge the market and sales, the few that are made, are arranged by telephone.

This is the readjustment to a vengeance. What say the rest of the labor of the world to the conditions to which our greatest industry is reduced? Would you take a farm as a free-will offering and pay interest on the land value investment for what you'll get out of it this year?

MUSCATINE GIRL CROSSES CHANNEL IN AN AIRPLANE

Muscatine, May 5.—The thrill of a voyage, via airplane, from Paris to London, is described by Miss Florence Martin of Davenport and Chicago, daughter of C. D. Martin of this city, in a letter just received by him.

Miss Martin, who is in charge of the interior decorating department of the Marshall Field store, Chicago, has been abroad since the first of the year, and is at the present time on her return trip home.

In telling of her very interesting aerial trip, Miss Martin writes:

"We flew from Paris to London in two and three-quarters hours, averaging 85 miles an hour, and flying for the most part at an altitude of 5,000 feet. We cut from Paris to Beauvais, then fifty miles or so along the coast and crossed the channel at Dover, making directly for London. We crossed the channel in about twenty minutes."

STAY OUT OF RUTS ON COUNTRY ROADS

Jim Cullen, who owns a farm one mile west of the city, on the new Airline road, is a firm believer in the theory that if farmers and others traveling country roads would keep out of the ruts the roads would be better. He has put a sign, illustrative of "The Faith that's in him," on his automobile, which reads: "Help make better roads—keep out of the ruts." Mr. Cullen says the roads are made into one or two ruts, chiefly because the traveling public follows the "line of least resistance," by going along in the same track made by the man just ahead. If everyone would stay out of the ruts, Mr. Cullen opines, the country roads would soon be in good shape.

COAL VEIN TRAPPED ON NEW HI SITE

A considerable vein of coal was uncovered by the workmen doing the excavating for the new school building at the Adams school yesterday, it is reported. Though the coal is of the surface variety and of not very great value, it is there in some quantity, it is said. A large truck load, in which some goodly sized chunks appeared, was hauled out last evening.

POPULATION OF IOWA FOR 1920 IS 2,404,021

Washington, May 14.—The total population of Iowa in 1920 was 2,404,021 of which 1,229,392 were males and 1,174,629 were females, the census bureau announced today. The population of the state increased 8.1 per cent during the decade since 1910, the male population increasing 7.1 per cent and the female population 9.1 per cent. The ratio of males to females in 1920 was 104.7 to 100. The white population in 1920 numbered 2,384,181; Negro, 19,005; Indian, 529; Chinese 235; Japanese, 29; Filipinos, 4; all others 8. The foreign born white population numbered 225,647.

1921

MAKES HUSBAND'S TIES

I think I save the most money with the least time expended by making my husband's ties. One-quarter yard of 36-inch silk makes a tie. At Christmas time when I am making several ties I buy three-quarters of a yard of silk and this makes four ties. I use an old tie for a pattern. I also watch the styles and see if they are making them wide or narrow.

MRS. C. W. M'CLANNING

EPWORTH LEAGUE ENTERTAINMENT

Tuesday evening a very unusual program will be given by the Epworth League of the First M. E. church in the social rooms of the church. An Americanization sketch "Lessons in English" will be a feature of the evening. A talented darky family will furnish some real fun. Wib F. Clements, a well known resident of Agency and Wapello county and father of Mrs. W. H. Perdew will portray the aged grandfather and as he recalls the activities of his younger days will deftly handle the banjo and 'fiddle'. A southern darky family looks upon the penny as far superior to the quarter and everyone is invited to attend and come prepared to please the darkies. You are invited.

General Pershing becomes chief of staff of the American army and takes charge July 1, succeeding General March. The honor and responsibility is passed to a deserving and competent military leader no doubt, but the government adds one more of the most pronounced influences for larger army expenses in the appointment. Pershing is ALL war in his ambitions and the 150,000 authorized will probably fall far short of pleasing him as he assumes command.

Arizona's Practical Joke

"A bill, introduced in the current session of the legislature of Arizona to prohibit smoking in public dining rooms and other public places, was first amended to prohibit the consumption in public of peanuts, chewing gum, tea and coffee and then defeated by the senate. The questionnaire returns from that state were 92 per cent 'no.'

"In Iowa where the 'no's' were 95 per cent a bill to repeal the anti-cigarette law has been passed and signed by the governor.

"A bill to repeal the anti-cigarette law in Kansas, with 89 per cent 'no's,' is receiving the attention of its legislature. Last year a petition for a referendum in Oregon to prohibit the use of tobacco failed of sufficient signatures to bring the question to a vote, and 95 per cent of the editors declare their public against legislation. In Oklahoma an anti-cigarette bill has been reported unfavorably in the house. The editors of that state reported 94 per cent against its public support.

"Outside of Utah, where Mormon influence predominates," the article concludes, "the anti-tobacco movement appears, as in the case of Tennessee, Arkansas and Iowa, to be losing ground and is not to any considerable extent supported by the people."

The friends of tobacco feel particularly elated over this showing, inasmuch as 1920-21 was a maximum year in legislative circles with 42 state legislatures in session and the tobacco subject relieved an unusual amount of consideration.

DICE ROLLERS GET FAST IN COILS OF LOCAL POLICE

A squad of police, in charge of Night Captain Criswell, last night made a raid on the home of John Campbell, colored, where they found an African Golf game in progress, it is alleged.

Campbell and seven others, all colored, three of them women, were taken to police headquarters. Campbell this morning paid a ten dollar fine on a charge of conducting a disorderly house, while Frances Carson, Tom Bolton, H. B. Bright, William Hicks, Charles Nichols, Dolly Bright and Madeline Long, each contributed $5 to the city exchequer on charges of being inmates of a disorderly house.

110 In 1921 O.H.S. Class to Graduate June 9th

The Ottumwa graduating class of '21 will number 110 as the list now stands, according to authorized statement made to The News this afternoon.

The commencement exercises will be held the evening of Thursday, June 9, with speakers selected by the class and faculty from the graduating list, according to scholarship and credit marks.

This is within two of the highest number that has graduated any Junetime since 1913. The number that finished the O. H. S. each year follows:

89 in 1914; 87 in 1915; 71 in 1916; 112 in 1917; 72 in 1918; 82 in 1919; 86 in 1920; 110 in 1921.

1921

Crime Wave Increases with Appalling Speed—1920 Had Worst Record in 23 Years

Forgery Becoming Greatest Crime in Point of Number—"Prohibition Is Indirectly to Blame," Says Chief Moran, of U. S. Secret Service.

By HARRY L. ROGERS

International News Service Staff Correspondent

Washington, D. C., May 13.—There was more crime in the United States during the last year than in any year since 1897, according to William H. Moran, chief of the United States Bureau of Secret Service. Though this increased activity of criminals extended to practically every phase of illegal endeavor, bank robbers, counterfeiters and forgers were particularly active.

Unsettled conditions following the war, and prohibition, Chief Moran believes, are in the main responsible for the great increase in crime.

"It has been stated by prominent observers that the returned soldier is responsible for the crime increase," said the veteran Street Service man. "Personally I do not like that manner of stating the situation. While it is undoubtedly true that discharged soldiers have in many instances been implicated in crime during the past year, it is incorrect to infer that there was something in the military experience of our soldiers abroad that made them criminal.

The time may come within your lifetime, when many housewives in Dubuque will receive daily, through wireless telephone, such things as food prices, weather forecasts and even fashion tips.

Ottumwa Daily News

OPTION ON GRAND OPERA HOUSE IS REPORTED TODAY

An option for the purchase of the Grand theatre building was closed this morning In the event the deal is successfully consummated, it is understood the building will be converted to other purposes than amusement, possibly first-class, up-to-date apartment house.

The building is one of the old type of the Grand opera house which is fast disappearing. In all this region there has not been one of the type built in the past twenty years. The old style one-night stand show troops, so frequent in early days, have ceased to exist, on account of high transportation rates, the advent of the movies, and it is now a three night or week engagement system.

The building originally cost around $60,000, but could not be duplicated today, probably, for less than $150,000.

WOMEN GET RULING TO KEEP OFF JURY

Erie, Pa., May 11.—Just how much suffrage women of Pennsylvania are entitled to under the nineteenth amendment was a question raised today by Judge Joseph Bouton in common pleas court when he ruled that women are not eligible to serve on grand or petit juries in Pennsylvania.

Mayor Miles B Kitts was indicted for neglect of office by the February grand jury, following an investigation of vice conditions in this city. The grand jury included seven women, one of whom was foreman.

Counsel for the Mayor attacked the indictment on the ground that women are not entitled to serve on juries in Pennsylvania and the court sustained this view and asked that an immediate appeal be taken to the Superior Court to settle the question finally.

In Schuylkill and other counties decisions have previously been rendered by the courts, individual and en banc that women could not sit on trial juries. That issue has never been decided by the upper courts.

FALSE MOVIE ADS AND CRIME
(By International News Service.)

Washington, May 11.—Fradulent motion picture concerns, promising girls fame and fortune, are responsible for the beginning of much of the waywardness among young girls which is causing the police departments of American cities so much trouble at this time, according to Mrs. Mina C. Van Winkle, head of the Women's Bureau of the Washington Police Department.

"The concerns are to be found in all the large cities," said Mrs. Van Winkle, "and they catch their victims through advertisements in local newspapers." Mrs Van Winkle is the prime mover in the plan to have Attorney-General Daugherty establish a bureau of missing persons under his department. "Women form the major part of the 65,000 missing persons in the United States today," said Mrs. Van Winkle.

1921

Extra Attachments for cleaning mattresses, pillows, portieres, upholstery, etc.

The Electric Cleaner Simplifies Housecleaning

Household labor is greatly lightened with the aid of the Electric Vacuum Cleaner.

Rugs can be thoroughly cleaned on the floor without the necessity of taking them out on the line for beating. The same is true of mattresses, pillows, etc.

Thus, the use of a Cleaner prolongs the life of your furnishings.

Get your Electric Cleaner now—in time for Spring housecleaning.

Ottumwa Railway & Light Co.

Ottumwa Daily News

BOY OF 10 IS HELD AS INCORRIGIBLE; ENTERED HOME

Marion Murphy, 10, son of Mr. and Mrs. William Murphy, 423 Randolph, was arrested today, charged with delinquency and being incorrigible. He is alleged to have entered the Hartley home, 930 West Mill, Wednesday afternoon, and appropriating the contents of two small toy banks. The banks are said to have contained about $1 each, principally in pennies.

Mrs. Hartley, it is said, had been away from the house, and on her return saw the Murphy boy running away. Thinking something was amiss, she gave chase, but the boy eluded her. On investigation, she found that the boy had entered the home via a screen door by using a wire hooked to a corncob to lift the latch.

The boy is to be given a hearing in juvenile court before Judge Cornell at nine o'clock tomorrow morning.

POLING ELECTRIC CO. AND ELECTRICIANS IN AGREEMENT

The Poling Electric company announces that an agreement has been reached with the electricians employed in which the men accept a ten cent an hour reduction, receiving $6.00 a day of eight hours and agreeing to remain on the job with any other craft whether union or non-union. This latter clause in the contractural arrangements reached is of major importance, assuring as it does to the Company, it is stated, a more satisfactory working program and minimizes largely the danger of suspension should non-union men be employed of other crafts.

FINISH PAVING JOB ON NORTH COURT; OPEN IN 3 WEEKS

What is regarded as perhaps the best paving contract completed since West Second street was built with creosoted block is the new piece which extends around the Ottumwa cemetery and finished at noon today.

Just three weeks ago today the firts concrete was poured and marvelous performance of the equipment used by the McCarty Improvement company was a revealtion to local people for expediency and labor-saving.

The scene presented little heavy work being done by men, the crushed rock, cement materials dumped into the giant mixers and poured out in sulshes that spread for yards on the prepared base, then the straight edge to level it pulled by the mechanical power, leaving little for the men to do but keep the system going.

It will be three weeks before the street will be opened to traffic, bringing the thoroughfare back to the public June 17th.

In the meantime detours will be made over streets and roads that have been made passably good by the city.

1921

OFFICERS GET MASH IN RAID

Sheriff George Giltner and Deputy John A. Bright, this morning, located four barrels of mash, composed of corn and molasses, in a high state of fermentation, in a tenement house on the Andrew Swansonplace, south of the Milwaukee terminal. The property had been rented to Bob Huff, and there was nothing else about the place except the mash.

Huff and a friend, J. E. Cummings, were seen about the place recently. Cummings was arrested in January, charged with operating an illicit still, and paid a $200 fine. Huff, however, was the man who had the house rented, and he could not be located by the officers. The mash was dumped.

DRIVERLESS AUTO CAUSES SMASH, ONE IS INJURED

A most peculiar and somewhat serious automobile accident occurred at the corner of Fourth and Market streets, at about 9 o'clock last night when the big Olds car of J. P. Cummings struck a Ford touring car blonging to the E. H. Emery Co. The Cummings car had ben parked at the curb in front of the Ben Ellsworth home on Market above Fifth, and in some manner started up and went down hill, a distance of a block and a half, where it struck the Ford, which was also parked.

Mr. and Mrs. Ed Brewer who were sitting in the Ford, heard the big car coming down the hill, and realizing that something was amiss, started to jump to safety. Mr. Brewer succeeded in extricating himself without injury before the crash, but Mrs. Brewer was not so fortunate. She jumped and was partly hurled by the impact, into a nearby telephone pole, sustaining painful injuries.

The Cummings car was driven to the Ellsworth home by Miss Alice Cummings, daughter of Mr. Cummings, who parked it in the usual manner by setting a front wheel into the curb and applying the brakes. After alighting from the car, Miss Cummings stood for some minutes chatting with frieneds, before going into the house. The car was still at the curb when the party went indoors. It is presumed small boys released the brakes, causing the car to start on its journey.

The big car struck the Ford at the rear, breaking a wheel and smashing in the back end and damaging the top. The Olds was not so badly damaged, the radiator being put out of commission and minor damage done the engine.

Ottumwa Daily News

PARKER, SKY-MAN ALIGHTS AT NOON, TO RESIDE HERE

Fred Parker, piloting the Curtis type biplane of the Ottumwa Aircraft Works the first of four ships to be assembled for that corporation, arrived in the city from Des Moines at noon today.

Mr. Parker started from Mankato, Minn., yesterday morning and expected to arrive in this city yesterday afternoon, but ran into a rain storm in the air which forced him to land at Des Moines and remain last night.

The arrival of the sky ship caused much comment at the noon hour. It is a first-class plane, equipped with all the latest devices and improvements. It is expected the machine will begin making student practice flights soon. A number of prominent men have signified an intention of "going up" at the earliest opportunity, among them Police Judge Kitto and Chief of Police Harry Blizzard.

ALBIAN WILL FLY; BUYS PLANE HERE

M. Plunkerton, of Albia, former garage owner at that place, has purchased a two-seater Curtis biplane from the Ottumwa Aircraft Works, for immediate delivery. Lieut. Powers, pilot of the Aircraft Works, will accompany the plane to Albia, and remain as pilot instructor until Mr. Plunkerton has been taught to pilot the plane. Mr. Plunkerton, it is understood, has had some previous experience in the aerial game.

MAKE DANDY TRIP IN LOCAL PLANE; TO ALBIA TONIGHT

Fred Parker and Willard Bridgeman, aviators of the Ottumwa Aircraft Works were up last evening in the new Curtis ship of the Aircraft corporation, which was piloted to the city yesterday from Des Moines, on a relay stop from Mankato, Minn.

Messrs. Parker and Bridgeman found it necessary to move the plane from the second field in which it landed, on account of being unwelcome in the field. In the first field in which Mr. Parker landed near the city, he was all out of luck, as the farmer who owned the place got all "het up" about it and but for the interevention of Mr. Bridgeman and a third party, might have cut loose at the aviator with a shotgun.

However, the aviators managed to find a field on the Rabbit Track near the Ogg schoolhouse, in which they were welcomed, and everything is running smoothly with them once more, so to speak.

At about four or five this evening, the aviators will go up and make a trip to Albia on business matters connected with the Aircraft Works returning tonight.

RAIL WAGE CUT AFFECTS 2 MILLION; 12 PER CENT MAXIMUM SAY UNIONS

New York, May 18—Samuel Gompers today denounced the decision of the Railway labor board to cut the wages of the employes as unwarranted. "There's no proper justification for the wage cut."

Affects Over Two Millions

Wage reductions for 2,000,000 employes, totalling approxibately $300,000,000 annually, are recommended yesterday by the United States Labor Board.

The new scale is to become effective July 1.

It is expected, according to the board's ruling, that by that date all roads which have not filed wage petitions will have done so to come under the same ruling. These roads have been given until June 6 to file.

Announcement of the decision, which was unexpected, was followed last night by predictions of an early and general reduction in both passenger and freight rates. It was felt that pressure from Washington had hastened the recommendation and that the administration would use this order in formulating and putting into effect the rate cuts.

No exact figures were named in the decision, but the general impression was that the cut would be 12 per cent, the maximum reduction favored by the unions. The unions have sought to hold the cut to 10 per cent, while the roads have been striving to make it 15.

Ottumwa Daily News

JUNE 1921

May 31-June 1 - Tulsa Race Riot (Greenwood Massacre) Mobs of white residents attack black residents and businesses in Greenwood District, Tulsa OK. The official death toll is listed at 36 but later investigations suggest an actual figure between 100 and 300. 1,250 homes are destroyed and roughly 6,000 African Americans imprisoned in one of the worst incidents of mass racial violence in the US.

June 3 - Sudden cloudburst kills 120 near Pikes Peak Colorado

June 6 - Detroit Stars' Bill Gatewood pitches first no-hitter in Negro League history, defeating the Cuban Stars 4-0

June 15 - Bessie Coleman becomes the first African-American to earn an international pilot's license

CONSCIENCE CENSOR FOR BATHING SUITS

Terre Haute, June 4.—"Chest to thigh," is all that a woman's bathing suit has to cover, according to a ruling today by Jack Beattie, police chief.

"Let your conscience be your guide: dress accordingly," is the admonition of the police chief.

"If women want to use a shoe horn to put on their suits, I cannot help it."

SENATE LIMITS ARMY TO 150,000

Washington, June 9.—Rejecting committee provisions rying approximately $354,000,000, and providing for an authorized enlisted strength of 150,000 men, passed the Senate today without a roll call. By a vote of 36 to 32 the Senate had rejected the amendment of the Senate military affairs committee for an enlisted strength of 170,000. The amendment had been adopted yesterday, 44 to 30.

1921

ATTACK ON WHITE GIRL INCITES MOB

HUNDREDS ENGAGE IN BATTLE AT TULSA WITH THREE COMPANIES OF NATIONAL GUARDSMEN CALLED TO QUELL RIOTERS—DEATH LIST REPORTED TO BE SCORE OR MORE.

Tulsa, Okla., June 1.—Continuous gun fire broke out shortly after daylight near the Negro quarters of Tulsa, the scene of all night race disturbances in which hundreds of armed white men and Negroes took part and which resulted in the death and injury of an unknown number of persons and the calling out of Oklahoma National guards to put down the disorders.

Many Believed Dead.

Late reports placed the number of dead in the neighborhood of fifteen.

The firing came from a spot where thruout the early morning hours five hundred men and a thousand Negroes faced each other across railroad tracks. First reports to police headquarters said that the bodies of from six to ten Negroes could be seen lying in a space described as "no man's land." The police also had a report that three St. Louis and San Francisco switchmen and a brakeman had been shot to death. The trainmen were killed, it was reported, because they refused to permit members of the opposing crowds to ride on a switch engine passing between the lines. The engineer was reported to have escaped.

Officials had hoped that with the coming of dawn the trouble, which began over the arrest of a Negro late yesterday for an alleged attack on a white girl, would die out. On the contrary, however, the early morning gun fire was taken as an indication that the riots had been renewed.

NEGRO SECTION ATTACK.

As the dawn broke sixty or seventy motor cars filled with armed white men formed a circle completely around the negro section. Half a dozen airplanes circled overhead. There was much shouting and shooting. A row of houses along the railroad tracks was fired, but lack of wind prevented the flames from spreading. A party of white riflemen was reported to be shooting at all negroes they saw and firing into houses. The negroes were said to be returning the fire dispiritedly.

In a fresh outbreak at 7:30 o'clock in the extreme northern section of the negro quarter Mrs. S. A. Gilmore a white woman, was shot in the arm and side. Mrs. Gilmore was standing on the front porch of her home when she was picked off by a negro, one of a score or more barricaded in a church.

Hundreds of armed white men are being rushed to the district in automobiles. An open battle is believed imminent.

Ottumwa Daily News, FRIDAY, JUNE 3, 1921

WHITES SEEK $500,000 FUND, GRAND JURY INQUIRY IS ORDERED

Tulsa, Okla., June 3.—Grand jury investigation of the race riots here Tuesday night and yesterday will begin on June 8.

Tulsa business men are preparing to rebuild the square mile of Negro homes and stores destroyed by fire.

Thus far the bodies of twenty-one Negroes and nine white men have been found. Local officials, anxious to minimize the losses, say all the dead have been found.

Governor J. B. A. Robertson expressed doubt that any good would result from the inquiry, pointing to a failure in Tulsa County in the case of a lynching.

Relief of Misery

An executive committee of seven appointed at a meeting of fifty prominent Tulsans this morning, announced the committee would undertake first to alleviate the miseries of the Negroes rendered homeless.

A subscription of $500,000 will be asked and the homes actually owned by the Negroes will be reconstructed. No attempt will be made to rebuild the business buildings or homes which were rented.

The committee of seven also voted to employ immediately as extra policemen fifty members of the American Legion.

Speakers blamed the rioting on city and county police officers, whom they accused of an apatheite attitude toward lawlessness. The lax law enforcement by the citizens themselves they found a contributing factor.

Thirteen Negroes Buried.

Thirteen Negroes were buried in the city cemetery without ceremony, for fear of renewd trouble if the burials were attended by any ostentation.

No bodies were found in a preliminary search of the devastated district. It had been believed that many Negroes were shot to death and their bodies burned and for that reason the deaths were placed at 100.

Tulsa tonight had regained its normal appearance, with regular policemen patrolling the downtown district. The martial law declared yesterday was relaxed sufficiently to permit business houses and theatres to operate as usual.

A hard rain that fell all the afternoon and early evening added to the miseries of the hundreds of homeless Negroes.

THE RACE RIOT

Tulsa jumped right in with a frightful vengeance when one of the young women of that community was attacked by a Negro. In Ottumwa it is not so very surprising when the police find a black man and white girl consorting in violation of the moral code.

The north has much to learn about standards of race and assertion of discipline that the white woman may be kept from such association even though she raises no objection to such contact. Our best Negro people contend for this social segregation, to the extent that the backs and whites keep within their own racial boundaries. At that, and particularly in the south, the claim is made the white man has radically transgressed multiplied times over compared with the calendar of sex crimes charged to the black man.

Tulsa has rioted and murdered because of the crime of a Negro and with disregard to law. The question might be reversed to ask how many of the whites in that southern mob can say their family name for generations is stainelss of crime against the black woman?

The other day a prominent Ottumwan returned from Mississippi and after several weeks in a city of 20,000 he reports then nine of every ten Negroes are of mixed blood, that seldom the pure Negro strain, the majority being quarter and eighth blood white.

LEGAL NOTICE

BIDS WANTED

Notice is hereby given that the Board of Education of the Independent School District of Ottumwa, Iowa, will receive sealed proposals up to the hour of 7:30 p. m. on Tuesday, June 28, 1921 at the office of the Secretary for the Repairs and Alterations to the Adams School, in accordance with the Plans and Specifications prepared by Croft & Boerner, Architects and Engineers. Separate bids will be received on the following:

(a)—General Construction.
(b)—Flooring.
(c)—Painting and Decorating.

Bids will be received only on the form of the proposal supplied by the Architects and Engineers and no other form will be considered. Bids must be accompanied with a Certified check for the amounts noted below, made payable to the secretary of the above School Board, to be forfeited to the Owner if the Bidder does not enter into a satisfactory contract and furnish the required bond within five days after acceptance of the bid.

General Construction Cert. Check for $500.

Flooring Cert. check for 5 per cent of bid.

Painting and Decorating Cert. check for 5 per cent of bid.

The successful bidders will be required to furnish the above Board with an approved surety bond in the amounts called for in the Specifications for the above items.

Copies of the Plans and Specifications may be seen at the offices of the Architects and Engineers, Secretary of the Board of Education and the Resident Architect on the site. Bidders desiring blueprints for their own use may obtain same from the office of the Architects and Engineers upon making a deposit of $5.00, which amount will be refunded upon the return of plans and in case a bonafide bid is submitted.

The Board reserves the right to reject any or all bids.

J. A. WAGNER, Sec.
C. D. EVAN, President
Board of Education Independent School District, Ottumwa, Iowa.
CROFT & BOERNER,
Architects and Engineers, 1006 Marquette Avenue, Minneapolis, Minn.

When is the band to play? The public has an $8,500 bandstand and a pretty, recently newly sodded park illuminated with bright lights and the evenings are enchanting. Why not some music? Is it possible that we are to disregard the opportunities to make the best of life? Nothing more charming and restful and prideful than to hear the town band, this big city First Cavalry band, in the twilight hours of an Iowa summer night. Give us music, Mr. Director Cleve. We will appreciate it more than ever with things as they are to enhance the glory of it.

HOUSE BURGLE FREQUENT, POLICE COURT IS BUSY

Quite a number of thefts have been reported to the police department within the past week. In this number is the complaint from Mrs. Ada E. Pelham, Grant and Cooper streets, who reports the loss of $4.50 and a quantity of clothes. The victim is a widow with three children.

1921

SOLDIERS' BONUS SPEEDS UP BY SENATE ASSENT

Washington, June 3.—Definite promises that soldier bonus legislation will be passed at this session of Congress were made today by members of the sub-committee of the Senate finance committee.

Representatives of the American Legion, including its national commander, F. W. Galbraith Jr., appeared to urge action and were assured by Senator McCumber, North Dakota, that leaders in Congress, regardless of party, favor speedy enactment.

ICE CREAM CONSOLIDATION INCREASED 800 PER CENT

Chicago, June 6.—Ice cream, until a few years ago considered a luxury, is today recognized a very nutritious delicacy and it is claimed that in Chicago the increase in output has been 800 per cent in three years. This big increase is enjoyed by manufacturers in all parts of the country. Ice cream is now freely prescribed by physicians where nervous systems need building up and in the summer seasons many homes have ice cream for dessert regularly.

One company in Chicago is reported to make two million gallons of ice cream annually.

WANT ADS

HANDSOME, CONGENIAL YOUNG lady, worth $100,000 is anxious to marry honorable, worthy gentleman. Mar— 508 Lankershim Bldg., Los Angeles, Calif.

Time was when Ottumwa had great multitudes and as a convention city ranked high. Today we have better facilities for handling conventions as to hotels, and just as commodious places for assemblages as in the past. The railroads are running and there is also the motorized mode of travel. Why is it Ottumwa is so shy of public functions? Horace Boies was nominated in Ottumwa and there was a day when we had a coal palace and county fair and features of this character to gain renown. Is Ottumwa a city grown indifferent to her possibilities?

PERSONALS

Mr. and Mrs. R. F. Moroney and Mr. and Mrs. Frank Daggett left this evening for Des Moines to attend the Undertakers' Convention to be held June 7, 8 and 9. The trip will be made overland.

ANNOUNCE TULSA DEATH LIST

Tulsa, Okla., June 7.—The first official list of casualties occurred during the race riots here, made public last by the national guard officials, places the number of white dead at nine and the Negro dead at twenty-six. known white severely injured is given as 16 and the ly injured at 63; Negroes severely injured 72, slightly 163.

CONFERS WITH CABINET ON HIGH PRICES MAINTAINED BY SINISTER INFLUENCES

Washington, June 1.—President Harding and cabinet have discussed certain interests whose activities through organization have kept prices high. The charge of price-fixing is heard.

It is a grave question in the minds of the President and his advisers whether certain "big business" interests have made themselves liable to the anti-trust laws.

Attorney-General Daugherty participated in the discussion and it was indicated that his department is fully prepared to go ahead.

Many big industrial organizations that were turned over to the government with their personnel during the war obtained a vast amount of information concerning production and distribution.

According to information lodged with the President, some of these organizations have since the war utilized the information thus obtained by the government to their own ends, to the general detriment of normal conditions.

It was stated at the White House that no definite, hard and fast policy was decided upon today.

The object of the movement, Mr. Daugherty stated, was to have the law definitely determined so that both the department and the business men would know where they stood.

In some instances, he said, the distribution of trade information within an industry made for uniformity of prices which stifled competition, and while there might not be definite agreements, "a wink of the eye and a nod of the head," were sufficient to accomplish desired results.

Mr. Daugherty said he had discussed the matter with Secretary Hoover, who is holding a series of conferences with representatives of leading industries to obtain co-operation in publication of comprehensive trade statistics by the government and that information and advice on the subject had been exchanged.

In connection with Mr. Hoover's proposal for the formation of combinations of exporters to compete in foreign trade with their rivals abroad, Mr. Daugherty said he thought such organizations could be reconciled with the antitrust laws as long as there was nothing effected which would cause the fixing of prices in this country.

Why Editor: Why is it Ottumwa sent in no report on the state-wide rat killing contest in which according to the big morning Des Moines paper netted one and a half million executions? Isn't Ottumwa ratty? o rdo we just now and then think so?
—"Clean Sweeper."

ROSS MUST STAND GRAND JURY QUIZ ON SEX CONDUCT

In the preliminary examination into the case of Charles E. Ross, charged with assault upon Mrs. Hazel Anderson, the accused this morning was bound over to the action of the grand jury under $2,500 bonds, in default of which he was returned to his cell at the county jail.

Ross did not offer extended defense but introduced a general denial. The prosecuting witness, Mrs. Anderson, testified that Ross had attempted liberties with her and after his alleged offenses sought to secure pledges of secrecy that the husband should not learn of his actions.

The English girl next door stated Ross had taken an affectionately petting attitude toward her, patting her arm and chucking her under the chin, until he was asked to go away.

ANOTHER BRUTAL ATTACK ON CAPITAL CITY WOMEN; PEACH PEDLAR ACCUSED

Des Moines, June 7.—While the web of evidence was being tightened around Tom Lewis, Negro, suspected of the murder of Barbara Thorsdale last Thursday near Valley Junction, word was received at the sheriff's office yesterday that another Valley Junction woman had been attacked.

Mrs. Dorothy Winger, about 24 years old, and the mother of a child, was found unconscious, bound and gagged in the bedroom of her home on Sixty third street at the Rock Island tracks.

She was found between 4 and 5 o'clock, by a man named John Wright, 70 years old, who lives across the street from the Winger home. Wright removed the ropes that bound Mrs. Winger and assisted in restoring her to consciousness. He had heard her scream a few moments before.

Screams Heard By Neighbors

Mrs. Phillip Dale and Mrs. Harry Hall, neighbors, also went to her assistance. Mrs. Dale stated that she heard screams, but had thought little of it as vehement arguments in the Winger home were not unusual.

On regaining consciousness Mrs. Winger told her story. She stated that at 10:30 yesterday morning a man came to her house offering to sell her some peaches. He had no peaches with him at the time, but left and returned in fifteen minutes with a dozen, which he offered for ten cents.

At 4:30 she went out to the house of a neighbor, J. E. Tyler, and telephoned the Valley Junction police, telling them she was suspicious of the fruit peddler.

Coloroform Used Is Belief

As she stepped into her house on her return the man came from behind the door and put his arms about her, she says. He then took a bottle from his pocket, the contents of which she said looked like alcohol. From that moment she remembers nothing more. Police are inclined to the belief that the bottle contained chloroform.

Mrs. Winger describes the man as tall and powerfully built, 5 feet 10 inches in height and weighing probably 180 pounds.

Sheriff Robb stated yesterday that he is convinced that in Tom Lewis he has the slayer of Miss Thorsdale. However, the latest out rage, occurring near the scene of the Thorsdale crime presents new possibilities in the case.

The evidence confronting Lewis is such as to thoroughly convince Robb of the Negro's guilt.

AUTOMOBILES AND HOMES

With many of our states showing an automobile to every sixth and seventh person and an increasing per cent of families non-home owners is it not time to take inventory of conditions?

The automobile is the greatest mechanical gift to the race in the past half-century as demonstrated by it universal service. Many odes have been written to the gas-wagon and too much cannot be claimed for its importance in the marts of trade.

But the country has gone drunk on automobiles. They are starving themselves, denying themselves, worrying themselves, do almost anything to become an automobile owner, or lessee on the partial payment plan. Which would not be so deplorable were it not for the fact that in many instances the purchase should not be made, and the earning capacity of the household be first applied to the acquisition of a home, the institutional investment that must ever occupy first place in the scheme of a useful and orderly life.

---o---

Three women in Des Moines maltreated, one murdered, and the criminal is still at large. Yet we have had such men as Havner and Terrill come to Ottumwa and complain with the charge that Ottumwa was the crime center of Iowa. Of all that is bad Des Moines seems to give forth the worst. Could it be any worse with saloons running as they did in the old days? We read that Iowa is soon to be covered with an army of prohibition enforcers. But it might be quite as helpful for morality and decency of every sort if all these agents be let loose were assigned to the capital city for the next six months.

Ottumwa Daily News

HOW ABOUT OUR ALLEYS?

Yesterday a policeman pointed out piles of boards and inflammable materials in the alleys back of our stores. He explained to us that this was the business of the fire chief. It ought to be somebody's business if the perils of a conflagration are removed to reasonable bounds.

The alleys of Ottumwa are generally paved. They make good runways for delivery wagons in a hurry. Less congestion. And the alley should be kept as well policed as the rest of the street spaces. The thought is presented for what it's worth.

First Cavalry Band Plays

Cleveland Dayton, Director, Concert Program, City Park June 10.

1. March, "Sons of Uncle Sam" .... McCoy
2. Overture, "The Beautiful Galatea" .... Suppe
3. Fox Trot Novelty, "Rose" .... Magine
4. Suite, "A Love Episode in Birdland" .... Bandix
   (a) The Magpie and the Parrot, Humoresque
   (b) The Gentle Dove, a love song.
   (c) The Merry Lark. A joyous flight.
5. March, "Poziers" .... Lithgow
6. Sacred, "Providence" .... Tobani
   A collection of the world's most famous sacred melodies.
7. (a) "A Bit of Syncopation" .... Goldman
   (b) "Wyoming Lullaby" .... Williams
8. Fantasie, "Gipsy Life" .... Thiere
   Morning, In the Woods, La Zingara.
   Gipsy love song, Tarantella.
9. March, "American Legion," .... Parker

THE BONDSMAN

In Ottumwa we have no man engaged in professional bonding of accused men who must either give security for appearance for trial later on or be confined in jail until the trial is held.

Ottumwa will hear more about a new isolation hospital after the meeting this evening in which the Lions, Kiwanis, Rotary membership will listen to suggestions from the local medics. It is a long-time need, a decently equipped and sanitary place where contagious cases may receive proper treatment. In other days, during the flue epidemic, this newspaper urged for the purchase of what is now the Legion building, but objections were advanced, chiefly from the doctors. Today there is a growing sentiment for the investment that will be worth much to our city. It will mean less quarantine and more life conservation. Possibly escape damages that might be adjudged against a city that compels registration at the pest house, which it is and all of that. Ottumwa has needs, many of them, but this is a humane idea and materialized will contribute great benefit to those who must take city care when contagiously afflicted.

-Orpheum-

BILLY BUNGE'S

SO-LONG MARY CO.

Starting Sunday

SNOWBALL JAKE

IN

**TROUBLES OF A MARRIED MAN
FEATURES TRIO**

12 People—Entire Week

Change Program Three Times Weekly

With the season now well advanced it may not produce any additional contracts in the buliding line whatsoever the wage agreement. Ottumwa is in need of better housing conditions and this is only possible with a half-thousand new ones. And there are plenty of places to build, choice sites, either for the residence palatial or the cottage and bungalow. To pass through another winter of high rents will prove a hardship on many families. A dearth of habitation means high level rentals.

OIL FOR STREETS IS MUCH CHEAPER

Commissioner Keefe has been taking oil prices today. He is marking down the best prices of oil supplied from Cushing to be used in oiling streets of Ottumwa, in response to petitions by citizens.

The prices are lower than last year. Now delivered and applied at 9.66 cents a gallon and it will take approximately 30,000 gallons for the streets proposed. Moore, Richmond, Willard, Vine and Vogel. The agent here figured that the total cost would be $2,898 to treat the 44,756 yards.

Keefe stated that there would be no oiling done even where the petitioners have filed, except they are willing to pay the price after being advised of same. Last year the oil was quoted at 12 to 13 cents and on top of this came the freight and the expense of application.

Admittedly the East Main street travel lane in the most deeply ocrrugated highway in this section of the state. Time and again this road with its bumps has been filled and leveled and tons of cinders used, but there is the grinding out of all that has been used for filling until today it's more than a shame, it's a disgrace. The city administration will explain and say that it does little good to patch with temporary filling, and that it were better to wait and do the thing right and save money by such policy. Many who have given the subject anxious study and suffered the shocks of driving over it are in agreement with the waiting plan, until permanent work can be done. There is a slight promise that the paving will be started this autumn, from Iowa avenue to the city limits. The project is a vital proposition and merits the earliest possible action.

The Daily News-- That Great Little Newsy Newspaper

You Enjoy--are You Getting it at Home or Office?

Take Note of This Offer

Ten Weeks

$1.00

This pre-war rate for city delivery by carrier is effective at once.

She Wants Electrical Things

Make no mistake about this—if every bride could tell you what she wanted, she'd name the useful electrical appliances that make housekeeping easier and living more enjoyable.

Electric Gifts are Handsome, Practical, Different

You know that what you give will be admired for its good looks, and daily used for its convenience.

See your dealer.

Ottumwa Railway & Light Co.
Second and Market Street.

1921

VIADUCT OUT OF QUESTION SAY RAIL HEADS TO MAYOR IN CHICAGO CONFERENCE

Will Make Another Appeal To State Board at Once

Mayor Chilton and City Solicitor Hunt returned from Chicago where they manifested their entire good faith with the Iowa board of railroad commissioners by holding conference with heads of the railroad Burlington and Rock Island systems with regard to the Vine street viaduct.

"The viaduct plan is entirely out of the question and yet we stand ready to do anything else the city will ask to make the Vine street safe to the public," was the united statement of the two sets of officials. They pleaded absolute lack of funds to entertain such a project at this time and declared a number of other appeals of similar character had been re- tion of the transportation business.

Wig-Wag Signal Is Suggested.

The Burlington representatives told the Ottumwans that they would have no trouble in getting co-operation for flagmen, for gates or for an electrical wig-wag system to warn of approaching trains at the Vine street crossing. This statement unconditionally made and in event the Ottumwa commissioners are unable to secure the order for the viaduct from the state railroad commissioners then the signal propositions are to be considered, particularly the wig-wag gong with its late devices that is proving in some cities, as at Hinsdale, Illinois, more serviceable than the gate or flagman safeguards. It gongs and at night also flashes a red light on approach of trains.

CITY HEALTH IS A RIOT OF NERVE

Officer Kapp has a map of the city before him. He used vari-colors to stick in spots where contagious disease prevails. His score today was eight pins, and that looks pretty good for the old town. Ottumwa has long enjoyed the reputation of being the healthiest spot on earth, a real nutriment for the nerve jaded. Live in Ottumwa a few days and you're all there for the most daring enterprise. Nerve is Ottumwa's other name. And the chief supply is to be found with our brave fire laddies, Chief Sloan, nd the police boys, and Chief Blizzard. Ottumwa's nerve seems to keep us in fine fettle, health and all.

MOTOR DRIVERS! BEWARE OF NEW LAWS OF IOWA

Des Moines, June 18.—Provisions of the new motor vehicle law, which becomes effective July 1, require that drivers in no event drive at a greater rate than as follows:

Thirty miles an hour if the weight of the vehicle and load is less than three tons and the vehicle is equipped with pneumatic tires and twenty-five miles an hour if the vehicle is equipped with solid rubber tires.

Twenty-five miles an hour if the weight of the vehicle and load is more than three tons and less than six tons weight of the vehicle and load is more and the vehicle is equipped with pneumatic tires, and twenty miles an hour if the vehicle is equipped with solid rubber tires.

Ten mile an hour if the vehicle or any trailer is equipped with two or more metal tires.

Provision is made that local authorities of any city or town may establish a suburban district in which the maximum speed of any vehicle shall not exceed twenty miles an hour, and a business district in which the maximum speed of any vehicle shall not exceed fifteen miles an hour.

The total maximum load on any one wheel of any motor vehicle, including the weight of the vehicle and the load it carries, shall be four tons, profided the total maximum weight of the vehicle and load hall not in any event exceed fouteen tons.

The total load on any wheel of any motor vehicle is limited to eight hundred pounds per inch width of tire, measured between finges of the rims. The enforcement of this provision is entrusted to the state highway commission.

The maximum width of any motor vehicle and its load is limited to eight feet, except loads of loose hay, straw and similar farm products.

Ottumwa Daily News

Ottumwa will have the finest park in this section within five years, along the river from bridge to Myrtle street, as now being prepared in the new acreage acquired by the city. Later on and in due season perhaps the River Front Commission will complete that boulevard around the bend of the river and to make a circle driveway, returning by Blackhawk bridge. This would be a change from what is now being done for drives, out West Second street to the end of the pavement and then right back on the other side the street, scores and scores of pleasure cars every night. It is a sad sight, the drive monotonous.

THE FIGHT PURSE

Iowa Legionaire: It is estimated that the Dempsey-Carpentier purse will reach $1,000,000.

A tidy sum, is it not, to be spent for two men to maul each other for twelve three-minute rounds at the most. And, chances are, with either man capable of scoring a knockout with one punch, the fight won't go the limit.

Think of what could be done with all that money!

It would build several hospitals for disabled ex-service men—men destitute because they cannnot work with shattered bodies and limbs, gassed lungs and shell shocked brains. Thousands of hospital beds are needed, and needed a lot more than prize fight seats.

BLACKHAWK BRIDGE OPEN TUESDAY; MORE GRADING

Commissioner Keefe announces the Blackhawk street bridge will be opened for traffic Tuesday morning. The bridge has been given a re-flooring job and a closure order has been effective for a week.

The News interviewed Henry Mudge, one of the three Center township trustees this noon, with regard to the topping of those hills on the Blackhawk road, just beyond the Cullen home. He said:

"This work could be done to good advantage, but there are no funds available this year to do enough of this grading to make it worth while." Then supplemented with the statement that he had said to Joe Manro, the other trustee, hundred dollars to lowering two hills, this season, if the land that he, Mudge, would be willing to appropriate five or six owners along side would contribute a like amount, thereby spending more than a thousand dollars and getting enough off the top of the hills to make it worth while.

"We, as township trustees, have only enough money to maintain the roads and not authorized under the township levy to grade and build highways. The conuty should look after the extra work to be done."

The outlook for this improvement is not very promising for this year, according to Mr. Mudge, unless the community out southwest of the city raise "dollar for dollar."

But Mr. Cullen is securing several hundred city and rural signatures to a petition to insist as far as consistent for the grading and the township or county at large paying the bill.

IOWA'S NEW CIGARETTE LAW
(Burlington Hawkeye)

On the fourth of next month Iowa's new cigarette law becomes effective. It is a marked departure from the requirements of the statute it supersedes and there is exception that the results will be much more satisfactory. The old law was strictly prohibitive of the sale of cigaretts in this state. The new law is designed to control the cigarette business in Iowa—something the old law signally failed to accomplish. Having in mind the prevention or sale or gift of cigarettes to minors under twenty-one years of age, the new law concentrates upon that one proposition and does not undertake to prohibit the use of cigarettes to adults. The new act was drafted upon the plan of the former mulct liquor law, enabling th eauthorities to get a grip upon practical enforcement of its provisions. To this end, prohibition, restraint and revenue to the state, are combined. It is made to the interest of evrey dealer to conform to the law—to refuse sale to minors rather than be penalized by the revocation of his license and by fines and imprisonment. He has every inducement to be law-abiding —whether he wants to do so, or not.

1921

PLATES SUPPLY GOOD FOR YEAR

A total of 250 auto license plates with 300 truck licenses remain on hand at the office of the county automobile license department. The plates, it is estimated, will just about take care of the demand through purchase of new cars until the end of the year.

"MEDICINAL" BEER

Washington, D. C. June 11.—More than 100 brewers are preparing to seek a court order to force the issuance of permits for the manufacture of medicinal beer, according to testimony of Wayne B. Wheeler, general counsel of the anti-saloon league, before the rules committee of the house.

Wheeler appeared Friday in support of the measure offered by Representative Volstead of Minnesota, which would make it illegal to manufacture or sell beer for medicine.

He urged prompt passage of the Volstead measure, so the breweries would not be able to go to court.

Washington, June 11.—Home distillers and wine makers used up more than 16,000 tons of raisins in 1919, W. M. Giffen, president of the California Associated Raisin Company, estimated today in giving a Senate subcommittee his views on the pending bill to authorize collective bargaining by farmers. He placed the raisin grape crop of 1918 at 167,000 tons and of 1919 at 183,000 tons, the difference, in his judgment, representing demand for fermenting. This demand was now decreasing, he added, the "hobby" apparently having worn itself out.

Co-operative associations to market crops would improve farmers' prices, Mr. Giffen thought. He urged that such associations should be restricted to dealing in products of their own members.

Senator Walsh, Democrat, Montana, said the company was a complete monopoly, and insisted co-operative associations should not be permitted to expand into monopolies.

CITY COUNCIL IS ANXIOUS TO PAVE EAST MAIN STREET

There is no question that the city council is interested in getting East Main street into a passable condition. Mayor Chilton, commenting on the prospects for this year, said the board of supervisors had practically agreed to allot $20,000 out of the automobile fund to apply on improvement up to a width of 18 feet, which added to the seven feet that would be taken care of by the street railway company, leaves only 1 feet more width to consider. At the best, with the $20,000 from the auto fund, and the one mill tax levy, and the benefit tax to property, there would still remain ten to fifteen thousand dollars of deficiency. In the succeeding year, an dperhaps for a half-dozen of them, the mill levy would be required and used in its full proceeds on this street, from Iowa avenue to the city limits.

"It might be just as well to put the street in best paved condition all the way while at it. But it would mean no money for other streets from this special mill for a time."

HAD BOOZE UPON HIS PERSON

John Ross, colored, having liquor upon his person and generally investigated found to be a suspicious fellow, as a possible booze dispenser, was placed under $300 bond by Judge Kitto last evening, in lieu of which he was remanded to the county jail.

Ottumwa Daily News

OTTUMWA, IOWA, MONDAY, JUNE 13, 1921   NUMBER 295

FROST KILLED IN CAR OVERTURN

JOE LINK; BAGG BROTHERS ESCAPE SERIOUS INJURIES SUNDAY A. M., ALBIA ROAD

Blinded by Headlights

Thomas E. Frost, 726 Wabash avenue, died at 10:30 this morning at the Ottumwa hospital. His death occurred as result of injuries received at 1:45 Sunday morning when a car in which he was riding overturned on the Albia road, about three miles west of the city.

There were four in the car, a Case, and coming toward Ottumwa when, according to Joe Link, who was riding in the rear seat at the time, an on-coming car must have blinded the driver, Herbert Bagg as the road was fairly level and no occasion for a slip down a declivity or into a ditch. The accident occurred while the car was running at about 15 miles an hour, it is stated, and all over in a fractional second, the car pinning some of the men underneath and the heaviest section of the machine upon Frost who was later brought to the hospital by a car that came along.

The two Bagg brothers were uninjured and Link was bruised somewhat but able to be around this morning.

Frost was one of the well known young men of the city, single, a brother of Bob Frost at the fire station, and although one of the four was killed the accident might have been more of a tragedy as the car was of the heavy type.

The body of Frost was taken to the home and funeral services will be announced later.

Link, after the accident, started to walk to town for help but before he could call a doctor his friend, who was also one of the employed at the Palace, Main and Green, had been picked up and hurried to the city in another car that happened along.

$30,000 RADIUM LOST FOR IOWAN

Council Bluffs, Ia., June 25.—Radium worth $30,000 was lost in the office of Surgeon Donald MacRae today.

It was applied to the fact of a patient with a bandage. The patient once visited the lavatory and it is feared the radium may have gone into the sewer.

1921

Unitede States Marshal Reed reports a considerable number of bankruptcies in his district and any amount of federal law violation having relation to the 18th amendment. "We are putting many of these people behind bars for manufacturing and selling liquor but in the majority of cases the penalty afflicts the family more than the offender," was the official comment. That the average man engaged in illegal traffic in liquor leaves his family destitute the moment his arrest takes place is the most regrettable phase of the prosecution. The guilty are not alone the punished in name of law.

C. D. Githens Coal Co.

has jus treceived a carload of hard coal. Also supplied with Illinois coal from Franklin county.

Place Your Order Now

Phone 742

CEMENT SIDEWALKS ARE ORDERED

You will find that a few cement, permanent, sidewalks will be laid this season. No turged upon the public, but where there is obvious necessity and the community requests, sidewalks will be built even though the cement trusts does pull down pretty heavy. Ottumwa is doing very well in this line, conservatively, sensibly.

In the report of City Engineer Brady on the North Court street paving everything shows O. K. and the bill of accounts totals slightly in excess of 53,000. It is a good job, says Mr. Brady. But The News wonders why they left that triangle projection just beyond the cemetery. It's a very awkward looking plan, but perhaps when full of flowers and carpeted with rich grasses like velvet laid, we'll modify this view somewhat.

NEW SEWER FOR SOUTH OTTUMWA

Responsive to petition the city council this morning took action on the petition for a sewer to extend west on Keota street one block from South Willard, thence south on Schuyler street a quarter mile to Mary street. Commissioner Keefe expects to put this work through this season. The anticipated cot will be in excess of $5,000 it is estimated in advance of the bids advertised.

AUTOS MAKE FAST TIME

Galesburg, Ill., June 13.—Ray Lampkin won a one-mile auto race here yesterday in 53 1-4 seconds. A three-mile race was won by Lampkin in 2:57. Tray Claypool and Leon Duray tied in a five-mile event, the time being 4:48 1-2. In the official time trials for the mile Cliff Woodbury and Duray tied at 53 1-4. In the run off Woodbury won at 53 seconds flat. Claypool captured a five-mile race for cars of 300 cubic inches or less in 4:57 1-5.

Editory Why: I read the Blakesburg Excelsior every issue and isn't it strange that Fred Raymond is getting by with a statement like this: "We had planned to make a trip to Illinois in our auto this week but it rained and we haven't had a vacation in fifteen years." Isn't that going some? Fact is, Fred wouldn't work if he had to and his wife publishes the paper and keeps her hubby outdoor deceiving himself with the idea that he can fool the people when Lincoln said it couldn't be done. Mrs. R. is one of the brightest newspaper women in the state and does most of the writing of course."

Poster Blakesburger.

SPLENDERS HOLD CROWDS AGAPE

Action, color, music, wild animals, beautiful horses, clowns, bands—all were features of the Hagenbeck-Wallace circus parade seen in Ottumwa today. The largest show in the world to retain a street parade as part of its daily program is entitled, in addition to that distinction, to the credit of giving a street pageant worth going a long way to see. Judging from comment heard on all sides, the public enjoyed it hugely.

JULY 1921

July 2 - US President Warren Harding signs a joint congressional resolution declaring an end to America's state of war with Germany, Austria, and Hungary.

July 11 - The Irish War of Independence (aka Anglo-Irish War) comes to a halt after a truce is signed between the belligerents.

July 11 - The Red Army captures Mongolia from the White Army and establishes the Mongolian People's Republic under Communist rule

July 14 - A Massachusetts jury finds Nicola Sacco and Bartolomeo Vanzetti guilty of first degree murder

July 18 - First vaccination against tuberculosis is given

July 29 - Adolf Hitler becomes Fuhrer of Nazi Party

$5,000,000 3 DAYS AFTER HE IS JILTED

Detroit, July 8.—On July 4 E. C. Cox borrowed $2 from the proprietor of the hotel where he worked to buy a shirt.

He then proposed to a pantry girl at the hotel, but his proposal was ridiculed because he made but 40 cents an hour.

Today Cox received word that he was one of three heirs to an estate of $15,000,000 left by Dr. Samuel Shaw of Hollister, Cal. He left immediately for the coast.

A pantry girl was left behind.

DESIRE SATURDAY HALF HOLIDAY

Our corps of faithful superior officers and especially the deputy division at the courthouse wnder why it would not be as well to have Saturday half-holidays during July and August. One of them asked what might happen to a petition circulated to suggest the closure the last half day of the week until the first of September and those present wanted to sign right away. Very little call for county office service during the hot weather at the week-end.

1921

POLICE COURT.

The police court fines this month amounted to $609.25, according to police judge Kitto. This according to the judge is the lightest month for some time. The fines total for the same month last year was $812.00. March of this year was the banner month since the saloons went out of Ottumwa with a total of $927.

Why, Mr. Editor, can't we have Turkey Island, a heavily wooded tract across from the boathouse, made a pasture for a hundred head of goats and in a few hundred days the weeds and undergrowth will have been masticated to a finish? I understand the city owns this Island in the waterworks title but surely Mr. Brown would not object if Superintendent Weidenfeller turned loose a herd of goats to clean up things and then pontoon the river to those concrete steps Julius Fecht put in a few years ago with the very best intentions and planning for a wonderland for visitors. We would buy the goats in the spring raise some wool and some lambs, then sell the whole caboodle in the fall with repeat the following year until there remained only those lofty trees which will carry a swing for the kiddies a hundred feet in the air. Great recreation spot, Turkey Island, don't you believe with me?

—An Island Friend.

FEWER CARS UNLESS MORE PATRONAGE IS HAD SOON; OUTLOOK NOT FLATTERING

Too Many Autos; Band Loss Affects; Other Deterrents

Mr. Fahrney stated this morning that a plan for diminished service had been under advisement for some time and would be carried out unless conditions would make further demand for the use of the street railway system.

"The Ottumwa Railway and Light company will increase service or decrease it as the demand is made" stated Charles Fahrney, manager of the company in an interview today.

It is not known by Mr. Fahrney just whether the decrease in the amount of "jitneys" operating after the first of the month will make for an addition in number of street cars or not. The manager of the railway company did promise service in a fair ratio to the demand. For the past two years according to Mr. Fahrney the street railway has been operating at a loss to the company. The increase in the operating costs and no increase in the fare has made the railway business extremely unprofitable but, as Mr. Fahrney stated a naffection akin to relationship grows up between a public utility company and its patrons which will not permit discontinuance of service.

Mayor Chilton stated this morning that anyone operating a "jitney" without a license would be picked up immediately by the police and turned over to the district court. Mr. Chilton said, "Now that we are in possession of the facts relative to the 'jitney' law which was passed by the last state assembly, we are going to co-operate to the last letter with the state authorities in enforcing the law.

Th slaw as passed by the late assembly carried a penalty of not less than $50 nor more than $100. This I think will be the means of ridding the police of the trouble of arresting offenders, for, with a penalty such as the law provides staring them in the face it would be folly for them to attempt to evade it."

Mr. Fahrney in speaking of the "jitneys" said that they have been a means of annoyance to the railway company ever since they started to operate. They impede the street car's progress and are a general nuisance to traffic. Mr. Fahrney said, "In the past two years we have noticed a falling off in our daily receipts. This is due to both the "jitneys", and to the increase in the number of privately owned cars. I have figured that in the past two years we have lost on the average of $50 every Friday night from the increased number of cars owned by members of the Ottumwa Country Club who attend the Friday night dances there. Since the "jitney" law is going to be enforced it may be necessary to put on several more cars, if necessary to put on several more cars. If such is the case, we will do so. I couldn't promise right at this time for I haven't had the opportunity of observing the effect the decreased number of "jitneys" will have on the number of people who will patronize the railway company."

Only one bond has been put up to date. William Hoogewoning being the only "jitney" driver having complied with the law by putting up a bond of $3000 yesterday with the clerk of the district court.

The reason for the delay in bringing the new law into effect according to Mayor Chilton, was the city's ignorance of the publication of the law as passed by the last state assembly taking effect in April, 1921. The publication was made in Des Moines and Cedar Rapids papers but city solicitor Hunt was never supplied with a copy of the law.

RIVERVIEW IS SOON A BEAUTY

You are noting daily improvements in the appearance of Riverside Park as the program goes forward under the direction of Superintendent Weidenfeller who is attaining to measures of proficiency deserving of acclaim.

The south section of Riverside, the new area now being put into fertile state, will be seeded at once and the 700 feet of a 20 feet slopeing embankment from the Church street walk to the park level will be sodded right away and with plenty of water available it is though tthe sod laid will thrive and become a bit of pretty fringe to the rest of the people's grounds.

"And I think it would be something of a crime now if the band organization should lose out," said Mr. Weidenfeller in an interview today.

BODY OF OVERSEA SOLDIER ARRIVES—

The body of Thomas S. Hardesty, cook with Co. G 16th Infantry arrived here last night escorted by a military guard. The body was taken to the Sullivan-Jay undertaking parlors from which the funeral services will be held at 2:15 o'clock Sunday afternoon.

From the Sullivan-Jay undertaking parlors the body will be taken to Kirkville for burial. The local American Legion post will have charge at the grave. Rev. Warren of Kirkville will officiate.

Thomas Hardesty was killed in action overseas February 28, 1918.

UNDERGOES SERIOUS OPERATION TODAY

Frank Grimes, a well known farmer residing 3½ miles northeast of the city, underwent a serious operation this morning when surgeons attended a leg trouble which may yet cause amputation. His condition is one that causes his family and friends much apprehension, stated a brother, H. Grimes, of Agency at noon today. Five incisions were made in the treatment given totay.

WILL START THE BIG TOWER CLOCK

President Knox of the Board agrees with everybody that the courthouse will look much better and be benefited generally when the repairing and cleaning jobs under way are completed. "Yes, we are going to the top, to the tower, and look after the big clock today," said the official. Which is in line with what wehad been "Really Ottumwa ought to have something musical near the City Park, don't you think?" was his comment. Did the Honorable Supervisor have in mild allusion to the band that was and is no more?

GERMANY'S DEBT ONLY PART CASH

Berlin, July 1.—The inter-allied guarantees committee has decided Germany will only be asked to pay 300,000,000 gold marks in money out of the second installment of 1,000,000,000 marks. The balance, due May 2, 1922, may be settled in good and from the proceeds of the export levy.

Double-Duty Sockets
Bring Greater Convenience

How often have you found it impossible to use a second labor-saving electrical device through the lack of another socket?

You will practically double the pleasure and convenience from your single outlets by adding inexpensive double or triple sockets. They save time—and cost of extensions.

Be sure that your **dining room, kitchen** and **laundry are** provided with **double sockets** so that you can use two or even **three appliances** from the same convenient fixture.

ODDS SUBSIDE IN GEORGES' FAVOR, WILL BE 5 TO 2

BY JACK VEIOCK

New York, July 1—Stage is set for the great international battle between Jack Dempsey and Georges Carpentier. Both are under cover until the hour arrives when they meet. There is more than a million dollars in the coffers.

Along Broadway last night $50 seats were to be had in some instances for $40 and $45. These seats, for the most part, were bought back from outside points where ticket agents contracted for more than they could dispose of. Ten dollar seats were offered for $9 in several instances.

Of course the big news for tomorrow's papers, both in this country and France and England, is the outcome of the Dempsey-Carpentier setto. We are advised that this evening many of the sport expers of the world will present their forecast to the press, and a lot of fellows will rely upon the judgment of these "experts" to some extent, but The News has only this prediction to make, the affair is ognig to return Jack Dempsey the winner, and we are hoping it oges the Georges. That may seem odd to the average fan, but them's our sentiments.

FAIR WEATHER FOR DEMPSEY FIGHT

New York, July 1.—Fair weather and normal temperature for the big fight on Saturday was forcast today when the heat wave which descended upon New York on June 21 ended.

The battle will be postponed only in case it rains hard Saturday morning and the storm lasts until early afternoon. If postponed it will be held at 3 p. m. July 4.

If it should rain Saturday when most of the crowd is gathered in the stadium at Jersey City the fight will go on with a special umbrellalike apparatus over the ring which will not obstruct the view of the spectators.

COLOR LINE IS OBSERVED STRICTLY BY DEMPSEY

Omaha, July 9.—Jack Dempsey, world's heavyweight champion pugilist, who passed through here on his way to Salt Lake City, denied that he is willing to fight Jack Johnson, "or any other Negro fighter."

"I will never fight a colored man," Dempsey said. "There is nothing to this talk of me meeting Jack Johnson. I am confident the public don't want this fight, and while I will govern myself to a large extent according to the public's wishes, I can't see my way clear to fight Johnson, or any other colored man."

1921

COUNCIL TAKING ACTION ON CROSSING PROVIDES FOR AMPLE PROTECTION

The City council today introduced an ordinance the purpose of which is to protect pedestrians from the dangers attendant to railroad crossings. It specifies a flagman at the Iowa avenue crossing to give twenty-four hour service and the signalman at Wapello to give sixteen hour service. A flagman is also specified to give sixteen hour service at Wapello street.

Nothing as yet has been done concerning the footbridge at Iowa avenue which was promised to be built by John Morrell and company in conjunc- In discussing the matter of the footbridge this morning the councilmen were dubious of the practical qualities of a footbridge. It was the general opinion that the footbridge would only be used as long as a train was passing, but that when none was in sight the pedestrian would take the easiest way at hand and use the regular crossing thereby thwarting the purpose of the footbridge.

Street commissioner Thomas Keefe stated that a subway would be impractical at Iowa avenue for reason of the closeness of the river, making some means of drainage necessary at an expense that would be prohibitive.

There never has been a flagman at the Wapello street crossing and the placing of one there will be a boon to those who must use this street. The traffic on Wapello street while not so heavy as that at Iowa avenue or Second street is quite enough to warrant the railroad companies placing a man there for signal purposes.

If you had a hundred thousands dollars and built a coliseum with the same, don't you actually believe Ottumwa would be greatly benefited? It would mean thousands of visitors to Ottumwa annually for conventions and state affairs and that would mean more publicity for Ottumwa, more money spent here, more business, more prosperity of community extent. A coliseum in Ottumwa would be worth ten times its cost to Ottumwa whether or not within itself it ever paid a dollar directly on its cost as dividends. Every self-respecting and thrifty city demands a place for public assemblage.

OUR MONSTER AIRSHIP

The British-built R 38, the largest airship in the world, will shortly become the property of the United States. There is a considerable crew now with the monster ship getting in readiness for the trans-Atlantic voyage. Beside the passenger and other commercial uses to which the ship will be dedicated, there is provision made for a heavy armament. She is expected to make 5,000 miles at full speed of 70 miles an hour, a 6,500 "cruising speed" at 60 miles an hour.

THE OTTUMWA DAILY NEWS

BOLD STEAL BAFFLES LOCAL OFFICERS

ROB GO-GAS STATION, $600 CASH AND CHECKS; WAS AN EASY GET-AWAY

Up until 4 o'clock this afternoon no definite clue had been found by officers who are tracking the man who early this morning robbed the Hawkeye oil station at Richmond and Church streets of $600 in cash and $60 in in checks.

The robbery according to the conclusions of chief of police Harry Blizzard was "pulled" by someone having accurate knowledge of the oil station. The office is not equipped with a safe and the money was kept in a box shelf in one of the little closets within the station. The thief made his entrance through the window in the rear of the station.

Smashing the glass, he was able to make a hole large enough to permit him to reach the catch. Exit was made through the same window.

The robbery was discovered this morning by the station man when he came on duty and he immediately notified the police. A thorough examination was made by the police department before calling in at a suggestion from the victims of the robbery, Rodibaugh's bloodhounds from Agency.

Several well defined tracks in the mud at the rear of the building furnished the dogs the scent and they started west on Richmond avenue. Turning off the street after they had gone about a block, the dogs took to the river bank finally bringing up at the back of Oscar Leedom's property 618 North Ferry Avenue. The dogs lead the men to an old boat tied up to an improvised dock. Here the trail ended.

The dogs with their keeper Rodibaugh, were rowed dacross the river and picked up the scent on the north side. Central addition was thoroughly scoured but with no success. The trail then lead west and the hounds were followed to the Milwaukee terminal where they suddenly halted near a pile of railway ties. The sudden stop baffled the officers for up until this time the trail as shown by the speed the hounds displayed in following it was clear. By this time sheriff Giltner had joined the party and the posse searched the west yards arresting Joeseph Geslenz, vagrant who was found there. He was taken to the county jail and will be held there pending investigation.

Sheriff Giltner in conversation admitted having a clue to the identification of the thief but would give no information as yet concerning his theory.

Charles Maddy, finger print expert of the olcal police department, was on the scene of the crime early this morning with his Bertillion camera. To his disgust he ofund that his camera was not o fthe type used fro securing prints of this nature and immediately wired the State Bankers Association officers 2OAlbm wbmw bmw bmw bmw in Des Moines in an effatrt to secure a camera to take some clear prints.

1921

DRAINAGE MEET TOMORROW

The Cedar Creek project will be up for another hearing with the board of supervisors tomorrow. This is a proposed improvement affecting thousands of acres of rich farm lands in Pleasant and Competine townships, reducing tortuous channel from 21 to 7 miles, approximately, costing probably in excess of fifty thousand dollars, the cost taxed to the owners benefited.

This county has few waste acres especially in the north half of the county. This northeast section is traversed by a stream that goes into high rampages the least excuse, and in some places the valley is a half-mile wide and subject to such a depth of overflow that traffic is suspended for days, roadways and bridges damaged and a most expensive state of affairs because the waters do not get away fast enough.

10,753 ADDED TO CITY'S GENERAL FUND

The City Clerk this morning announced the total of last month's gross receipts as being $13,320.68, the largest amount to be taken in at the city offices for many months. Of the $13,320.68, $10,753.16 goes to the general fund. The list in detail is as follows:

Poll tax, $4.27; license, $300.50; fines, $609.25; dog tax, $26; fumigating, $635; ambulance, $22; refunds, $1,605.41; building permits, $128; cigarette permits, $3,200; park, $27.50; special trust, $2,546.02.

$2,500 of the special trust fund was paid by the Ottumwa Cemetery Association to apply on the paving which was done on North Court street.

IRELAND IN ARMISTICE

News that Ireland and England are about to reach such an agreement as will stop the war between these two peoples and sober, high-minded, humanitarian rule modeled after the Canadian plan, giving practically home rule to the Emerald Isle, soon to come, is good news to the world.

Peace sentiment is increasing everywhere in Ireland as it is in England. The Irish voter will no doubt be premitted to pass judgment on whatever the overture may be, as a result of the conference being held in hope of peace, and indications today are that such a settlement will be offered as will find approval.

The dominion character of government appeals as a compromise yet more than just that, it will mean the Irish Republic is granted self-government in the chief essentials and principle of self-determination firmly recognized in the realities.

The dominion character of government appeals as a compromise yet more than just that, it will mean the Irish Republic is granted self-government in the chief essentials and principle of self-determination firmly recognized in the realities.

There has been a powerful American influence swaying the lives of all men, both England and Irish, of recent months, and July Fourth found the American principles of freedom symboled with many demonstrations, especially at Dublin. All of which but demonstrates the mighty service that has been given to the great cause by the Irish of America, by millions who are not catholics but wishing Ireland a fulfillment of its dream. This, too, without the accusative finger from any authoritative source pointing to an offense of intervention.

The interest manifest in Ottumwa as an example, for the recognition of the Irish republic, has been so so profound and Christiann and preservingly consistent as to contribute no small part in bringing the Irish problem close to the hearts of all.

The hope of Ireland may not be realized to the fullest measure but practical success for the plans cherished for 600 years is now apparently assured.

THE OTTUMWA DAILY NEWS

COUNCIL ACTS ON EAST MAIN PAVING

RESOLUTION IS FOR BRICK SURFACE FROM IOWA AVE. TO FOOT OF BIG HILL

The new pavement will extend from Iowa avenue on to the bottom of the big hill adjoining Foster park. The width of the roadway from Iowa avenue to Van Buren avenue will be 42 feet and from Van Buren avenue on to the city limits the street will be 24 feet wide. The wearing surface as specified in the general specification calls for a vertical fibre paving blick laid so as to make a three inch wearing surface. The filling is to be of asphalt.

The new paving will be a boon to travelers who must navigate the series of ruts and bad places which now form the roadway out of one of Ottumwa's most traveled streets. Paving the big hill which lies just to the north of Foster park will also be a benefit to travelers especially after rains. The hill which has a wearing surface of clay is practically impassable at certain times of the year.

Work will start on the new paving at the earliest possible moment contingent upon the allotment which the mayor and commissioners asked for this morning.

As passed by the last state assembly, twenty per-cent of the gross receipts from the auto tax in each county goes to the county to be applied up roads. Applications for aid by any city or town is made to the county board of supervisors who pass upon the merits of the petition. It is not thought by the commissioners that the allotment can be refused. Wapello county's share of the auto tax amounts to approximately $100,000.

The U. S. census figures claim there are 2 million more men than women in this country. Now where is the excuse for the maid that permits herself to become a spinster? There are plenty of the male gender and they need care and attention. And despite the numerical handicap it is claimed women are taking jobs away from men in the populous centers and doing it with sweeping success. Immigration is advanced as one reason for the excess of the man citizen.

TAKING OUR STRIDE

It sounds almost too good to be true, this story about paving East Main street with the job under way this season. If a city ever had a serious handicap in the way of bad roads Ottumwa has experienced the worst possible. From each of the five directions it has been years of intolerable conditions. And East Main is perhaps the most conspicuous offense to the traveling public.

Of course it will cost a lot of money. When West Second street was paved with creosote block a number of years ago the protests were vehement. Owners of property fought it to the finish, which finish was in favor of the paving, and today Ottumwa has in West Second the best paved street in the state and not a penny of expense since the work was laid.

The people will extol the achievement in compliment to the present city council and board of supervisors if the East Main project gets by all O K and there is small question now but the thing is as good as done, lacking only the Highways sanction of the plans that will be presented for inspection.

This improvement, that extends from Iowa avenue to the city limits at the bottom of the big hill, will cost a pile of money but when it is considered $20,000 the first year will be derived from the primary road fund made up from auto money it is readily seen not a considerable more than in a decade ago will be taxed to the property owners. The city railway is interested in the enterprise because it will mean a considerable expense to them, but Manager Fahrney is taking no exceptions, is willing to do all possible as his part in making Ottumwa a bigger and better city.

Indications are that Ottumwa is getting ready to make a race for goals that will be a merry clip for other centers to equal. It is high time, yet how very gratifying to know that we have in reserve the powers of purpose and resources of plenty to accomplish the best when once started.

1921

RIVERVIEW PARK TO BE OPENED SOON

The Riverview Park site is fast rounding into shape and with the sowing of grass seed yesterday and the continuation of the sodding work Ottumans wil lsoon be able to enjoy one of the best park sites that the City of Ottumwa affords.

Park superintendent J. N. Widenfeller stated this morning that the bathing beach would not be opened for some time yet owing to the high stage of the river and its muddy condition. Mr. Widenfeller promised the opening of the beach as soon as the river recedes to such a stage as to make it safe for all swimmers.

R. R. EMPLOYEES HERE AFFECTED BY 12 PER CENT CUT

The railroad wage decrease which will be out to a vote next Friday will be met with opposition from the railroad employees here ni Ottumwa and cording to Edward Hale, chief clerk to J. P. Cummings superintendent of the C .B. and Q.

The decrease averages 12 per cent and will affect all departments said Mr. Hale. The local railroad offices have been supplied with data to be used in preparatory work on the new schedules which without a doubt will be effective July 8.

COLLECT TAX FOR SPECIAL LINES DURING JULY

Special intenal revenue taxes beY come due and payable after July 1 and not later than July 31 to the Collector of Internal Revenue for Iowa, Lars Bladine. The announcement of special tax collection was made on Friday.

Forms for filing returns of special taxes upon business and occupations are now available at offices of collectors fo internal revenue and branch offices. These taxes are due July 1, adn ae held by the bureau of Internal Revenue to be delinquent unless paid on or before July 31. The list includes the tax on brokers, pawnbrokers, museums, theaters and concert halls, circuses, bowling alleys, shooting galleries, riding academies and automobiles operated for hire.

Editor Whys: I see that a minor may not buy and smoke the cigaret. Why so. Some of them just under 21 were good enough to go into war for us, cigarettes and all yet in time of peace they are ruled out as ineligibles. Who owns this country anyhow?

—Under Twenty-One.

THE OTTUMWA DAILY NEWS

CASH AND JEWELS ARE TAKEN IN LOOT

REEVES APTS. RANSACKED BUT INVADERS OVERLOOK VALUABLES AND PURSE

Only Two Night Patrolmen

Thieves entering the apartents of George Reeves over the Sullivan and Jay undertaking parlors early this morning stole $60, two gold watches, two revolvers, a diamond ring valued at $150 and made a safe "get away."

The robbery is thought to have occurred between the hours of 5 and 6 o'clock this morning. Mrs. Reeves, who was up at about 5 o'clock, noticed nothing wrong and returned to bed ignorant of the visit of the thieves. The robbery was committed in the Reeves' bedroom. The money and guns were taken from a dresser drawer.

The robbers also made off with two cantaloupes and a pound of butter, but in their haste to escape they left the butter on the front steps.

John Drake, employed at the Sullivan and Jay parlors was in the undertaking office at the tiet the robbery is supposed to have been committed. He said he noticed no one ntering or leaving the building.

The burglars ransacked all the dresser drawers but failed to note that one contained a pocket book with $70 n cash together with two diamond rings belonging to Mrs. Reeves.

The police were notified of the robbery and are now at work on the case. This is theboldest robbery which has been "pulled" in Ottumwa for many years. According to Harry Blizzard, chief of police, not since the days of the porch climbers here has such a daring theft been eported.

WHAT IT COSTS

According to figures just given out it's going to cost each citizen of the United States the sum of $82 to keep the government running next year. That ooesn't mean that every man and woman in Ottumwa, for instance, will pay that sum, because not all of them are taxpayers. But it does mean that those who do pay taxes will have to make up an amount equal to $82 for every man and woman living in this countrp. This is based on a budget of $6,500,000,000, which would mean a per capital of about $60. But state and county taxes average up another $22, so it really means a tax of $82 on every citizen to run his government one year. It's a lot of money. There's no getting away from that fact. ut when we stop to compare this nation with any or all of the others we're forced to admit that $82 a year is pretty cheap for the privilege of living in the best country on earth.

It is become a vital question with the rural townships whether the consolidated school is a good thing. As the rule we are finding the leading educators of the country enthusiastic over the plan, but when the proposition gets down to the working basis farmers are skeptical about the economic and general utility virtues of the moment. In this county will be found all the points pro and con in liscussion, as instanced in the Competine township proposal. This much at least can be said of it locally, it affords more material for community antagonisms than all the religions rolled into one.

ANDREW CARNEGIE LEFT $22,151,011

New York, July 1.—The state controller's office today appraised the estate of Andrew Carnegie at $25,933,014 gross and $22,151,011 net. The principal items are securities valued at $17,543,538.

1921

BATHING BEACH TO OPEN SATURDAY

Yo! Ho! Skinney! Did ye hear about the smimmin' hole? J. N. Weidenfeller, superintendent of parks, announced this morning that the Ottumwa bathing beach would open next Saturday afternoon at ' o'clock if the weather permitted.

The pontoon bridge has been laid across the river and the life lines secured. The lights will be ready by Staurday. Mr. Widenfeller stated that a charge of 25 cents would be made for two swimmers with an aditional 5 cents for towels. The beach will open at 1 o'clock in tch afternoon on week days and remain open until 9:30 at night.

On Sundays the beach will open at 10 o'clock in the morning and close at 9:30 at night.

SUNDAY NIGHT SERMONS

Ottumwa is privileged, whether permitting, to hear an outdoor sermon in the City Park Sunday evening. This is quite a treat and room for everybody. You will enjoy the preacher no doubt tomorrow night and the singing, too, will be by a choir from the church with which the preacher is identified, so that you get the spiritual inspiratoin delivered from a new range each succeeding occasion.

The excuse that "It's too hot to go to church" has been put out of business by the park sermon arrangement. Attend and get something different and for your own personal needs.

THE BONUS WILL LOSE

President Harding, under advises of his secretary, Mellon, is convinced that to vote a cash bonus now for the ex-service men would bring about national disaster.

Preceding his statement to this effect by one day the President tells the world he would like to have a conference held looking to disarmament, limitation on expenditures, and this preface to the negation for the soldier is supposed to indicate the necessity of utmost economy.

But there is something the matter with the county because things are going bad, and millions and millions of cash in banks and in the treasury at Washington.

It is reported that one-third the gold of the world is now in the U. S. vaults, and more than debt, or a bit of speculation that might bring harm, is this menace of hoarded monies, immense gold reserves, so much more than is needed to hold in reserve, and which ought to be discharging its natural function in trade, having circulation with our industrials to benefit.

What is the policy of this administration? Hoarding riches and the people deprived of money with which to carry on business?

Does it mean that a bonus to the soldier is denied because it would release all this useless money? And why is it the New York Chamber of Commerce, standing sponsor for the attitude the smaller C. of C. of a thousand U. S. cities is to exert such influence as will not only deny the debt we owe the solicitor but as well perpetuate this depression in business due to lack of money in circulation at a fair rate of interest?

Not many will be able to clearly understand, much less generally agree with Harding, that it would be a catastrophe to do anything for the bonus cause. It is regretable that this ultra-conservatism is decided upon at a time when we have millions in surplusage and idle and an estimated five million American citizens in need of employment, which number of course includes the ex-service man.

So it goes down in history for the future politicians to recall and campaign. President Harding has had his way. The senate capitulates. The soldiers' bonus appreciation from a grateful nation denied. Such is the action of a Republican administration and under the command of a Chief Executive whose word is getting to be law with the people's representatives. Is it too much to expect in matters of taxation that the public voice should be the only one? What right or privilege has been delegated to the New York Chamber of Commerce to tell Mellon what kind of report to make from the United States treasury? If this nation continues in such attitude patriotism is liable to take a slump along with the rest of our material assets.

MRS. KENDALL QUITE ILL; APPENDICITIS

Des Moines, July 16—Mrs. N. E. Kendall, who was taken to Methodist hospital Thursday afternoon with an attack of acute appendicitis, was reported last evening to be seriously ill.

An operation is to be performed as soon as her condition will permit. She was reported to be suffering great pain. Dr. C. B. Luginbuhl is the attending physician.

Ottumwa will be fortunate if no other "Eakins Family" cases are campaigned necessarily for home and food supplies. It is not a case of being out of the woods while seeking a path back to "normalcy" for the American public. President Harding has not yet demonstrated any special capacity as a leader and his most conspicuous acts to date, it appears, are those not receiving the indorsement of the people. We need employment for several million workmen today. There will be more idleness when the winter months arrive.

YOUR SHARE, $238 AS INCOME TAX, $1,268,000,000

Washington, uly 25.—The government obtained a total of $1,289,000,000 in revenue from personal income taxes in 1919—an increase of $141,900,000 compared with 1918—according to a preliminary report of income tax returns made public tonight by Internal Revenue Commissioner Blair.

The commissioner's report showed there were 5,338,700 personal returns filed in the calendar year 1919, representing a growth of 97,646 from 1918, while the total amount of net income reported for 1919 was $19,859,000,000, an increase of $3,934,000,000 over the previous year.

The average net income per return for 1919 was $3,722.05, the average amount of tax $238.68 and the average tax rate 6.39 per cent.

There were had sixty-five returns of net income of $1,000,000 and over, and the "million a year" men paid practically two-thirds of their earnings in taxes.

There were 189 returns on incomes of $500,000 to $1,000,000; 425 of $150,000 to $300,000; 2,983 of $100,000 to $150,000; 13,320 of $50,000 to $100,000; 37,477 of $25,000 to $50,000; 162,485 of $10,000 to $25,000; 438,851 of $5,000 to $10,000; 1,180,488 of $3,000 to $5,000; 1,569,741 of $2,000 to $3,000 and 1,924,871 of $1,000 to $2,000.

Wives making separate returns from husbands numbered 58,534; single men, heads of families, 362,797; single women, heads of families, 88,595; single men, 1,602,277; single women 361,960.

Warning against fake income tax "experts" was issued tonight by Internal Revenue Commissioner Blair.

1921

THE OTTUMWA DAILY NEWS

OTTUMWA, IOWA, WEDNESDAY, JULY 13, 1921

$200,000 HIGHWAY BY DECEMBER FIRST

BLOOMFIELD ROAD TO CITY BIGGEST GOOD ROAD IDEA OF ALL SOUTHERN IOWA

By December 1 the great Ottumwa-Bloomfield highway will have been formally dedicated to the world, all grading and bridging completed by this date, according to statement by President Knox of the Wapello county board of supervisors this afternoon.

This is a great work in behalf of good roads. For always and down through the later busy yesterdays this up and down roadway has been famed for the grades, in days when teams were used almost impossible without going double horse power to negotiate the ascents with an average load of farm products, and as a route for general travel avoided if possible, teamsters preferring to drive miles detour to avoid the hills.

Will Cost At Least $200,000.

This is the second summer with civil engineers, workmen, power shovels, dredges, bridge builders, going at top speed through all sorts of weather and many hours overtime. Cox Brothers' firm from Wapello had the grading contract for this county, then secured the Davis county job and have been months in the big enterprise, which in completion will cost at a fair estimate not less than $200,000, the biggest thing done outdoors of its public character in all this section as one attest it; biggest thing in road building and next to the Keokuk dam in importance for southwestern Iowa.

Great Thoroughfare For Traffic.

With grades cut down and the 21 and a fraction miles between the two city limits, and this an automobile age, what else can happen than a fifty-mile newly acquired patronage will be won on the Ottumwa retail stores and general markets by reason of this highway, under the state board requirement, not exceeding six per cent grade at any point?

Supervisor Knox remarks that the full significance of this wonderful new short line road, with its low grades and Wabash bridge overhead, and curves eliminated, really means to Ottumwa is not yet known. "It is going to prove the biggest card in bringing trade to Ottumwa of anything that has happened in years," was the forecast of Knox.

How much closer does it bring Ottumwa to Bloomfield, West Grove, Ash Grove, Moulton, Coatesville, Lancaster, and a score of cities and towns south and east? It is probably safe to estimate time will be halved and the expense of travel per tonnage practically as much for economy and for scenic delights there is all the rugged and picturesque one will be able to find in the state.

Ottumwa will exchange congratulations with the capital of Davis county when the dedication is formally arranged. The occasion should be the biggest affair of its sort known to local history.

CHEAPEST MAN IN CITY IS DISCOVERED

He's found. The cheapest man in Ottumwa. By the merest chance he was discovered today by a reporter for the News.

A neatly typewritten letter on Micheal Shoehan's desk at the city hall disclosed the fact that a certain well known man in Ottumwa took out a dog license three weeks ago, the said dog license costing the man $1.00. Two days ago the dog was poisoned and the discomforted owner has written to the city clerk asking for a refund of $1.00 license tax and 75 cents extra for a leather collar which was on the dog at the time he was taken away by the city.

NO CRIME TAKING BOY TO BALL GAME EVEN ON SUNDAY

New York, July 21—Taking a boy to a ball game on Sunday is neither a crime nor evidence of moral turpitude, according to Vice Chancellor Backes of New Jersey.

Mrs. Grace Lines, who is suing her husband for separate maintenance, asked the vice chancellor to forbid Lines to visit their small son because "Lines took the boy to ball games."

The vice chancellor refused her request.

Why doesn't Chief Blizzard conduct a school for his patrolmen? Why place a novice on duty without so much as instructing him in his duties? The Civil Service rules don't say anything about that phase of the business but never-the-less whey wouldn't it be the logical thing to do?

TAX PAYER

"BEATING PROHIBITION"
Chicago News

Three men were dead in Chicago Friday morning and a fourth was dying as the result of a "moonshine" party held early in the week. The "moonshine" was purchased at "a blind pig in Dearborn street near Randolph." The keeper of the blind pig probably will not be punished or even more closely identified, since the city authorities take the position that enforcement of the prohibition law is the business of the federal government, and not of the Chicago police.

Before prohibition a certain whisky was advertised as containing "not a headache in a barrel of it." Of much of the illicit booch that has been sold since prohibition experience has proved that there is a death in a swallow of it.

To say nothing of the moral side of the matter, men who buy and drink the illicit liquor offered for sale in Chicago and elsewhere run terrible risks. Even though they may know the bootlegger who sell it they do not know that the bootlegger knows where and by whom the stuff was made and what it contains. Buyers must remember that they are dealing with men who are willing to do business in violation of the law and that some of them have not hesitated to sell poison for profit.

A good many men have paid with their lives for the fun of "beating prohibition." Any patron of a bootlegger or a blind pig takes the chance of paying the same extortionate price.

Children's Gingham Dresses--
Pretty Plaids $1.49 and $1.69
SIZES 7 TO 14 YEARS

A galaxy of pretty styles and so attractively priced mother can't afford to make them this hot weather. Delightful plaids in blue, pink, lavender, yellow and their combinations. Fancy styles every one a pleasing selection and colors that will launder perfectly. Wide choice, 7 to 14 years at $1.49, $1.69, and $1.98. Sizes 2 to 6 years at only 98c

---

FORD, 1924 POSSIBILITY AS LEADERS SEE THINGS; IS STRONG WITH FARMER

Washington, D. C., July 26.—Political astrologers, with whom every up-to-date administration is these days adequately equipped, announced discovery of an important phenomenon in America's political and industrial skies.

They see Hery Ford moving increasingly rapidly and ever more brightly through the path of their vision. They further report that the Ford star is showing marked attraction to numerous other bodies, such as the agricultural element and labor.

1921

In fifty years there has been no news as important to this country as that describing the destruction on Thursday of the German fully armored dreadnaught Ostfriesland. The great battleship was sent to the bottom in twenty-five minutes by two bombs. They did not touch her, simply fell in the water near by and destroyed her by the impact of the water itself forced against steel armor with sufficient force to open the seams and sink the boat.

The New York Times, reporting the destruction by two inexpensive bombs of a ship that cost millions quotes Gen. Williams: "The bombs that sank her will be heard around the world."

The Times asks: "Is the battleship obsolete?"

It is indeed obsolete, as has been said in this column many times during the last two years. To build forty-million dollar battleships is a stupid waste of money, done only to please shipbuilders that want money. The entire engineering and mechanical intelligence of this country should be devoted to flying machine construction.

The President is to be especially congratulated upon the fact that army and navy, under his control, are manufacturing bombs three times as great as the 2,000-pound bombs that sank the German dreadnaught. These bombs carry each 4,000 pounds of T. N. T.

This country should have as quickly as possible 5,000 first-class flying machines to carry the mails in time of peace, and drop bombs upon the enemy in case of war. Five thousand flying machines would make any attack by a foreign fleet preposterous. The 5,000 machines honestly built, without aid from grafting $1 a year patriots, would cost less than one $40,000,000 battleship and could destroy a thousand such ships if possible to build so many.

The battleship has gone by, a joke. The President knows it. Under his direction, the Postmaster General, Mr. Hays, can and will usefully produce and use flying ships that will take care of natural protection, with a good fleet of submarines to back them up.

Phone Exchange Latest is Move By Physicians

A phone exchange for physicians in Davenport is the latest plan. The exchange which will be installed within a few months is the last innovation for getting your family doctor in a hurry. The plan has already received the hearty support of the Scott County Medical Society and many Davenport physicians have already signed up. Dr. N. S. Bradfield of Ft. Madison was in Davenport today completing plans for the installation of the exchange here, which in time will no doubt take in the tri-cities. Exchanges have already been established in Sioux City, Des Moines, Cedar Rapids, Omaha, St. Joseph, Mo.; St. Louis, and several other cities and have been pronounced a success.

Under the system you merely call the number of the physicians' exchange and the exchange operator locates your doctor. When Dr. Phil leaves his office to call upon a patient, play a game of golf, hurries out to lunch or goes on some kind of an errand he merely notifies the exchange operator where he is going. When a call comes in the operator knows just where he is. In the event, however, the physician should forget to state his whereabouts to the exchange operator there is a card index system at the exchange which lists his favorite haunts and locating him is an easy matter.

ECLIPSE RANGES

THE GAS RANGES WITH A COLLEGE EDUCATION

AUGUST 1921

Summer - Research on the pancreases of dogs at the University of Toronto, led by Dr. Frederick Banting and Charles Best, leads to the first crude use of the substance which later comes to be known as insulin

Aug 2 - Italian operatic tenor Enrico Caruso dies at 48

Aug 2 - Chicago jury acquits 8 Chicago White Sox accused of fixing the World Series

Aug 3 - Despite being acquitted, Chicago White Sox players are banned from organized baseball for life

Aug 3 - First aerial crop dusting, to kill caterpillars, in Troy, Ohio

Aug 5 - KDKA Pittsburgh airs first radio broadcast of major league baseball; Pirates beat Phillies 8 to 0

Aug 5 - Treaty of Berlin officially ends WWI (then called The Great War, or the World War) as U.S. and Germany sign

August 10 - John M. Martin, last living Confederate Congressman, dies

Aug 24 - R38 class airship ZR-2 explodes on her fourth test flight near Kingston upon Hull, England, killing 44 of her 49 Anglo-American crew

Aug 25 - Franklin Roosevelt is diagnosed with polio at age 39, following a two-week illness characterized by paralysis and fevers; he becomes permanently disabled

Aug 25 - Battle of Blair Mountain, largest labor uprising in United States history, begins in Logan County, West Virginia

Aug 26 - Rising prices (caused by inflation post World War, and exacerbated by reparations demanded by Allies) cause major riots in Munich

Aug 26 - Assassination of German politician Matthias Erzberger causes the government to declare martial law

HERO SOUGHT; BABY DEAD

Chicago, Aug. 5—The American Legion post at Chookston, Minn., yesterday appealed to police here to locate William Kaiser, war veteran, taking automobile work at a Chicago vocational training shop. He is asked to communicate with his wife at once as their child has died suddenly.

1921

LANDIS IS SURE MEN BARRED

The Baseball Organization Is Through With Men Who Consort With Crooked Gamblers.

Chicago, Aug. 3.—The "Black Sox" despite their acquittal of charges of conspiracy to throw the 1919 world's series to Cincinnati, will never play in organized baseball again.

Judge K. M. Landis, higher commissioner of baseball, made this emphatically clear in a statement issued today. He declared that no players who associate with a "bunch of crooked gamblers" are wanted in the national pasttime.

REGARDLESS OF VERDICT

"Regardless of the verdict of the jurors," Judge Landis said, "no player that 'throws' a baseball game, no player that undertakes or promises to throw a ball game; no player that sits in conference with a bunch of crooked players and gamblers where the ways and means of throwing games are planned and discussed, and does not promptly tell his club about it, will ever play professional baseball.

"Of course, I don't know that any of these men will apply for rein-statement, but if they do, the above at least are a few of he rules that will be enforced.

"Just keep it in mind that regardless of the verdict of juries baseball is entirely competent to protect itself against crooks, both inside and outside the game."

A jury in Superior court here has said that the "black sox" committed no crime in connection with the alleged conspiracy to "throw" the 1919 world's series of Cincinnati Players and gamblers accused in the scandal that turned the baseball world topsy-turvy a year ago have been exonerated. The law has no further terrors for them.

Eddie Cicotte, Joe Jckson, Claude Williams, "Buck" Weaver, "Happy" Felsch, "Chick" Gandil and "Swede" Risberg, however, still must face the bony, pointing finger and the piercing eye of Judge Landis, the big shiek of the baseball tribe. The arbiter of all disputes that arise in the national game must say whether they shall again be permitted to participate in organized baseball.

JURY OUT FOUR HOURS

The verdict of the jury that ended the famous scandal trial came just before midnight. The jurors had deliberated four hours and had taken but one ballot, it was announced. The clerk of the court read one by one the names of the defendants and the decision of the jury that they were innocent. Besides the ball players, David Zelcer, of Des Moines, Ia., and Carl Zork, of St. Louis, alleged gamblers and "fixers" of the series, were exonerated.

Demonstrations of joy followed the verdict. The ball players pounded each other on the back and fought to shake hands with the jurors. A crowd of 500 men that packed the courtroom stamped and cheered despite the warning of Judge Hugo M. Friend that no demonstration would be permitted.

Ottumwa Daily News

FINAL ACTION ON PAVING

Monday the city council made the action final in adopting resolution of acceptance for the North Court street paving. "We believe with the adjustments conceded on protest to a number of the taxpayers, who claimed there was not 25 per cent benefit to the actual value of the property appraised, that now nearly every one is satisfied," stated Mayor Chilton in commenting on the matter today.

In some instances a review of the valuations fixed upon which was computed a 25 per cent benefit the figures were found too high and revision made accordingly. And there are some pretty heavily assessed. Mabel Beck, $1,236, Russell Harper $1,150, W. H. Robinson $1,020 and the Ottumwa Railway and Light Co., $7,223.34, as instances of expense incurred in the large amounts and affecting a total of 44 properties. Total cost in excess of $53,000.

The city will be obliged to make up the deficit, $31,000 plus, and of course every dollar reduced from the private property owner adds to this deficit.

"The city now has a first class road to the city limits, north, and the county and Country Club interests might well join and extend this paving to the gold ground entrance, then by the county for at least a mile and a half from the city limits," commented the mayor.

OTTUMWAN BAFFLED; PLAYMATES LEAVE HIM WITH 37 CENTS

Chicago, Aug. 3.—"Hey! We don't play poker with our feet out in Ioway," shouted Jess Lee, who hails from the Iowa metropolis of Ottumwa, as he looked under the table and saw 5 aces, 3 duces and 2 kinds assorted between the bare toes of James Johnson, one of his partners in a "friendly" little session, in which Jesse had just kissed $62 goodbye.

Jess, with $62.37 in his jeans to spend judiciously taking in Chicago's pageant of progress, fell in with three very sociable men and got into a poker game. Two hours later he had 37 cents. Then he discovered the toe play. In court today Jesse retrieved $34 from his playmates and got this advice from the court:

"Better leave town before they get your pants."

LOCAL SCHOOLS HAVE EFFICIENT METHOD OF RECORD KEEPING

Superintendent H. E. Blackmar stated today that Ottumwa now has one of the most efficient methods known for keeping record of pupils. It has been worked out under Mr. Blckmar's supervision in the past four years.

The card index system is used now in contrast to the cumbersome book method formerly used. In refutation of the argument that nothing but live records should be kept for reference, Mr. Blackmar stated it is a common occurance for people to ask for records for 25 and 30 years.

M. Blackmar stated school will begin September 5. Ottumwa High school still lacks one history teacher and bookkeeping teacher and these positions probably will be filled soon.

SHOOT FAMILY DESERTERS IN LEGAL ADVICE FROM CO. ATTY. AT DAVENPORT

Davenport, Ia., Aug. 3—Men who desert their wives and families, leaving them penniless and on the verge of starvation, should be treated the same as an army deserter in time of war and stood up before a firing squad, according to County Attorney John P. Weir.

"Take them down to the levee and make them look like a sieve," says the prosecutor. "The punishment is about what they deserve. It would only be necessary to treat about two cases in this manner before the habit of deserting one's family would become mighty unpopular and wife desertion would go out of style."

Movie Artists Will Resist Salary Slash; War Impends

Washington, Aug. 3—Without any due publicity the stage is now being set for a bitter struggle between the managers and owners of the theatrical and motion picture industries, on the one hand, and the artists and employes of those industries on the other. The opening gun of the conflict has, in fact, already been fired, and the beginning of the new theatrical season this fall is likely to find the opposing forces contending for supremacy.

The theatrical and film industries are in a state of rather pronounced depression, a part of the "deflation" process. Things have been going badly with the theatre since last fall, a contributing factor in its trials being the high rates which made travel almost prohibitive. Some of the smaller companies, indeed, even attempted touring by automobile.

Spokesmen for the motion pictures have made it evident that there will be a general readjustment of salaries in the industry, even affecting the high priced stars. Those whose weekly stipened has been measured in the thousands will have to show good reason for the continuance of such salaries or submit to a cut.

Meanwhile there has been a disturbed labor condition in the Pacific coast studios, which recently burst into a strike. The studio employes walked out, but the actors—members of the Equity—decided that they could not afford to come to their support. The status of the actors themselves was so precarious that they could not afford to jeopardise their contracts and the studio workers agreed that the actors' course was proper.

How very odd that the Republican administration can pile up taxes to build useless dreadnaught battleships, raise postage to 3 cents, and so very little complaint is heard? But something did happen when Mellon proposed ten dollars levy against every automobile and truck in the country. That was going it a bit too strong as these cars today average a tax cost of nearly forty dollars annually.

20 SUNNYSLOPE BONDS NOW READY

Sunnyslope bonds were delivered to County Auditor Fred Prosser this morning. Each was a valuation of $500 to bear 5 pe rcent interest per annum and falls due in 1941.

The bonds were subscribed for last year. The certificates are in two sheets, the first describing the bonds and the last containing forty coupons which will be detached as the interest falls due and is paid. There are twenty bonds.

If the working people of this country who have repeatedly voted for thirty, forty, or fifty years to bring about the present conditions are satisfied with results as they are, they are then what we understand as one hundred per cent plutocrats.

For what purpose have we a congress? Why do we need a United States Senate? What have they done for the country since the war, but to levy and collect taxes from the people?

OBITUARY

GEORGE DOYLE SHORT

George Doyle Short, 3 year old son of Mr. and Mrs. Roscoe Short, who died this morning at 11 o'clock will be buried tomorrow in Shoul cemetery.

The funeral services will be held from the Short home, 1702 Mabel St., at 10 a. m. with Rev. R. B. Fisher officiating.

The deceased is survived by his parents, two brothers and two sisters.

As you witness the put-over of the Fordney bill be convinced it is framed to meet the slightly reduced budget and that the only relief this affords is so designed as to make those most able to pay the chief beneficiaries. One writer with keen analysis pared the thing to the bone and says it might well be designated "a bill to relieve the profiteers and owners of largest incomes."

Do Your Kitchen Work in Comfort

Think of the hours you'll spend there this summer—the long days canning fruit, the afternonos when you iron, the Saturday mornings when you bake. And at least an hour preparing every meal and straightening things away.

Goodness knows, it's hard enough work in the winter time. You deserve every possible aid to make kitchen work more bearable in summer. It's a joy to prepare good things to eat when there'a a cool zreeze blowing. Makes the meal more appetizing for you too. You're rested and refreshed when you go to the table.

WANT ADS.

BE A NURSE

WANTED—Young women to study nursing. Two years course of training and instruction in accordance with Illinois new law. Accredited training school. Graduates of this course are eligible to registration in Illinois. Modern fully equipped general hospital. New modern nurses' home. Class now forming. State age and preliminary education. ENGLEWOOD HOSPITAL, 60th & Green Sts., Chicago, Ill.

TO HOLD SERVICES FOR LT. SCHAEFER IN CENTRAL PARK

Funeral Services for Lieutenant Walter Beaumond Schaefer, who died in a German prison April 22, 1918 from wounds received while leading a raiding party in No Man's Land in the Champagne sector in France in the World War, will be held in Central park next Sunday afternoon at 3 o'clock.

The deceased hero was born October 1, 1893.

Announcement was received here yesterday by Lieutenant Schaefer's parents Mr. and Mrs. John M. Schaefer, 402 Chester that the body left Hoboken, N. J. yesterday and is expected here tonight.

The American Legion will have charge of the funeral services with Rev. E. J. Snook D. D. of Mount Pleasant officiating. If the weather will not permit of the services being held in Central park they will be held in the First Methodist Church corner of Fourth and Market streets.

FILE CHARGES OE MURDER TODAY; THREE ARE HELD AS PLANS NOW POINT

At 2:30 this afternoon Sheriff Giltner stated: "We will file charges this afternoon against three for complicity in the murder of W. H. Armstrong, and Bill Jackson is to be held as an accomplice."

The official did not name the two of the three because "there may be some change in the plans after a conference with Chief Blizzard and Coroner Hammer."

Jackson was arrested Monday morning and has been held with no information filed against him for more than 48 hours.

One physician speaking of the death stated that it would be quite possible that Armstrong received the blow on the head while outside and coming home was able to partially undress for bed when a collapse overcome him, ending in his death. "There are instances where ball players, struck in the temple, resume playing and it is some time before they succumb to the injury. It might be that way in Armstrong's case, although this of course is purely supposition."

While it was stated by the sheriff that information will be sworn out and filed with the county attorney this afternoon, still in absence of the coroner's report it would be rather the unusual to file charges so serious in advance of the coroner's jury verdict. "There has been no urge from the prisoner Jackson or his counsel for arraignment," was the comment of Chief Blizzard.

There is no let-up on the part of the officials, both city and county, as they seek for clues that will lead to the guilty person or persons, and it appears a suspicion is entertained that at least three are involved in the alleged crime. Jackson, husband of the woman who had been keeping company now and then with Armstrong, is one who has been named to be held for arraignment.

Resume Work

Heavy rains visited upon Ottumwa the past week are responsible for damage to concrete form ditches on the new high school site at college and second street. Digging of ditches was completed some time ago and pouring concrete has occupied the greatest part of the building program. The crumpled condition of the walls made necessary the work of clearance which has now been completed and concrete pouring resumed on the foundation.

RELEASE JACKSON FROM MURDER CHARGE; DR. WILLIAMS SAYS MAN MET DEATH FROM BLOW TO HEAD

William Jackson and Lafe Johnson suspects in the murder of W. H. Armstrong were released last night by order of Sheriff Giltner. No further arrests have been made and none will be made it is alleged, until the Coroner's inquest which is being held today, shall have been finished.

The fact that Armstrong met his death by foul means was substantiated by the testimony of Dr. A. O. Williams before Coroner A. L. Hammer today. Dr. Williams conducted the postmortem examination of the body of Armstrong the morning of the murder. Dr. Williams stated that death was caused by concussion of the brain produced by a blow on the head from some blunt instrument. According to Dr. Williams, Armstrong's death was not due to congestion of the brain for there were no signs on the man's throat to indicate that his assailant had choked him. In the postmortem examination it was shown that a blow had been struck hard enough to break the bones in the nose where the nasal organ joins the skull.

Been Dead Several Hours

When asked if Armstrong might have received the blows on the head before reaching home and died from congestion of the brain, he stated that concussion was most profound at its conception and that death was almost instantaneous whereas congestion does not produce unconsciousness at once but it may follow from three to six hours after the rupture of an artery or vessel in the brain.

Rigorous mortis had set in before the body was turned over to Dr. Williams for examination and was so far completed to indicate that he had been dead several hours.

The examination, according to Dr. Williams, showed Armstrong to be in good health with heart and lungs normal, proving that he did not die of any physical defect. As to the probability of the man having an apoplectic stroke or heart failure, Dr. Williams stated that the posture of the man when found would not indicate this. Armstrong was found lying face downward and stretched his full length on the floor.

DUTTON ARRESTED

A raid on the rooms of Charles Dutton 330 East Main street last evening resulted in the finding of four pints of whiskey and two half pints of "corn." Dutton was taken before Justice Cremer. Waiving preliminary hearing he was bound to the grand jury.

Caruso is dead.

A little while ago that would have meant much to a few thousand that had seen and heard him, nothing to others. Now it means loss and sorrow to tens of millions that never saw Caruso but heard his voice.

A while ago the millions would all have said: "He is dead, and I never heard him." Now they will say: "He is dead. I have heard him often, although I never saw him."

And in years to come a thousand will hear Caruso, dead, for everyone that heard him, living. Such is the miracle of the talking machine.

COUNCIL TURNS DOWN SEWER BIDS; SCOTT LOWEST

The City council this morning rejected the bids of J. W. Scott, lowest bidder on the contracts for the Schuyler-Finley Avenue trunk sewer and the Keota, Willard-Schuyler street sewer. The work will be advertised for bids again soon and they must be submitted by August 15.

On the Schuyler street sewer from Finley Avenue trunk sewer to center of Glenwood Avenue, Mr. Scott bid $2 per foot for 10 inch pipe and $2.80 per foot for 12 inch pipe. The manholes were bid at $7.50 per lineal foot. Manhole tops were bid at $17 each. T and Y junctions were bid at $6.25 for 10 inch at $7.50 for 12 inch.

On the Keota-Willard-Schuyler street sewer Mr. Scott bid $2 per foot for 12 inch pipe and $2.00 per foot for $15 in. pipe. T and Y junctions were bid $4.75 for 12 inch and $6.25 for 15 inch. Manholes were bid at $7.50 per lineal foot while manhole tops were bid at $17 each.

Only one bid other than that of J. W. Scott was received, that of Harness Brothers' bid for $50 higher than that of Scott.

THE NEGRO MIGRATION

Later census figures follow the earlier ones with almost touching fidelity. Very early, when only municipal counts were given, it appeared that the negro population of the north had increased much more rapidly than the white, while in the south just the opposite was true. Now, with state statistics coming in, we find that the white population of Illinois increased 14 per cent in the last decade and the negro 67; while in Oklahoma, the negroes gained 8.6 per cent and the whites 26.

The race problem is no longer sectional yet it differs sharply on the two sides of Mason and Dixon's line. In the south, the color question seems quite as likely to be raised in the country as in the cities, and the disgraceful lynching of negroes occurs mainly in the smaller communities. In the north, race conflict is confined almost wholly to the cities, there are comparatively few isolated lynchings, but every few years, some northern town indulges in a riot with negroes for victims.

There is little to choose between the two regimes in the matter of injustice, but there is pretty good evidence that northern conditions hit the colored race, as a race, much harder than do those of the south. City life is not well endured by the negro. The high birth rate of the plantations is cut down, and the infant death rate goes up. Even among the whites, great cities are maintained chiefly by immigration from the countryside; and without such immigration city negro colonies would disappear in short order.

TEACHERS TO MEET AT COURT HOUSEE

A meeting of all rural teachers will be held in the little court room at Wapello county court house the afternoon of August 26 at 2 o'clock.

R. L. Gardner, Superintendent, of Schools stated today that there are more teachers for jobs this year than there have been since before the World War

JULY, 1921 HOTTEST SINCE 1916; 16 DAYS WITH MERCURY AT 90

July, 1921 will go down on the weather bureau record of Ottumwa as the hottest in many years. The record kept by Henry Eiler, official weatherman in Ottumwa shows that the temperature stayed at the 90 degree mark for 16 days in July and that upon July 11, 12 and 13 the mercury climbed to the 98 mark.

There have been only two other Julys with higher temperature average. That of 1916 as slightly warmer and had 17 days with 90 degree or above and three days with 100 degrees. July 1901 was considerable warmer andn had 22 days with 90 degrees or above and nine days with 100 degrees or more.

THE SALES TAX IDEA

The Ottumwa Chamber of Commerce is practically committed to the espousel of the sales tax and the larger newspapers of the country, headed conspicuously in the movement by the New York Herald, is bringing pressure to adopt this method of raising revenues for the government. And there is no doubt about the justice of such procedure as will pass the tax to the customer, that ultimate fellow who in all the ages of the past and for the future no doubt, stands to take the final count.

The News can appreciate the force of the argument in the claims that the customer sees the tax on his article, that he can buy or leave it alone, that it cannot be repeated on him except with his consent and under federal supervision there is equality in the distribution of the tax, but even so is there not a better way to ease the tax burden by eliminating programs for war xpenditures to the millions of dollars?

Ottumwa Daily News

NOTED SCULPTOR TO VISIT OTTUMWA LATE THIS YEAR

David Edstrom, noted sculptor and former Ottumwan, plans to pay this city a visit this coming fall in the interest of his work.

Mr. Edstrom several years ago when he was contemplating the creation of the Soldier and Sailor monument which now stands in Central park offered to move his collection of sculptured work reposing in various parts of Europe to Ottumwa if enough money could be raised to meet the expense of moving. This was passed up at the time for each 100 funds.

Los Angeles, Cal., has taken up a proposition now which will result eventually, according to advices received here, in the establishment in Los Angeles of a gallery devoted to Mr. Edstrom's works.

It is the thought of many that the bequest to the city of Ottumwa for library purposes by the late J. C. Hackworth may be diverted to some extent to help in a proposition which will enable Ottumwa to possess some of Mr. Edstrom's works and for a local art gallery to be located at the Hackworth home at the corner of Pennsylvania avenue and Court streets.

Nothing of a definite nature will be done relative to any of Mr. Edstrom's works until he pays his visit to Ottumwa this fall.

It was learned today that the first thought of the Public Library board in dispensing the interest from the $800,000 will be toward the building itself. Floors and walls will be gone over thoroughly in an effort to make the interior of the building more beautiful. The book shelves will also come in for a good bit of attention as they need replenishing badly.

CITY P.O. SELLS 2,999,000 2-CENT STAMPS ANNUALLY ---$33,000 MORE AT 3 CT.

Secretary Mellon advocates the three cent postage for all first class matter.

The News asked Deputy Grant Keyhoe of the Ottumwa office what this increase would mean to Ottumwans. He estimated it would reach $33,000 additional expense annually on the population basis and demand for the present year.

The local office however, under Postmaster C. W. McCarty's nearly eight years management, has shown constant increase of business and before the 3 cent postage rate would be lowered it is likely the excess penny charge would total not less than $50,000 a year within a short time.

The following figures will prove interesting, serving as they do as an index to the growth and thriftness of this locality, for number of two cent stamps sold for the year ending June 30, 1921:

July, 1920—155,000; August 1920—180,000; September 1920—205,000; October 1920—205,000; November 1920—205,000; December 1920—240,000; January 1921—200,000; February 1921—200,000; March 1921—204,000; April 1921—170,000; May 1921—150,000; June 1921—185,000.

Ottumwa sells 2,299,000 2-cent stamps annually. Receipts, $45,980. With the three center, it means $78,970. An increase of $33,000 estimated.

Land Tax Fairly Equalized Wapello Is Told Roberts Cites Merchandise as Low

"The assessment valuation of Wapello county's acreage at $60.26 with a 112 per cent increase for equalization purposes, I believe, is fair." Thus spoke County Attorney N. W. Roberts today.

The delegates of the Farm Bureau and Farmers' Union feel the same way about the valuation assessment after conferring yesterday with the Equalization Board at the State House in Des Moines.

1921

YOUTH GETS 5 YEARS FOR STORE THEFT

Judge Francis Hunter this morning pronounced sentence on Willard Travis, 18 year old youth who was caught last Thursday morning in the act of stealing a suit of clothes from Trott's clothing store in Eldon.

Judge Hunter sentenced the boy to five years in Anamossa. Travis first gave his name upon being arrested as Jimmy Barnes but later admitted to the officers his right name and gave his address as Blue Island, Ill. Travis' parents were notified and yesterday the father arrived here. He talked with Sheriff George Giltner but asked no clemency for his son.

CORONER JURY ADJOURNS TILL MONDAY MORN

After visiting the house at 507 Gladstone street where W. H. Armstrong, murdered man was found, the Coroner's jury adjourned yesterday afternoon until 9 o'clock Monday morning.

More than twenty witnesses have been examined and the officers are no nearer a solution of the mystery surrounding the death of the man.

A petition for divorce was filed with Clerk Dungan this morning by Mrs. Nathan Johnson, wife of the man who was with Armstrong on the night before the murder.

W. B. Griffith, state detective, is here today, conferring with Sheriff Giltner on the matter. He was sent here at the instigation of Attorney General Ben Gibson.

Hupmobile

Prices Reduced $200 to $325

Effective immediately, Hupmobile prices reduced on open cars, and $315 to $325 on closed cars.

The five-passenger car and the Roadster are now $1,485; the Sedan, $2,485; the Coupe $2,400 all prices F.O.B. Detroit, war tax to be added.

What this reduction actually means is an increase in Hupmobile value that is worth far more than the revision in price.

The truth is that at its new price, and with its well known economy, low repair costs, life long and high grade resale value, the Hupmobile stands forth today as the best buy in the motor car market.

The revision represents the rock bottom figure at which the high quality of the Hupmobile can be maintained.

HUPP MOTOR CAR CO.,
DETROIT, MICH.

NOW $1485

We also have a number of USED CARS. Dodge, Maxwell, Velie, Ford Sedans. All late models. Bargain prices.

WAPELLO AUTO COMPANY
Distributors—Ottumwa, Iowa

11-13 W. SECOND ST.   PHONE 283

VIOLATION DIMMER LAW LOSE LICENSE, 3RD TIME

Beginning Sept. 1, drastic punishment for violators of Iowa's new automobile headlight law which went into force April 13, is promised by W. M. McCollaway, superintendent of the state motor vehicle department.

Until now no attempt has been made to enforce the law, for the reason that the state highway commission to which is delegated the task of testing all headlight lenses, has not been equipped to perform this function.

Three Times Are Out

Penalty for the first offense is by fine of not less than $5, nor more than $25. Second offense will entitle the bright light demon to a similar punishment.

But look out that you are not apprehended a third time for the same cause. Your license to drive an automobile will be revoked for a period of not less than one year. The new law very clearly provides this penalty.

Here are some of the things your headlights and spotlights must not do.

In the first place, they must not throw a light higher than 42 inches from the ground at a distance of seventy-five feet from the headlights.

Get An Approved Lense.

Spotlights must be adjusted so they throw all their light on the right side of the center of the road, and they may not be set to throw a brilliant light directly in the faces of drivers of oncoming cars, at penalty of the driver being prosecuted for a misdemeanor.

The state highway commission already has finished many of its tests of standard types and makes of lenses. Motorists desirous of obtaining a strictly legal lense may obtain the list of approved lenses from the motor vehicle department.

According to the county officials familiar with the automobile law, it is obvious that the use of plain glass lenses will be illegal under the terms of the law, and enforcement of the law is expected to do away with most of the dimmer troubles experienced on country roads and city streets.

ARMSTRONG SLAIN VERDICT OF JURY

"That William H. Armstrong came to his death by a blow on the head with some blunt instrument in teh hands of some person, the reason being unknown to the jury," such was the verdict of the coroner's jury delivered yesterday after an investigation lasting three days.

CATARRH OF THE STOMACH

YOU CAN'T ENJOY LIFE with a sore, sour, bloated stomach. Food does not nourish. Instead it is a source of misery, causing pains, belching, dizziness and headaches.

¶ The person with a bad stomach should be satisfied with nothing less than permanent, lasting relief.

¶ The right remedy will act upon the linings of the stomach, enrich the blood, aid in casting out the catarrhal poisons and strengthen every bodily function.

¶ The large number of people who have successfully used Dr. Hartman's famous medicine, recommended for all catarrhal conditions, offer the strongest possible endorsement for—

PE-RU-NA
IN SERVICE FIFTY YEARS

TABLETS OR LIQUID
SOLD EVERYWHERE.

1921

HOW TO FOCUS THE BULB IN A HEADLIGHT.

Drive the car to a place where the light from the headlights will be thrown on a wall, fence or screen at least twenty-five feet from the car.

Remove the front lamp glass, then cover or disconnect one lamp so that only the light from one lamp at a time will show on the screen.

FOCAL ADJUSTMENTS.

No. 1 Focal Adjustment—

The filament of the lamp bulb is at the focal point of the reflector. The resulting beams of light are almost straight ahead and of the smallest diameter. It is this form of beam that the majority of lamp glasses or lenses are designed to take and modify into a beam of more useful light on the road.

How to make No. 1 Focal Adjustment—

Move the lamp bulb forward or backward in the reflector until the circle of light on the wall is as small as possible.

No. 2 Focal Adjustment—

All of the filament is back of the focal point of the reflector. The resulting beams of light spread out as much as possible. This adjustment gives the greatest spread of light without black spots in the center.

How to Make No. 2 Focal Adjustment—

After making No. 1 adjustment, move bulb backward until a black spot appears in the center of the light. Then move bulb slightly forward until the black spot almost disappears.

No. 3 Focal Adjustment—

The filament of the lamp bulb is slightly back of the focal point of the reflector. The resulting beams of light spread out slightly from the lamp.

How to Make No. 3 Focal Adjustment—

After making No. 1 adjustment, move the lamp bulb backward toward the rear of the reflector until a black spot appears in the center of the light. Then move bulb forward slightly until the circle of light is larger than No. 1 and smaller than No. 2.

No. 4 Focal Adjustment—

All of the filament is forward of the focal point of the reflector. The resulting beams of light cross each other before spreading.

How to Make No. 4 Focal Adjustment—

Same as No. 2 except that lamp bulb is moved forward.

Do not neglect the focal adjustment of the headlights. It is the most important detail of the headlight.

Remember that the application of an approved device does not comply with the law unless:

1. A proper candlepower bulb is used.
2. The proper focal adjustment is made.
3. The proper tilt is given to the headlights.

Clothes for Active Boys

OBITUARY

GEORGE DOYLE SHORT

George Doyle Short, 3 year old son of Mr. and Mrs. Roscoe Short, who died this morning at 11 o'clock will be buried tomorrow in Shoul cemetery.

The funeral services will be held from the Short home, 1702 Mabel St., at 10 a. m. with Rev. E. B. Fisher officiating.

The deceased is survived by his parents, two brothers and two sisters.

BATAVIA MAN HAS FLIVVER STOLEN HERE

The police today are looking for a Ford touring car which was stolen last evening from N. E. Weitch of Batavia. Weitch alleges that he left his car on Main street in the block between Market and Green streets and discovered his loss about an hour later.

The car's license number is 104141 and had a blue laprobe in the rear seat. This makes the second car stolen in Ottumwa the past week.

Arthur Ransome, who has preferred giving facts, as he found them, to imagining things about Russia, reports that the bolshevist government is drifting back to capitalism rapidly. Tchitcherin revealed the drift of old times in a recent speech.

YOUR LIGHT FOCUS

Motorists are having considerable trouble to secure the proper and legal focus for headlights. It is a delicate operation and consists in getting the right adjustment by length given between the light bulb and the reflector. One authority writes that "usually the means for doing this is easily understood and consists of a threaded holder for the bulb with a lock nut for securing the holder in the position arranged.

"A method of finding out just how each lamp is operating, and of having a definite basis upon which to do the adjusting, is shown in the diagram, which explains itself, writes W. V. Relma in Farm and Fireside.

"It will generally be found that one of the headlights has a tendency to tilt in a certain other direction other than straight ahead. Some of the cars have provided a means of adjustment that will let this be corrected. Where such a method is not provided it will be necessary to use a heavy monky wrench for bending the lamp supports to the desired angle."

Sheriff Giltner will announce seven places where tests may be officially made of the lights, their focus, in this county and thus provide a means whereby the precise adjustment may be assured and throwing a clear, strong ray where desired.

Next Wednesday is the last day you will be permitted to operate a lensless car. This is not a new law, however, just the application of a law that has been ignored in Iowa to date.

40 BUSHELS CORN TO ACRE ESTIMATE FOR WAPELLO CO.

"Our idea at this time is that corn at cribbing season will be sold on the local market at about 45 cents. We are paying 50 cents for old corn today and there is not going to be much change in price. Probably a few cents lower when late in November or when the new crop is sold."
—Robinson.

A yield of 40 bushel to an acre is the prediction of local grain men for Wapello county's corn crop. The drought which was visited on the country in general during the last part of June and through July didn't hold on long enough to "fire" the maize.

The early potato crop is damaged and the yield is the lightest for several years. However, the rains of the past two weeks have helped the late potatoe crop and unless there is a drought soon, Wapello county housewives need not worry about "spuds." Reports from he northern part of the state announce a fairly heavy potato yield.

WANTED—3 COPIES

The News will pay 10 cents each for first three copies of June 22, 1921. Bring to News office.

1921

ROY CRABB BUYS BOAT CLUB LAND AFTER 15 YEARS

The club house and grounds, which in time gone by were the pride of "The Ottumwa Oarsmen," is now the property of R. L. Crabb, having been sold to him recently and the deed transferred last night.

The club was organized about 15 years ago and in 1910 the present club house was built. The property is located on the Des Moines river bank across from Turkey Island.

Mr. Crabb, the present owner, states that he will re-model the clubhouse and conduct a strictly up-to-date bathing beach and dance hall. Officers of the boat club are Judge Seneca Cornell, president; Anton Elliott, vice president; and James Winn, secretary.

FAILS TO MAKE NEGRO CONFESS

Des Moines, Aug. 29.—Sheriff Robb, so far, has failed to gain a confession from George Davenport, Negro, whom he claims murdered Sara Thorsdale. He also has failed to locate the rings which were worn worn by the pretty teacher at the time she was slain.

The negro has been grilled time after time, but he still sticks to his story that he was not at Valley Junction on the day the teacher was murdered.

James MacDonald, veteran detective, gave out a statement Sunday declaring that Robb was trying to fasten the crime on Davenport, despite the fact the evidence almost conclusively shows Joe Williams, Negro, the killer.

OBITUARY

Dardanella, one year, six months, daughter of Mr. and Mrs. Walter Walker, 420 Foster avenue, died at the family home at 12:25 Wednesday afternoon. She is survived by her parents and one brother, Jack Edwin Walker. Funeral services were held at the home this afternoon at 4 o'clock.

44 IN DIRIGIBLE TRAGEDY OF ZR-2. 16 AMERICANS; THOUSANDS IN WITNESS

London, Aug. 25.—The list of victims are now known to have numbered 44 with 16 of these Americans, it is reported. Early this morning divers began to search for bodies in the wreck of the ZR-2.

Spectators who witnessed the start of the buckle of the dirigible say it seemed a turn was attempted and that this was the cause of the disaster.

LIBRARY CAN'T USE $600,000 UNTIL JULY 1923

The money willed to the Ottumwa Library Association by the late J. T. Hackworth will not be available until 1923, according to the interpretation of John F. Webber, one of the attorneys for the Hackworth estate and president of the Wapello County Savings bank named as trustee in Mrs. Hackworth's will.

In the will of Mrs. Hackworth it is provided that the bequests it makes shall be paid in quarterly installment at intervals of six months during to years following her death which occurred July 9 this year. When the two year period shall have expired the trusteeship for which he codicil of her will makes provision will become effective, and it is under the trusteeship that money will be available for the libarby."

CITY NOT YET EXEMPT

Mayor Chilton, in commenting on the matter today said, "Mr. Webber's interpretation of the will of course admits of no question and it will be up to the city to supply the necessary monies the next two years to take care of the library. It is possible that the levy can be reduced in 1924, but not for the coming two years."

LOCAL CAVALRY MEN TO RECEIVE HORSES

Hostler Ben Crips of local Service Troop, First Iowa Cavalry, has been ordered to purchase forage for cavalry horses enough to last ten days.

Crips states the horses ar eexpected to arrive here within the next few days. When asked where the stables will be located he stated that Joe Blount has suggested a location on one of his lots, but this is thought to be too small.

It is the aim of the cavalry men to project the stables on a tract of land with at least ten acres for military practice, including hurdles.

This government has to date been a signal failure under President Harding. The slacker charge may well be laid at the door of these men who sailed into office nearly a year ago with a program that was announced as a curative to start the wheels of industry everywhere humming away and all groups of our citizenship provided with means to share in a restored prosperity.

Congress has done practically nothing to elleviate the hardships imposed on the nation, particularly the wage-earning classes.

Women now can hold office in Missouri, the question having been carried by a large majority in the recent state-wide election.

1921

But for reasons best known to republican politicians, congress has flopped about like a chicken with its head tied in a sack. Meanwhile the business of the country has been drifting. When money is not employed, men can not be employed. There need be no wonder that the secretary of labor reports that 5,700,000 workers are idle. Except for the patriotism and resourcefulness of hopefulness of hopeful business men the number would never be nearer 10,000,000.

U. S. SIGNS LAST OF PARTS WITH ALLIES

Washington, Aug. 30—Signautre of a treaty between the United States and Hungary, set for late today according to Budapest dispatches, brings to an end the peace negotiations entered into by the United States under President Harding with the central powers against whom the United States declared war in 1917. The treaty with Austria was signed last Wednesday at Vienna and that with Germany the following day at Berlin.

OBITUARY

DON EUGENE HOWARD.

Don Eugene Howard, 3-month-old son of Mr. and Mrs. Joe Howard, died Saturday night at the home of his parents, 903 West Barton street.

He is survived by two sisters, Ruth and Francis. Funeral services were held this afternoon at 2:30 o'clock from the residence. Mrs. Peters of Pentecostal church, officiated. Burial was made in Shaul cemetery.

LOCAL MAN IS TARGET —WOUNDED

H. E. Headley, Ottumwan, is suffering today from a gun shot wound in his left shoulder inflicted by one of four unknown men who fired upon him from the roadside near the Reveal schoolhouse west of Ottumwa on the Eddyville road last night.

Headley says that he was driving past the schoolhouse in his car and was accompanied by a lady friend. He added that he knew of no reason why he was made the target of the men's guns.

Five shots were fired according to Headley. One shot struck him in the shoulder and another ripped through the tonneau of his car.

Sheriff Giltner has been notified and will make an investigation.

Ottumwa Daily News

SEPTEMBER 1921

Sept 3 - Communist Party of Belgium forms

Sept 3 - American reporter, war correspondent, and Pulitzer Prize winner Marguerite Higgins born

Sept 6 - The inventor of the bar code is born in Atlantic City, NJ

Sept 7 - First Miss America Pageant is held, in Atlantic City NJ

Sept 8 - Margaret Gorman, 16, wins the pageant's Golden Mermaid trophy and $100 and later is dubbed the first Miss America

Sept 13 - White Castle hamburger restaurant opens in Wichita KS, the foundation of the first fast food chain

KISS YOUR WIFE 3 TIMES A DAY; IT'S THE .... ROYAL ROAD TO CONNUBIAL JOY

Chicago, Sept. 1.—Kiss your wife three times a day. That's just enough. So say the experts. Three kisses a day will maintain happiness in the home and the proper amount of avoirdupois on the wife.

More than three every twenty-four hours is too much, experts say, citing the case of Mrs. Lillian M. Cummings, wife of a six-foot, 200-pound policeman, who wants a divorce, because she lost forty-four pounds as the result of the frequency and ardor of the osculatory activities of her husband. Her weight fell from 145 pounds to 101 pounds.

ARMY TO RESUME RECRUITING

Washington, Sept. 7.—Recruiting for the regular army which was practically stopped when it became evident that Congress would reduce the army to 150,000 men, was ordered resumed today by Secretary Weeks.

1921

MARCONI RADIOS WITH MARS TOLD

New York, Sept. 2.—J. C. H. MacBeth, London manager of the Macaroni Wireless Telegraph Company, Ltd., today startled members of the Rotary Club of New York by the announcement Signor Marconi believed he had intercetped messages from Mars.

The wireless inventor, he said, while making atmospheric experiments aboard his yacht, the Electra, in the Mediterranean several months ago discovered wireless wave lengths far in excess of those used by the highest powered radio stations. These led him and other wireless experts to believe Mars or some other planaet was trying to communicate with us.

MacBeth said the maximum length of waves produced is 14,000 meters. He said those picked up by Marconi were about 150,000 meters. He said their regularity disproved any belief they are produced by electrical disturbances

CREIGHTON HELD ON LIQUOR COUNT

Leonard Creighton was arrested last night for maintaining a liquor nuisance at his home on Hayne street. He was arraigned before Police Judge Kitto this morning and entered a plea of not guilty. His bonds were fixed at $300, which he furnished. His trial will be held next Friday afternoon at 2 o'clock.

Did you ever see such fine crops for this state? True we are short of fruit and potatoes but the big items, corn and hogs, are crops quite up to the highest average. Today the housewives are canning peaches shipped here from the far west, Colorado, Utah, Idaho, and they will go a long way to make up the shortage. Prices are a trifle higher pretty well up toward $4 a basket, but sugar is considered as cheap and it might be worse indeed. The advice is to can all you can. It is the last canning chance you have for putting in the winter supply. It is a long time until they grow again.

LOCAL P. O. HOURS LABOR DAY; G-D OPEN 7:30 TO 10:30

The hours of service at the Ottumwa, Iowa, post office for Monday, September 5, Labor Day, will be as follows:

The General Delivery and Stamp windows will be open from 7:30 to 10:30 o'clock a. m.

There will be no delivery of mail in the city or on the rural routes, but the carriers' windows, both city and rural, will be open from 9:30 to 10:30 to accommodate patrons who wish to call for their mail during that hour. All windows will be closed at 10:30 o'clock and remain closed for the balance of the day.

The regular collection will be made from the street letter boxes.

CHAS. W. MCCARTY,
Postmaster.

Columbia University is establishing a new course in motion pictures, the first of th ekind given in the United States.

Morals and ethics are among the new studies to be added this fall to the curricula of the public schools of Chicago.

SCHOOL STARTS NEXT TUESDAY SAYS BLACKMAR

Superintendent H. E. Blackmar announced today that the Adams school will not be ready for the pupils at the opening of the school next Tuesday.

The following arrangement has been made for those pupils who are in the Adams district:

8-A pupils will go to Lincoln school; 8-B pupils in Franklin and Garfield districts will go to Franklin school; 8-B Adams and Lincoln pupils will go to Lincoln school; beginning 8-B pupils will have their choice of going either to the Douglas or Lincoln schools all pupils in grades below the eighth will go to Garfield school at 10 o'clock beginning next Tuesday; Garfield district pupils in grades below the eighth will go to Garfield school beginning at 8 o'clock next Tuesday.

There will be no school next Monday on account of Labor Day.

Electric Breezes Keep the World Moving

You recall how thousands of speakers condemned as utterly inefficient the Democrat regime that for two terms in the White House was giving rather good business service to the country. About all you can claim for the "business" talent of the Republican powers at Washington is the announced sale of 205 wooden ships for $450,500, or a salvage of less than one-half of one per cent of the cost.

1921

THE OTTUMWA DAILY NEWS

OTTUMWA, IOWA, Friday, September 2, 1921

16 INDICTMENTS; 8 LIQUOR CHARGES

"RED" ELLIOTT, DUTTON IN FATEFUL LIST; GIVE BOND FOR TRIAL APPEARANCES

H. Bukowski for Contempt

The grand jury, August term of District court, returned 16 indictments late yesterday evening. Eight of the returned indictments were for maintaining liquor nuisances.

Charles (Red) Elliott was indicted on a charge of accepting bribes while on duty as an officer. The true bill names him as having received money from Louise Bryant, who maintains a rooming house at 303 West Main street. Elliott furnished $500 bonds this afternoon and was released pending his trial. A similar bill was returned against Elliott during the October term of court, 1920, but for want of sufficient evidence the case was dismissed.

Charles Dutton, who is also in District court on a charge of contempt of court, was named as defendant in a true bill charging him with maintaining a liquor nuisance. Dutton gave a $400 bond and has been released.

John Jaicl, arrested last Sunday for larceny of a car belonging to W. R. Phillips, is indicted on a charge of grand larceny. He is lodged in Wapello county jail.

Thomas Keen and Harold Postum (both colored) are in Wapello county jail, having been indicted on a charge of breaking and entering Burlington railroad freight cars and with larceny of goods therefrom.

Johnny Ross, Charles (Slim) Trainor and J. L. Brockenbrough are named in separate true bills, alleging maintenance of liquor nuisances. Trainor gave bond of $400 this afternoon for his appearance in court.

Hans Bukowski, who faces a contempt of course charge, is indicted for maintaining a liquor nuisance. He is now in Wapello county jail. Bukowski was in District court last year on a charge of maintaining a liquor nuisance and was found guilty, serving a short time sentence in Wapello county jail. Recently he was charged with violating an injunction placed against him by order of court and warrant issued for his arrest. At the time the warrant was issued Bukowski was in Chicago. He voluntarily gave himself up to the authorities yesterday.

Henry Davis and Thomas Sexton are indicted for liquor nuisances. Both men are in Wapello county jail awaiting trial.

Tony Naraccio and John Ward are indicted on charges of wife desertion.

The indictments against Lester Proctor for rape and against Charles Ross for assault with intent to commit rape were ignored by the grand jury.

Walter Simon is indicted for breaking and entering the J. M. Shindley grocery store at the corner of Ash and Main streets. Simon is in Wapello county jail.

David Cobler is indicted on a charge of robbery committed against one George E. Leedy.

GROUP NO. 1 MEETS NEXT TUESDAY EVE

Group No. 1 of the local Chamber of Commerce, which is given over to advertising Ottumwa, will meet next Tuesday evening in the Chamber of Commerce rooms. Sixty new members have been added to this group, making a total now of 160.

MADDEN REPORTS PROGRESS ON WHITE WAY PETITION

According to T. J. Madden, chairman of the White Way committee, the scheme is not to be abandoned. In a report before the directors of the local Chamber of Commerce, Mr. Madden is quoted as having said many more are ready to sign the petition and a majority of Main street property owners will secure for Ottumwa a White Way.

CITY PHYSICIAN'S REPORT SHOWS SMALL POX ON DECREASE

City Physician Dr. Margare Mill's report to the city council for the month of August shows a decrease in the number of smallpox cases to one case in quarantine. Eleven cases of scarlet fever were quarantined and 14 cases were released from quarantine. Two diptheria cases were confined to the city isolation hospital, two were released and one case was quarantined. The sanitary officer made 49 trips to attend to fumigation work; 123 notices were served on vaults and 21 notices were served commanding new vaults be built. Dr. Mills made 29 professional calls. Four typhoid fever cases were reported and three venereal cases were reportd. The total numbr of deaths last month numbers 32.

SAYS SUNNYSLOPE BEST IN IOWA STATE

Did you ever know that Ottumwa affords the only isolation hospital for disabled ex-service men that is acceptable by standards set by the American Legion?

State Commander Daniel F. Steck, in a talk yesterday before directors of the Chamber of Commerce, declaredd that Sunnyslope was the only sanitarium which measured up to specifications.

FINISH FOUNDATION ON NEW HIGH SCHOOL

The concrete foundations for the new High school building are now all in place and masonry work will soon begin. The Adams school is being thoroughly "overhauled" and will be ready for grade pupils within the next two weeks.

BLACK OPPOSES PAVING HALF OF FOSTER HILL

County Supervisor B. F. Black declared himself today in opposition to the plan of Satte Highway Engineer F. R. White to pave East Main street to the foot of Foster Park hill.

In commenting on the proposed paving Mr. Black said, "I am not in favor of the county paving half of Foster Park hill. We need all money we can get for road grading. The allotment we have made for 1922 grading will not cover the proposed work for next year and in all probability we will have to issue more certificates.

"The city should take Riverview into the corporate limits and get from property owners there for the paving. We cannot afford to make a gift."

Mr. Black admitted the ned of paving the hill all the way and didn't deny that some day the work will be dnoe.

1921

THE ALL-YEAR SCHOOL.

When Professor Hammitt was in our public schools of Ottumwa he advocated the all-year school. He introduced his system at Mason City. His ideas caught the attention of many national educators.

Isn't it about time to have a change in our school system with respect to the length of term? To have the doors of learning over at least eleven months in the year?

Briefly, it is plain to keep the high schools going forty-eight weeks of each year, four terms of twelve weks each, with a week's vacation betwen each term and the next.

The considerations in favor of this plan are obvious, and some of them are stated by the correspondent. It saves time—a pupil by continuous work can graduate in three years instead of four. It saves money—a given school equipment will suffice for a third more pupils than now, assuming that all or most take advantage of the full year sessions. It avoids the dangers, whatever they may be, of long vacations, and doubtless by sheer continuity would induce more pupils to take a high school course. Business goes on throughut th eyear, an dso does the universities of many cities. Why not the high schools, too?

Ottumwa factories are doing some business. The Morrell plant leads off as usual with a good showing of men on the payroll, then in turn comes the smaller enterprises with increasing demand for their products, it is claimed. Ottumwa has weathered along very well compared with many another city. While the crisis is not passed by a considerable, still there is a hope possible things will improve right along with the change of season and a measure of the 1921 crops put into the market. The coming national conference to relieve the unemployed situation may bring about some comfort. But it is certainly to be a trying time of it for the next six months in America, do what they may down at Washington.

SHELLY ARRESTED ON MURDER INTENT INTENT CHARGE

Alva Shelley, who was arrested last Wednesday on a charge of assault with intent to do great bodily injury and later released under $700 bonds fixed by Jdge C. W. Vermilion, was arrested again last night for assault with intent to commit murder.

It is alleged that Shelley beat his wife and threatened to kill her. Shelley, when arraigned on the first charge, pleaded not guilty.

GERMANS BUILD AIR LINER TO CARRY 500

London, Sept. 13.—Germany is building a super-air liner which will carry 500 passengers, according to a Berlin dispatch. The air ship is to have a promenade deck covering its whole length and isbeing built for passenger traffic between Germany, America and Portugal.

Ottumwa Daily News

LEGAL

Mechanical Equipment For
OTTUMWA HIGH SCHOOL

Notice is hereby given that the Board of Education of the Independent School District of Ottumwa, Ia., will receive sealed proposals up to the hour of 7:30 p. m., on Wednesday, September 14, 1921, at the office of the Secretary, for the erection of Mechanical Equipment of the new Ottumwa High School, in accordance with the plans and specifications prepared by Croft and Boerner, Architects and Engineers. Separate bids will be received on the following:

(a) Heating, (b) Plumbing, (c) Ventilation, (d) Electric work, (e) Temperature control, (f) Pipe covering, (g) Elevator, (h) Various combinations as indicated in bid form.

Bids will be received only on the form of the proposal supplied by the Architects and Engineers, and no other form will be considered. Bids must be accompanied with a certified check for the amount of five per cent (5 per cent) of the bid, made payable to the Secretary of the above School District.

The successful bidders will be required to furnish the above Board with an approved surety bond in the amounts called for in the specifications for the above items.

Copies of the plans and specifications may be seen at the offices of the Architects and Engineers, Secretary of the Board of Education and also at the Builders' Exchanges of Minneapolis, Des Moines, St. Paul, Chicago and Omaha. Bidders desiring blue prints for their own exclusive use may obtain same from the office of the Architects and Engineers, and such bidders will be required to pay the net cost of blue printing. A deposit of $35 will be required for all copies of plans and specifications, which amount, minus blue print cost, will be refunded upon the return of plans and in case a bona fide bid is submitted.

The Board reserves the right to reject any or all bids.

J. A. WAGNER, Secretary.
C. D. EVANS, President.

Board of Education, Independent School District, Ottumwa, Iowa.

CROFT and BOERNER, Architects and Engineers, 1006 Marquette ave., Mpls.

F. D. ROOSEVELT HAS INFANTILE PARALYSIS

New York, Sept. 16.—Franklin D. Roosevelt, Democratic candidate for vice resident at last year's election, is suffering from a mild case of infantile paralysis, his pysician, Dr. George Draper, announced today. Mr. Roosevelt is nearing recovery after an illness of four weeks. He is slowly regaining power to control the muscles of his lower legs and feet.

One of the most common cases in all our courts is that of illicit trafficking in liquors which is an outlaw enterprise. The accused, convicted, goes to jail and the world moves on. In a recent local instance of considerable prominence both jail and fine punishment was meted to the defendant. There is no right to criticize, but it is quite true that the one in a hundred caught in these liquor prosecutions makes it 100 to 1 a farcical proposition. The country is full of these bootleggers. Their number multiplies in many sections and the thrill of adventure, the daring, the profit, and the opinion of many engaged in smuggling intoxicants that personal liberty has been invaded and outraged incidentally serve to keep the rest of the fellows in line for the vacant place when one is caught and imprisoned. Funny world. Getting a wrong start and using the worst possible system to challenge a constituent citizen by execution of a loosely conceived policy and we have created thousands of culprits read to dare and do.

Bootlegging is a big income proposition. The chiefs in the industry say they can make 500 per cent, pay all costs, fines and bribes and then finish on the fortune-winning side. So long as there is big money the distillation of beverages and distribution thereof will continue, time without end and in the future until something amendatory to the Volstead act takes place our courts will have a congestion of litigation on the subject.

Why don't somebody start a K. K. K. in Ottumwa? Might prove an antidote to the N. P. L., of which a few fellows stand in mortal dread. —15-CENT OATS.

WHY?

WHO SAID FALL FESTIVITIES AND IF SO, WHEN?

Is Ottumwa to have a Fall Festival or will the matter be dropped as have others in th epast for want of support from recognized community leaders?

This question loomed up in the discussion of a Community Day for Ottumwa last evening in the Chamber of Commerce rooms in the meeting of Group No. 1.

Eleven members, a puny representation of the 160 active members, who associate themselves with Group No. 1 for the Advertising of the City of Ottumwa, were present at the meeting last evening. For want of a majority representation at the meeting action on the proposed plan for the Fall Festival were shelved.

A committee working on the details of the matter have not reported any progress as yet.

LAND VALUE AT $94.44 IS CLAIM OF ATTY. GENERAL GIBSON

Attorney General Gibson is authority for the statement that land values of Iowa are at an average of $99.44 an acre and not $216.

Runs Like a Sewing Machine

Smooth action, light draft, effective operation, long life—that is what roller bearings stand for. That is why roller bearings are used at seven points in the new INTERNATIONAL TIGHT-BOTTOM MANURE SPREADER.

The load is carried on roller bearings on both rear wheels, the two beaters spin on roller bearings, and the rear axle eccentric which operates the walking-beam rachet-drive manure conveyor works on a roller bearing. These are the points where ordinarily there is heavy wear—the places that stand the brunt of hard service. Roller bearings are provided on the new INTERNATIONAL SPREADER to offset the effects of stress and hard service, and it is no great exaggeration to say that this spreader runs like a sewing machine.

You will be interested in the many good points of the International. Why not have a look at this spreader when you are in town? You know where we are located, and know we are always glad to see you.

FABRITZ, BLACK & FABRITZ
"Where Your Dollar Has More Sense."

Phone 2161　　　　　Ottumwa, Ia.　　　　　301-3 Church Street

22ND CHILD TO THIS WIFE AT 43; TWICE MARRIED

Cedar Rapids, Iowa, Sept. 12.—Mrs. Eve F. Rowray is the proudest mother in Cedar Rapids, and if Col. Theodore Roosevelt were alive he doubtless would exclaim, "dee-lighted," for Mrs. Rowray has just given birth to her twenty-second child, a daughter. The mother is only 42 years old.

Mrs. Rowray became a bride when she was 14 years old and her first child was born when she was 17, and she was a grandmother before she reached the age of 40.

Mrs. Rowray was born in Valley Junction, Ia., and was one of eight brothers and sisters. She was married there to William Barker and to this union twenty children were born. Her husband died a few years ago and four years ago she was married to William Rowray, a 22-year-old machinist, who is employed in the Rock Island shops.

The children of the first marriage were born at intervals varying from one to four years. Ten of the children are dead, some dying in early childhood and others at more mature years. There were three pairs of twins, but only one pair is living. They are now in a home in Davenport.

"I always liked to have children around me," said the proud mother when she was congratulated on the birth of her newest child. "When I was younger and lived on a farm, my children and I always played together and had good times. I do not believe I will ever get tired of having children around me."

Mrs. Rowray is in good health and mothers her several children at home just as if she had not given birth to more than two score.

NO HOUSEMAIDS; BLAMES BEAUX

New York, Spet. 10.—Young men don't like to call at the back door and therefore girls don't like to go into domestic service.

This was one explanation given by social workers for an acute shortage of household help which exists in Brooklyn, notwithstanding that thousands of women and girls are idle because of factory shutdowns.

Director Metcalf of the Y. W. C. A. employment bureau said she had abandoned efforts to supply general houseworkers.

"Men don't care to escort a girl through the rear door or be entertained in the kitchen," she explained.

SAVES DAUGHTER IN MAIN STREET CAR ACCIDENT

What might have resulted in one and possibly two tragedies at 8 o'clock Sunday evening was narrowly averted when O. S. Dimmitt, 708 East Main, rushed to the aid of his daughter, Olive, 20, as she was placed in imminent peril from an oncoming street car and automobiles from two directions, opposite the Empire theater.

Miss Dimmitt started across the street between crossings and was closely followed by her parent. In endeavoring to escape an approaching automobile and a street car the girl stepped in front of the rail car and would have been ground to bits, believe bystanders, had not her father plunged forward, grabbed his daughter and swung her clear and into the space that was left as the automobile met and passed the street car. Miss Olive was not injured, but Mr. Dimmitt did not get into the clear, the corner of the street car hitting him and throwing him violently to the pavement, breaking his shoulder and inflicting serious injuries to his right arm.

"Don't make much of a story about it, but be sure to say the Ottumwa Railway people were mighty fine about it. I told them they were not in the least accountable for the accident yet they insisted in taking care of my doctor's expenses just the same. Which was mighty good of them."

SMALL TAXPAYERS' PLAN UPHELD; MELLON LOSES

Washington, Sept. 13.—The Senate finance committee today voted unanimously for increased income tax exemptions for heads of families and for dependents.

The provisions of the House revenue revision bill increasing the personal exemptions from $2,000 to $2,500 for heads of families having incomes of $5,000 or less and the exemptions for children and dependents from $200 to $400 each were approved.

All of Secretary of the Treasury Mellon's tax recommendations that came to a vote tday were rejected by the committee, and the committee expects to reject the remainder of the administration program when it votes on making the excess profits tax retroactive.

Rate Schedules Up.

Consideration of the rate schedules will be completed by the finance committee Friday, Chairman Penrose announced.

The bill, in its final form, will be virtually the same measure that passed the House. Senator Penrose predicted today the finance committee probably will refuse Mr. Mellon's request to make the excess profits tax retroactive.

If this is done, Senator Penrose said, Mr. Mellon's recommendation that $250,000,000 in addiitonal taxes be levied on small taxpayers to make up for the loss of the excess profits tax would not have to be carried out.

The finance committee today fixed 32 per cent as the maximum individual income surtax rate. Mr. Mellon had recommended that surtaxes be reduced to 25 per cent.

Rearrange Suraxes.

The schedule of surtaxes will be rearranged. Senator Penrose said the committee was working on a plan to have the surtaxes start at 1 per cent on incomes of $6,000 instead of $5,000 and increase the surtax 1 per cent for each additional $2,000 of income instead of 2 per cent as at present.

The plan, if adopted, would mean a reduction of surtaxes on incomes from $5,000 to $72,000. The 32 per cent tax would be levied on incomes of $72,000 and over.

The committee today also apprved the provision of the House bill permitting taxpayers to deduct net losses against their income for the succeeding year.

The committee tomorrow will vote on Secretary Mellon's recommendation that one-half the present transportation taxes be retained for another year and htat the existing tax on capital stock be repealed.

OIL EXPLOSION BURNS LOCAL MAN; HOME TOTAL LOSS

Homer McFarlane was badly burned about his arms and legs last evening about 6 o'clock when the two-room shack in which he lives caught fire from an explosion of kerosine.

The shack is located on the river bank near the old ice house above the boat club. McFarlane, returning home about 6 o'clock, attempted to start a fire with kerosene. Gases generated and as he struck a match an explosion through the burning oil over him and the room.

McFarlane ran for the river and plunged in, extinguishing the flames, but not before he had been badly burned. He was taken to Ottumwa hospital, where it is reported he is better.

BURNS ARE FATAL TO MC FARLANE; DIED IN HOSPITAL TODAY

Albert Homer McFarlane, who was severely burned by an explosion of kerosene at his home on the Des Moines river bank west of Ottumwa, died this morning at 4:15 o'clock in Ottumwa hospital.

McFarlane was 57 years old and is survived by his father, Thomas McFarlane, 84; his stepmother, Mrs. Thomas McFarlane, one brother and one sister.

1921

HOMES IN OTTUMWA

Strange how we are prone to arrive at conclusions with so little regard for our opportunity to know what is what. Yesterday, The News carried a story setting out figures from the tax records to show that the owner of a home in Ottumwa is required to pay less taxes than in Eddyville and Eldon and Oskaloosa. You should read the story. It is worth while.

Today we place this inquiry: If it be unquestioned that taxes on a $4,000 home property in Ottumwa is $155.40 annually while Eddyville home owners to that value must pay $175.10, Eldon $195.90, then why are rents double in Ottumwa as compared with these other cities?

The statement is made to The News that rents are much higher and in many instances practically twice the Ottumwa schedule for a modern house, as in the small cities named.

Landlords in Ottumwa would ask not less than $40 a month for this $4,000 modern house. For a $2,000 home at least $25. It is quite interesting to note two things, first, that the larger city property owners needs, asks, for more rental because his personal expense are higher.

He pays more, as the rule, for his general living necessities and luxuries. They live more lavishly, therefore more income is demanded.

Basically, right down on the fundamentals, why should a $4,000 house in Ottumwa, at the same tax, rent for ten to twenty dollars more than in the smaller town? Your answer anticipated that the demand is keener in Ottumwa than Eldon does not make the complete explanation.

BUY STEAM BOILER TO HEAT CO. HOME, TOTAL COST $1,100

The supervisors have contracted to purchase and transport a huge boiler in disuse at Bidwell. It is to be placed in the County Home, and being a ten-tonner capacity, will be ample to supply heat to the citizenship of the Home, now populated by about 75, many enfeebled by advanced age and other ailments.

"We are assured this one boiler, used only a year, will more than make up for the two that it displaces and that the inmates of the Home will be well protected against the winter chill," said Mr. Knox.

The boiler will be loaded on a flat car at Bidwell and taken to Rutledge and then unloaded to be conveyed the rest of the way, work to start at once.

It is estimated that the cost, complete, will be about $1100, or fully one-third less than a new boiler.

RAID OF SHERIFF AT EDDYVILLE GETS RESULTS

Sheriff Giltner was the central figure in a still raid one-half mile east of Eddyville this morning when he followed the tip from Sheriff Henley, Oskaloosa, who had found 24 quarts and three one-half gallon jugs of hootch in a car at Eddyville, then, securing information from two men where the still was located. State Agent Griffin was with Giltner in the raid.

6,200 STUDENTS AT UNIVERSITY OF IOWA

Iowa City, Sept. 26.—More than 6,200 students will be enrolled in the University of Iowa this year. Last year the total registration was 5,343. In medicine it has become necessary to restrict registration to Iowa students.

Ottumwa has consumed more ice this season than in any year of its history. It has been a long and very hot summer and extending into September with still more of it. Ottumwa will be interested to know that we are promised a hard winter and this may mean a reduction in price. So while the coal bill goes up the 1922 ice account may shrink.

CHILD FALLS IN CISTERN SHAFT; WILL RECOVER

Harold Gilman, 3-year-old son of Mr. and Mrs. E. D. Gilman, south of Ottumwa, narrowly escaped death from drowning this morning when he accidentally fell into an open cistern shaft on the George Wycoff place near the Gilman home.

The accident occurred about 10 o'clock this morning. Mr. Gilman, accompanied by the child, went to the Wycoff home to obtain water from a well. Finding the well needed priming, Mrs. Gilman went to the Wycoff house to get some water for this purpose. The small boy wandered over to where a new cistern was being built on the Wycoff place and losing his balance, fell.

About three feet of water is in the bottom of the cistern shaft from recent rains. Mrs. George Wycoff heard the child's muffled cries shortly after the accident and found the little fellow struggling for his life.

A ladder was fetched and the boy was recovered in an unconscious state. Dr. Anthony was summoned to the scene and after working with the still, little form for more than an hour was rewarded by signs of life. It was learned this afternoon that the child is much better and will live.

BEGIN WAR ON KU KLUX KLAN, SAYS AIM OF ORGANIZATION IS TO DISCREDIT JEWS IN AMERICA

Chicago, Sept. 15.—A nation-wide movement to crush the Ku-Klux Klan was started yesterday with the organization of the National Unity Council, with former Edward F. Dunne Illinois committee chairman.

Hostility against the secret organization, crystallized immediately after publication of the first installment yesterday of its expose in The Herald and Examiner.

National Unity Council committees are to be organized in every county and community in which the Ku-Klux Klan gains a foothold, and through mass meetings, patriotic demonstrations and personal contact the danger will be pointed out.

Leaders in church, politics, business and welfare work are being invited to membership. State headquarters have been established at 419 Temple Building, 108 S. La Salle st.

AIM AT SUPPRESSION.

With the moral and financial support of the state's best citizenship it is expected that formidable opposition to the "Klan" will find expression in legislative action suppressing the "Invisible Empire."

Jewish, Catholic and Episcopal leaders throughout the country resent the charge that they cannot be loyal to America and the nation's ideals. Foreign-born citizens, who are also barred from membership in the "Klan" because of their alleged un-Americanism, point to the sacrifices made for America by thousands who were not born upon her soil and to the sterling Americanism displayed by the foremost educators, scientists and business men who left the lands of their birth to adopt America's ideals. Negroes throughout the country feel that the "Klan" is a menace, that it makes for racial unrest and creates bad feeling.

The council expects to unify the best citizenship in a stand against lawlessness and mob rule and to encourage amity rather than enmity between races, religious groups and political parties.

DINNER TONIGHT AT WILLARD STREET METHODIST CHURCH

All men who are interested in the Willard Street Methodist church are invited to attend the dinner to be given there tonight at 6:45 o'clock. The purpose of the event is to better discuss plans for the church program of 1922. No charge will be made for the dinner and a general social hour will be enjoyed.

1921

THE OTTUMWA DAILY NEWS

OTTUMWA, IOWA, THURSDAY, SEPTEMBER 15, 1921.

$204,905 O.H.S. CONTRACTS AWARDED

HEATING ITEM IS $54,253; VENTILATION COST SECOND AND PLUMBING IS THIRD

Six contracts were awarded by the school board this morning relative to mechanical equipment for the new High school. They are as follows:

Heating: General Heating and Ventilating Co. of Milwaukee, $54,253.

Ventilating: Mesaba Sheet Metal Works, Virginia, Minn., $51,975.

Electric Work: Carsten Bros., Ackley, Iowa, $35,974.

Temperature Control: Johnson Service Co., Chicago, Ill., $11,250.

Pipe Covering: Keasley & Mattison C., Chicago, Ill., $8,500.

Plumbing: Western Heating Co., Minneapolis, Minn., $42,935.

Bids were opened yesterday by the school board in a special session. Discussion and simmering of the different bids received started at 9:30 o'clock this morning and lasted until 11:30 o'clock. All local bids submitted for the contracts were too high.

The preliminary work on the building is already completed. Foundations have been erected and work will commence very soon on the super-structure.

The contracts let this morning will not be completed for two years the earliest it is estimated the new building will be ready for occupation.

The earliness which characterizes the letting of the contracts in the eye of the layman is in fact a very short time considering that many of the mechanical features of the work require special attention and special construction.

The Adams school building will not be ready for occupation for two weeks yet. Work is still in progress on interior decoration and re-finishing. The moving work has been completed for some time and the rough work finished.

Ottumwa Daily News

THREE CENTS PRICE FOR CORNHUSKERS

The farm bureaus in the seeral counties are already taking up the wages to be paid to corn huskers. In recent years the price has been from 7 to 10 cents a bushel. That was when corn was selling for from $1.50 to $2.00. Now conditions are quite different. The directors of the bureau in Poweshiek county have headed the procession by declaring three and three and a half cents as the standard rates for pickers this year. Three cents is considered the proper rate for farmers who have elevators at their disposal, and three and a half cents is thought to be about right for those who have to use scoops.

LIEUT. M'CREADY flew up 40,800 feet, seven and three-quarter miles. Up there the temperature, sixty degrees below zero, caused his engine to die. He glided down safely, sliding down hill on the air without an engine going, and established a new record for high flying on this earth.

He wore a fur suit, heated throughout by ecelricity, on his flight up into the space where the lightning lives. That amazes the world now.

It will seem the simplest thing in the world a little later, when the big airships all travel six miles or more above the earth, sending passengers down with smaller ships, not coming down themselves except rarely for important repairs.

In that future day men will go up to the low temperature heights to freeze out disease germs. GO UP EIGHT MILES AND KILL YOUR COLD, will be the doctor's advice.

With the exception of the school of mines, every school connected with the Pennsylvania State College, is giving degrees to women for the first time in the history of the college.

THREE MEN GUARD IOWA AVE.; PUBLIC WANTS POLICEMAN

That always dangerous Iowa avenue crossing now has three watchmen, eight hours shift, a complete 24 hours daily safeguard against accidents. The order became effective the first of the month and was given compliance by the rail companies in operation the fifteenth. This in response to a petition circulated some time ago and filled with more than 200 names, then filed with the city commissioners.

This week another petition is passing around that will ask for a city policeman to maintain a "beat" from Ash street east to the city limits.

President Harding has his finger prints taken. It is getting to be a furious pace between W. G. and Hays to see which can claim the spotlight on daily dallying with the frivolties of life. Great world this. Funny, too. In the meantime let us talk normalcy and praise the farmer with his overproduction and low prices while the protected manufacturer of the city stops work and cashes in on high.

1921

Long Distance Is at Your Service

To congratulate or extend sympathy to friends—to get information quickly and correctly—to promote sales—to avoid making needless trips—for any business or social purpose—"Long Distance" is always the quickest and best way. Here are a few representative rates:

TO	STATION-TO-STATION			PERSON-TO-PERSON
	Day	Evening	Night	Day, Evening or Night
Burlington, Ia.	$.50	$.30	$.25	$.70
Cedar Rapids, Ia.	.55	.30	.25	.75
Centerville	.25	.25	.25	.35
Des Moines	.55	.30	.25	.75
Fairfield	.25	.25	.25	.35
Galesburg, Ill.	.75	.40	.25	.90
Waterloo, Ia.	.70	.35	.25	.95

Evening rates apply from 8:30 p. m. to midnight; night rates from midnight to 4:30 a. m. Station-to-station calls for 25 cents or less are for a 5-minute conversation. All other rates quoted are for a 3-minute conversation.

When you will talk to anyone at the telephone called, it is station-to-station service; if you specify a definite person or persons, it is person-to-person service.

"Long Distance" will give you the rate anywhere.

NORTHWESTERN BELL TELEPHONE COMPANY

Ottumwa Daily News

OCTOBER 1921

Oct 1 - American actor James Whitmore is born in White Plains, NY

Oct 19 - "Bloody Night" massacre in Lisbon claims the life of Portuguese premier Antonio Granjo and others

Oct 21 - Peace conference between Ireland and the United Kingdom begins in London

Oct 21 - The silent film *The Sheik* premieres, propelling lead actor Rudolph Valentino to stardom

Oct 25 - Bat Masterson, American gunfighter in the Wild West, dies of a heart attack at 67

Oct 29 - American cartoonist and Pulitzer Prize winner Bill Mauldin, famous for his World War II cartoons of American soldiers, is born in Mountain Park, New Mexico

PERNICIOUS ANEMIA CURE DISCOVERED

PASADENA, Cal., Oct. 22—Discoverery of the germ of pernicious aneima by Dr Philip Rantjen, former professor of bacteriology at the University of California, was announced today on receipt of word from Washington that the American Association for the Advancement of Science had elected him a member. Dr Rantjen isolated the anemia germ and developed an anti-toxin and serum.

19 STILLS TO DESTRUCTION.

United States Marshal Reed and assistants have been breaking jugs, jars, kegs, bottles and other receptacles, including 19 stills, and pouring the illicit contents of moonshine and home brew into the sewers of Ottumwa today. The atmosphere throughout and around the big federal building is jaggy, permeating the environment as far as the various church corners and smellier than in the days of the licensed drink parlors.

"It's awful stuff," said the official. "I could never have believed men would drink such mixtures until the evidence came in from the local outlaw hiding places. It is rank poison. Judge Wade's order will be cheerfully obeyed."

1921

FIND STILL AND LARGE QUANTITY OF CORN MASH

J. D. Gates is in Wapello county jail and the officers riches by one brand new still as the result of a little sluething party's raid on the premises of Clara South's place on the Air Line road near Bear Creek.

Charles Hyatt and John Bright deputy sheriffs went to the South place this morning to foreclose a mortgage and before starting procured a search warrant from the court as the place was under suspicion

Arriving at the home the still was located and confiscated while Gates was taken into custody. No time has been set for his arraignment. A large quantity of mash was also found.

The day of natudal ice is passing Not only is the manufactured article superior in quality and more sanitary but it is certain to be cheaper later on than the river product ever has been, because the processes for the artificial kind are improved and capacity greatly increased. Many cities already have restrictions against natural ice, except for refrigerating purposes, and our local board of health might well contemplate something along this line in protection of Ottumwa. The cause had better be treated than the effect in the question of pure ice.

Why is the newspaperman telling only half what he knows when he charges full price for a subscription? Did the Daily News give the public the courthouse oratory from the at'orneys in closing "Red" Elliott's case and if not, why not?

—NEWS SUBSCRIBER.

(The News does not publish judicial instructions or closing arguments sof attorneys in cases of this chaarcter.—Ed.)

KEEP TO YOUR RIGHT WHEN DRIVING 'ROUND CITY PARK SAYS MOX

Drive to your right when circumnavigating the city park is the injunction issued to all car owners to lay by Traffic Officer Walter (Max) Ruckman. The city administration as seen fit to erect signs to tell those ignorant of the law to keep to the right side of the park. One sign as been placed on top the public horse drinking fountain at the Third treet intersecion of Court street. The other sign stands at the north nd of the park and at night will be lluminated by a red light.

Keep to your right when driving round the park fellows for if you on't well—Kitto and Ruckman ill get you.

ELLIOTT IS ACQUITTED OF BRIBERY CHARGE

THE NEWS WAS INFORMED FROM A VERY AUTHORITATIVE SOURCE AT NOON TODAY THAT ON THE RETURN OF LAWYER DUKE NECESSARY NOTICE WILL BE SERVED ON THE PROPER OFFICIALS AT THE CITY HALL DEMANDING THE RESTORATION OF CHARLES ELLIOTT TO THE POLICE DEPARTMENT SERVICE. "We will probably file these papers early Monday and believe there is every warrant for expecting compliance therewith under the civil service rules," stated this informant.

Charles A. (Red) Elliott, ex-policeman charged with accepting a bribe as an officer, was found not guilty in district court this morning.

The jury in the case was closeted in the juryroom from 5:30 o'colck yesterday evening until 6 o'clock this morning before obtaining a unanimous ballot.

The interest in the case has been widespread and long before court convened this morning the courtroom was filled with people anxious to hear the verdict. The jurymen filed into the courtroom shortly after nine o'clock and Foreman B. Y. Smith handed the sealed verdict to Deputy Clerk C. D. Githens. The verdict which was verified by the foreman follows: "We, the jury in the case of the State of Iowa vs. Charles A. Elliott, find the defendant not guilty."

It was alleged in the charges against Elliott that he had accepted bribes from Ida Bryant, keeper of a rooming house at 303 West Main street. On the night of June 8, Mayor Charles Chilton, Commissioner Thomas F. Keefe and Chief Harry Blizzard secreted themselves in the Ida Bryant house with a view to witnessing Elliott in the act of accepting money. Elliott is alleged to have entered the room and conversed with Mrs. Bryant about several raids which had taken place shortly before. Mrs. Bryant then, according to Elliott's testimony on the stand, asked him how much he expected from her and that an understanding was necessary. She is further alleged to have said that she had been friendly with other officers on the beat, and named William Simmerman, ex-patrolman. Elliott claimed in the trial that Mrs. Bryant dropped a ten dollar bill in his lap and before he could stop her she left the room.

While waiting for Mrs. Bryant to come back into the room Elliott thrust the bill into his pocket and was shortly after confronted by the city hall delegation.

Elliott is alleged to have refused to give the money to Mayor Chilton at first, but finally did turn it over. He was then asked to resign, which he did.

Information was filed by County Attorney Newton W. Roberts against Elliott gave himself up to the authorities June 8.

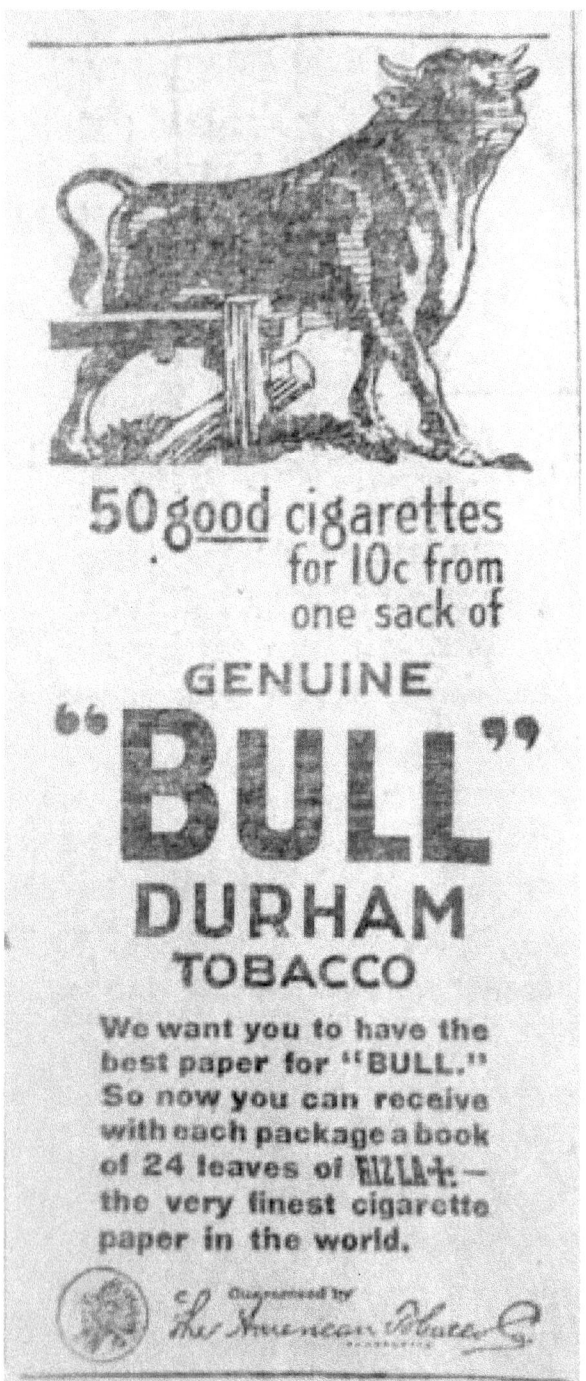

SHOULD A GIRL PAY HER OWN CAR FARE?

If a man meets a woman friend and they get on the street car together should he pay her carfare?

Of course, if he were her escort there would be no question to it, but should she let him pay her fare, just, because, of, the casual meeting?

Theoretically she shouldn't, but as a matter of convenience she permits it. A woman shows bad taste to do anything more than offer to reimburse him. She should not insist on it.

In the home town a chap who asks a girl to a party with him or to the theatre is many times lucky in having the family limousine placed at his service to take the young lady to the entertainment. The family feel safer and contribute the car as part of the evening's entertainment.

Why the plumber at $1.50 an hour and the experienced goods salesman getting 50 cents, or $24 a week and Saturday nights thrown in for good measure?

—COUNTER CALEB.

Ottumwa Daily News

OTTUMWA NEEDS ISOLATION HOSPITAL; COMMITTEE NOW WORKING ON FURTHER PLANS

Ottumwa is to have a new isolation hospital if the plans of the Lions, Rotary and Kiwanis clubs as adopted by them last night at the Chamber of Commerce rooms are carried out.

A committee has been appointed with full power to act and the three organizations will back whatever action they may see fit to take. The members of the committee are T. J. Madden, Dr. M. Bannister and J. E. Espy.

Emmett Work, who has been actively engaged in the work of organizing for a new isolation hospital, stated that funds for the work will be solicited from the residential districts and the business part of Ottumwa will not have to contribute toward the plan unless they are so inclined.

A concensus of opinion among the doctors of Wapello county is such as to warrant immediate action on the matter. The present pest house maintained by the county and city is not adequate for the needs of the town and is far too small to furnish rooms for patients should an epidemic strike the city such as was the case during the influenza epidemic which swept the country.

Some friction exists between members of the clubs and the city council, as voiced today by Emmett Work, but upon investigation of the matter by a News reporter it has been found that a complete understanding of the process of maintaining an isolation hospital is lacking. The present pest house was built by the city and maintained by the city until a few years past when the state legislature passed a bill which states while in quarantine all bills relative to the maintenance of the hospital and medical attention shall be paid by the county. When out of quarantine the maintenance of the hospital shall be paid by the city.

Mayor Chilton, in commenting on the matter this afternoon, declared that if an isolation hospital is to be given that it should be given to the county which maintains it in time of sickness and quarantine. He further stated that he is not in favor of locating the hospital on the Sneiling property on Elm street on account of public feeling and from the fact that it is in a place and one cannot be reached at times when rains have made the roads impassable.

From the tone of voice at the meeting last night in the Chamber of Commerce rooms there is no doubt but some property will be purchased and a hospital erected if necessary.

GROUP COMMENCE WORK

The different groups of the local Chamber of Commerce have taken up their organization's work where they left off at the beginnin of sufner and, soon, various civic improvement projects under consideration will be announced and pushed by the groups united.

Group No. 3 met last night with chairman T. J. Madden presiding. Royl Holbrook, expert combustion engineer from Iowa State College as Ames, spoke to the group on the matter of the "Smoke Menace In Ottumwa." Mr. Holbrook is making a point of addressing each group separately and at the meeting of group No. 7 tonight which meets with its chairman W. T. McElroy he speas in an effort to urge co-operation in elimnatng he needless waste of coal through the agency of better combustion methods.

1921

THE OTTUMWA DAILY NEWS

WALKOUT OF MAJORITY AT MORRELL'S

THE MAJORITY OF WORKMEN AT THE MORRELL PLANT WALKED OUT THIS MORNING AND THIS AFTERNOON AT LABOR HALL THE VARIOUS ASSIGNED CAUSES CONSTITUTING GRIEVANCES AS CLAIMED, ARE BEING DISCUSSED.

"WE DO NOT CARE TO GIVE OUT ANY STATEMENT WHILE THE MEETING IS BEING HELD," STATED ONE OFFICIAL, "BUT THERE ARE SEVERAL REASONS FOR THE WALKOUT."

FROM ANOTHER SOURCE THE NEWS WAS ADVISED THE SUSPENSION IS DUE TO EXCEPTIONS TAKEN WHEN A NUMBER OF MEN WERE DISCHARGED, AND THIS IN ADDITION TO REASONS AFFECTING WAGE AND TIME SCHEDULES. IT SEEMS THERE ARE A NUMBER OF REASONS ALSO DECLARED THIS EMPLOY...

FROM STILL ANOTHER INFORMANT WHO DECLARED HE KNEW THE "STRAIGHT" OF IT, THE TROUBLE STARTED WHEN WORK IN THE TRIMMING ROOM THAT HAD BEEN DONE BY GIRLS AND WOMEN WAS TAKEN FROM THEM AND GIVEN TO MEN. EXCEPTION TO THIS ORDER TAKEN BY BOTH MEN AND WOMEN PRODUCED THE WALKOUT.
ADD

At 2:45 this afternoon an official at the packinghouse called No. 111, police station, and asked for Chief Blizzard.

LAST TIME -- TONIGHT

Special Attraction at

NATIONAL THEATRE

in the apperance of

Flora Craig

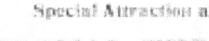

in person. Known as the daredevil of the films.

There is no advance in price of admission.

10 Cents and 5 Cents

Ward street and Chester avenue cars to the doors of the theatre.

DON'T MISS SEEING MISS CRAIG
also J. P. McGownan in Discontented Wives

The body of Vera McClure, 19 who died yesterday noon at St. Joseph hospital was removed to Eldon for burial. She is survived by her parents Mr. and Mrs. Henry McClure residing 9 miles southwest of Eldon.

Burial will be made Tuesday morning in Bethlehem cemetery.

THE OTTUMWA DAILY NEWS

MORRELL STRIKE GOES INTO 3RD DAY

"UNWARRANTED" CLAIM WHEN DEMANDS ARE MADE BY PARLEY COMMITTEE

FIRST BLOOD IS SPILLED

NINE P. M.— The strike goes into another day at Morrel's plant.

The committee of five, two of whom were women, were informed by officials a the packinghouse the strike was unwarranted and no settlement would be possible with the employes on strike, it is alleged.

he committee appointed to present the demands was composed of William Downey, J. Hillgethner, Hollis Neighbor, Edward Schoekrow, Fred Kreutgbroder, Mrs. H. Bargis and Mrs. R. B. Blizzard.

A big mass meeting is called for 3 o'clock Sunday afternoon in the City Park. J. C. Lewis state president to speak.

FIRST BLOOD IN MORRELL STRIKE

First blood flowed from the temple of Arthur Canny when a fight was precipitated on Vine street bridge at 4 o'clock this afternoon. Canny was in a battle with E. M. Taylor who had passed the odious word "scab" at Canny who had been working on the day previous, but later quit and joined the striker faction. It is reported Taylor did not know Canny was already an "out" when he assailed Canny.

The wounded man was rushed to Ottumwa Hospital and was soon restored to consciousness. The blow was a severe one, the cut in the head deep and painful. Canny resides on Route 7, Ottumwa. George Canny, a brother of the victim could not say just how the wound was inflicted, whether from a fist impact or from a more weighty instrument.

Secretary Muldoon stated the committee consists of five men and two women. Their demands it is stated, unofficially will follow the outline published in the News yesterday.

1. Guarantee of a 40-hour work week instead of the 32-hour week now prevailing.
2. A raise in wage of the common laborer fro mthe 30-cent an hour rate now prevailing to a determinate scale of 42 to 45-cent rate in force in other packing plants.
3. A raise in wages in branches of skilled labor to correspond with the average rate prevailing in other packing plants.
4. Return to rules governing the piecework trimmers prevailing until recently.

OTHERS WALK OUT

The truck drivers, machinists and carpenters walked out this morning bringing the total number of idle men to 1,200. Secretary Muldoon stated confidently today that he expected the entire force to walk out within the course of the next few hours.

A big mass meeting was held in Labor Hall last night and was featured by an address from J. H. Davis, of Chicago district president of the Amalgamated Butchers and Meat Cutters of North America. He declared himself in favor of the walkout as the only means to secure justice. He added that the Morrell workers were in comparison to workers in other packing plants throughout the country underpaid.

The Morrell company this morning issued a statement to farmers which states on account of labor trouble at the plant no live stock will be received until further notice. With only 200 men left to operate he plant the reason for the Morrell statement is apparent.

PAY MEN SATURDAY

A statement to employes today announces the paychecks will be given out at the plant Saturday starting at 8 o'clock in the morning withcheck No. 150 till three o'clock in the afternoon with check No. 1951 and up.

The press associations throughout the country are making inquiries regarding the strike and are keeping close touch on the situation which involves one of the largest institutions of its kind in the United States.

W. A. C. Brown, returning from the real corn county, northern Iowa, in answer to a question as to what he farmer will do with his crop in the cornbelt region, said he was t loss to kn w but believed considerable antity of will be burned in stoves and p housands of bushels not gathered.

OTTUMWANS VIEW ECLIPSE OF MOON

Many Ottumwans were stratled last night by a one-quarter yellow moon appearing out of the east as the Indian summer moon sank into the west. The phenomenon of eclipse was seen by numerous local people. Three-quarters of the moon's surface was darkened by the shadow of the earth and lasted for about an hour.

1921

THE OTTUMWA DAILY NEWS

NO CONTRACTS EXIST, SAYS FOSTER

POSTED RULES FROM OFFICE OUTLINES POLICY; MEN ARE WELCOME TO CONFERENCE

Expect Workers to Come Back 50 Per-cent Idle--Pickets

T. Henry Foster of the Morrell company at 1:15 this afternoon stated he was not in th city yesterday and therefore no committee asked to confer with him.

The News asked Mr. Foster if the charge made in the meeting of the workers last night claiming the Morrell company had repeatedly violated their contract with them in recent week was a complaint in any manner justified. In reply Mr. Foster said:

"The Morrell company has no contract with the men, in any form of agreement. We have had no agreement of any kind since the end of th war officially was announced from Washington. There have been rules of the company posted for several months about the premises and these rules have governed the operation of the plant.

"So I don't know what is meant when the reference is made to contracts and piece work agreements, as there is no contract whatsoever. Whn the trouble started in the trimming room and men and women quit work we asked that they return to their positions and permit an investigation to be made, which they declined to do. No committee called to see me yesterday, nor have they appeard today. We have a notice posted that states any person who wants t present long time.

"I will ask the newspaper to give my statements a correct appearance, not garbled as has happened in the past, because often a misrepresentation in print is harmful to both sides.

Wants Men to Return to Work

"We are operating but inconvenienced of course. I presume that half the men are employed but I don't know. At the gates there are pickets and while we are not going along as we would lik to do, we are operating as best we can and expect that the men will return, and we hopee they will."

Foster stressed the poin that rules are posted in the shop so as to keep the employes informed of wages, hours and other things attendant working conditions.

Clean Clothes for the Children

In homes where there are "kiddies" the need for an Electric Washer is even greater than in the ordinary household. Children will get their little frocks soiled—one after the other. Unless Mother has an

Electric Washer

—hers is indeed a hard task. With the aid of this great labor-saving device, however, it is always possible to have plenty of clean, fresh things for the youngsters to wear—and with little work on mother's part.

Ottumwa Railway & Light Co.
Second and Market Street.

1921

The news today that our troops will be withdrawn from Rhineland is interesting, but the fact that his administration has been seven months getting action on the treaty of peace is not complimentary to the to the ational authority at Washington. Soem of the days when it is deemed proper with tecnical ratifications completed, we shall read a g-l-o-r-i-o-u-s proclamation stating peace has come, now three years after the end of the war.

TRANSFUSION OF BLOOD SAVES HIM

What is said to be one of the few and successful blood transfusion operations performed in Ottumwa is that which is now believed saved the life of W. A. Harper who was near death Saturday from self-inflicted wounds in his throat and on the left wrist. Dr. S. A. Spilman, family physician, assisted by Dr. F. L. Nelson, who is accredited with being expertly familiar with this kind of emergency treatment arranged the infusion of the life fluid supplied by Henry L. Bell, the well known motor truck manufacturer. The reports today, and since the very hour of operation, are highly favorable. Mr. Harper will probably recover, is the statement given out this afternoon.

Beside the generous offering by Mr. Bell there were other men ready to make the sacrifice and the physicians were highly elated professionally at the apparent success of the work accomplished.

PEACE AT LAST--OH!

WASHINGTON, Oct. 19—By a senate vote of 60 to 20 the senate last night ratified the treaty for peace between America and Germany. The ballot counted eight more than the required majority.

Fourteen Democrats voted in favor and two republicans, La Follett and Borin, against it. Johnson of California moved back into line with his party by reasons of his indorsement particularly of the reparations reservations, being firmly opposed to this government joining an allied commission.

OBITUARY

Max Howard Dixon, infant son of Mr. and Mrs. W. E. Dixon, 1914 Emma St., was borne June 8, 1921, and died Wednesday evening, October 19, at 8:00 o'clock. The child had been ill for several weeks. Besides the parents he leaves two sisters, Ellen and Verlis, an done brother, Claude. Funeral services were held at the ersidence this aftrnoo nat 3 o'clock, conducted by Rev. Ella Miller of the Church of God. Interment in the Ottumwa cemetery.

* Why didn't President arding tell *
* the municipalities he advised to *
* supply work for the unemployed, *
* just how it was to be done? His *
* passing the buck getaway is not *
* making much of a hit with the Re- *
* publican mayors, and none at all *
* where the Democrats are in local *
* power. Why that promise of pros- *
* perity? Why not keep the faith? *
*   —Unemployed *

Anyone have an idea how much it is costing this country—and the southern district of Iowa, to handle these liquor cases? They seem to not only get the right of way as preferred cases for prosecution but also come in for a set series of admonitory lectures from all high places of legal authority. The fellow who gulps a swallow of liquor these days had better understand in advance that his days of freedom, if not of life itself, are numbered.

GUILTY OF WALKING STREETS GETS 15 DAYS

Martha Morgan who was arrested Tuesday night and arraingned in police court late yesterday morning was given trial late yesterday and found guilty of a charge of street walking. She has been sentenced to 15 days in Wapello county jail. Her home is Knoxville.

One of our business men got up at 5 o'clock yesterday morning and did some work of the common labor sort and actually believes common labor at 40 and 50 cents an hour is hard to get. "If you don't believe me, try to get it," he said. Well, it is indeed a strange delusion we are entertaining if men cannot be had by the hundreds in Ottumwa who will work for 40 cents an hour. How about it?

BALANCE IN CITY COFFERS OCTOBER FIRST $38,156.08

The city financial report for the month of September which has been recently completed shows a balance of $38,156.08 as total for all funds. The total receipts for the general fund was $15,430.36. The balance in the general fund beginning October 1, was $4,804.24.

The balances in the different special funds beginning October 1, was as follows:

Police equipment $83.66, fire equipment $2,700.53, police pension $874.65, fire pension $1,910.64, improvement $283.61, light $4,663.98, sewer $192.50, main sewer $4,652.72, grading $368.01, bridge $1,190.69, bond $178.02, cemetery paving $1,012.97, garbage $457.21, special trust $1,708.59, auto road $116.78. The total balance in the special funds was $20,394.56. The total balance in the general and special funds was $24,998.80.

The balance in the waterworks fund was $12,550.80, libraray $465.87, park $140.50. The waterworks disbursements for the month of September were $17,571.09.

Everybody's Heater

The Riverside Duplex Heater

Can truthfully be called Everybody's Heater since it is the one stove that successfully burns soft coal, hard coal, wood, slack, corn cobs, chips, or anything that burns. No matter what fuel you have, the Riverside Duplex is the ideal heater in which to burn it.

With uncertainty of the kind of fuel you are able to sucre, the variations in prices, the number of other reasons that might warrant a change in the fuel from time to time make the Riverside Duplex the one safe buy.

See us if you are in need of a stove—we will please you.

FABRITZ, BLACK & FABRITZ

"Where your Dollar has more Sense."

Phone 2161 301-3 Church St.

NOBODY HURT IN CLOSE CALL WHEN TRAIN HITS TRUCK

A loaded Morrell Company truck was struck by Burlington train No. 179 at 1:50 o'clock this afternoon and completely demolished it.

The accident occurred at Green street. "Red" Burke who was driving the truck said that he didn't see the rtain until it wa sabout ten feet from him. Harley Reece who was in the seat beside Burke called to him to "step on the gas" but too late to avoid being run down.

Neither occupant of the truck was injured which is considered nothing short of a miracle since they were enclosed in the cab of the ehavy truck which when struck by the train speeding at a rate of 35 miles an hour was totaly wrecked.

The truck contained lard, beef quarters an dother produce. Much of the trruck's contents was carried way by after the accident.

Mr. Bartch, life insurance expert of Omaha, tells you that human life has grown longer by ten years in the last half century. Two or three hundred years from now, with counsmption conquered by good food, and some other enemies put down, average life should be about one hundred. Men are learning how to live.

PEOPLE ASKED TO OBSERVE PERFECT PARCEL WEEK

Perfect parcel week will start next week and A. G. Peterson, secretary of the Chamber of Commerce urges everyone who sends parcels during the campaign to see that they are well wrapped and securely tied.

The campaign is sponsored by the railroad and express companies and is expected to be educational in that the results will tend to teach people to take more care in wrapping articles for shipment.

NEW SPEED RECORD BY PACIFIC LINER

San Francisco, Oct. 27—A new speed record for American pasenger liners on the Pacific was established yesterday when the steamer Golden State of the Pacific Mail steamship Company arrived, four days and seventeen hours out from Honolulu. The former record was made by the Empire State in four days betwenty-two hours.

1921

Now Comes The Electric Dishwasher

to take from mother's shoulders another unpleasant household task.

Housewives everywhere are welcoming this new Electric labor-saver with open arms.

Used as a table during the day, it becomes a priceless possession when meals are finished. It enables mother to rest in comfort after the dinner hour in place of toiling over the kitchen sink.

THE OTTUMWA DAILY NEWS

OTTUMWA, IOWA, MONDAY, OCTOBER 31, 1921

NEGRO LABORERS APPEAR AT MORRELL'S

USED TO BUTCHER; FOSTER SAYS HE WAS MISQUOTED ON IMPORT OF WORKERS

NOT IN STRIKE BREAKER CLASS; HAD CONFERRED WITH SHERIFF

* * * * * * * * * * * * *

Conditions are improving right along about fifty men came in to work today. Some of these were old employes and some were butchers that came from other packing centers where work is slack. We are expecting more as the word gets around that there places open here where men can find steady employment.

We are killing cattle every day and have resumed buying both car and local hogs and expect to resume the killing in our hog department tomorrow or Wednesday of this week.

T. H. Foster

* * * * * * * * * * * * *

ARE NOT STRIKE BREAKERS

Mr. Foster was asked by The News how he reconciled the public's understanding he would not bring in foreign labor with the appearance at the plant this morning of men from Chicago, or elsewhere. He replied: "I was misrepresented Saturday in a published statement that had said no labor would be brought from other cities. This mis-quotation, unfortunately, has caused me considerable embarassment. I had a talk with Sheriff Giltner a few days ago when that official agreed with me it would be all right to bring in some labor—butchers—and at that time I said I would not import strike breakers. We recieved a few men last night and they are butchers. They do not come as strike breakers. These men will butcher and allow us to go ahead with the increasing force that appears at the plant. I did not say we would not bring in labor. I said we had no intentions of bringing in strike breakers. We have not done so. No, there are no men from a distance expected tonight. We are running along and hope that all the local men will be back to work soon."

The News presents the Foster statement today as to imported labor with the undersanding that Mr. Foster does not regard a few butcher workers in the killing room as the strike breaker type.

CAVALRY HORSES ON NEW LOCATION

Sheridan avenue folk win in their objection raised to quartering First Cavalry horses at the site selected by the Armory representatives. The barns and livestock are to be quartered on Webster street lots, near Richmond avenue.

1921

Ottumwa Daily News

NOVEMBER 1921

Nov 1 - National Birth Control League and Voluntary Parenthood League merge to become American Birth Control League

Nov 4 - After a speech by Adolph Hitler in Munich, supporters physically assault his opposition

Nov 4 - Japanese Prime Minister Harar Takashi is assassinated in Tokyo

Nov 9 - National Fascist Party is founded in Italy

Nov 11 - During an Armistice Day ceremony at Arlington National Cemetery, the Tomb of the Unknown Soldier is dedicated by Pres. Harding

Nov 14 - Spanish Communist Party is founded

THIS MACHINE FLIES STRAIGHT UPWARD; MYSTERY OF MACHINE GUARDED

LONDON, Nov. 9.—Great Brtian has solved the helicoptor problem through Louis Brennan, the war inventor.

Air ministry experts succeeded in launching the helicoptor, which is an airplane that flies straight upward, at the Farnborough aerodrome, using a machine which had undergone tests under the direction of Brennan.

The machine rose vertically, hovering at a height of forty feet, decended gently and landed safely, proving the feasability of the gyroscopic principle, which gives the direct upward elevation.

No attempt was madt to test the machine for lateral flight, but according to Brennan, his will be easy. Experiments in lateral flying will be made in the ngar future.

The machine has been stationed at the government aerodrome and is guarded day and night. Only six engineers and designers know the mystery of the helicoptors construction.

1921

19 Come, Five Break Ranks Steady Today

Nineteen negroe laborers from Chicago unloaded at Agency last night and rushed to the Morrell plant by automobiles. One auto load nevr reached the plant, being stopped by strikers and the situation explained. Five negroes declared the matter had been misrepresented to them and they knew of no trouble in Ottumwa.

Fourteen of the nineteen are at work in the plant today. Those who were present at Labor Hall today said they had been hired in Chicago by Morrell agents who agreed to pay their transportation to Ottumwa.

Of the nineteen who were brought to Ottumwa last Monday morning seven have quit in sympathy with the men on strike and three of these have left town.

Dave Wilson, representing the press committee, stated today that nothing of importance has happened outside of the importation of foreign labor. He hinted at further plans for a conference but added hat nothing definite has been arranged.

The relief committee is aiding those who are in need and reports that as a whole the strikers are holding out well in face of a trying situation. oal for families in need has been furnished at a reduction through coal dealers in sympathy with striking employes.

MEN WANTED

For General Packing House Work Apply At Plant.

JOHN MORRELL & CO.

MR. FOSTER—TODAY

"I really have nothing to say today in addition to what I have said, that is, the gates are open to men who will return and apply for work. I am hoping they will.

"We are going along about the same, possibly showing a little gain. Working along.

"No, the drop yesterday in hogs was not due to anything but the general conditions of the Chicago markets."

A CORRECTION

In view of the fact that certain statements have been made which tend to create a wrong impression in respect to working conditions at our plant, we wish to make it clear that no change has been made in wages and that the 40c per hour minimum still prevails.

John Morrell & Co.

MILLIONAIRE SPEEDS TO ST. LOUIS; SHIP LIGHTS AT ELDON

Eldon was visited from above yesterday by a Chicago millionaire who arrived with his pilot in an airplane, enroute from Chicago to St. Louis. The News reporter gathered the information that Mr. Millionbucks had left Chicago at 7 a. m. and reached a point directly over Eldon at 9, two hours later. They needed gasoline and 35 gallons was purchased. "We expect to make Kansas City in an hour and a quarter," said the speedy gent as the ship lifted and in a few seconds was lost to view.

Three hours and 15 minutes, Chicago to St. Louis, is something in the way of a record.

CHANGES FAVORED ON ON DRAINAGE PLAN

At a joint meeting of the Wapello and Davis county supervisors here this afternoon it was decided that certain minor changes would be considered in the work that will give to the farmers along Soap Creek, for a distance of nearly five miles when channel is ditched to the shorter line, various advantages they would not otherwise obtain on previous platting.

The work was to have started the first of October but owing to filed of corn maturing the delay was occaisoned. The work will begin at the Eldon vicinity end of the drainage as proposed. The estimated total cost will be about $30,000, according to a statement of Supervisor Lockman.

SPECIAL TRAIN TO IOWA-MINN. GAME NEXT SATURDAY

IOWA CITY, Ia., Nov. 2—Special University of Iowa football fans will descend on Minneapolis in full force for the Iowa-Minnesota game next Saturday. A special train will be secured to carry the band and rooters and it is expeced that moer than 1,00 Iowa students and alumni will be in the stands for the Minnesato homecoming battle.

From Iowa City a special train will carry the crowd for $12.41 round trip, and many fans from nearby towns and the southern part of the state are expected to leave on the special Friday night. Tickets for the return trip will be good on regular trains up to and including Sunday night. There will be no reduction in Pullman fares, a berth costing $3.24 each way for a lower and $2.59 for an upper.

The Howling 300, men's pep organization on the Iowa campus, is conducting a campaign to raise funds for sending the band to Minneapolis for the game.

To assuer the special train 125 tickets must be sold at the general ticket office in Iowa City. Tickets must be paid for in advance and if enough are not disposed of for the special tarin the tickets will be honored on regular trains. owever, with the low rate order especially since fifty members of the band will be passengers, it is expected that the special will be oversold in short order. any are planning to make the trip north by automobile.

1921

SAYS 40c HOUR MINIMUM WAGE FOR ABLE BODIED; SOME NOT REINSTATED

"My Position Unchanged"

Mr. Foster Says:

"More men were at work in the packing house today than any day since we went out. Monday morning a number of men seeing a crowd did not go to work, but today's (Wednesday) number of employed was higher than any previous day during this strike period.

"We made a statement in your paper announcing that the minimum wage of 40 cents an hour still prevails. Of course there are some old men who are keeping the doors and gates who do not receive that much, as the rest of the men know, but abled bodied men who can do a man's work receive not less than 40 cents."

Asked concerning the statement quoted by the Mayor's committee to the effect that Foster had said "there are between thirty and fifty men who will not be taken back," Mr. Foster replied:

"I don't know how many and will not know until they make application for a job, and we talk with them, and I understand a number of men have left town hunting employment elsewhere. I presume the men we will not take back are those who know if they are the ones."

Ottumwa is figuring on the cost of strikes.

The employes at the Morrell plant have been out of employment 16 working days.

The loss thus far has been in excess of $100,000 and were they each to receive 25 cents more income per diem and resume tomorrow morning it would require two years to make up the loss already sustained.

You lose if you win, is the expression often heard. It applies both ways, for the employer as well as the employe.

Just to interest the reader of this, assume there a thousand men idle at Morrell's and they average an income of $3.00 each day. In round numbers that's $50,000 wage loss to date.

To this $50 loss to each worker must be added an incurred debt and money spent previously earned, and the general disadvantage in not having money sufficiently to buy when necessities are at lowest prices, this fairly showing a loss, total of $100 to the idle employe.

STRIKERS ON RELIEF LIST GIVEN AID; BUTCHERS 100 PCT. LOYAL TO UNIONISM

"WE'RE WINNERS UNDER 600 EMPLOYES" CLAIM OF MULDOON

STATEMENT

Conditions at our plant are very much improved, a number of old employees came in yesterday and went to work; a greater number came in today. In addition a number of new men have been employed.

A large number have made application for work on Monday. All applicants are now being hired as new employees, as those who have been working during the strike will be retained in the service of the company. Others, such as we can use, will be re-employed in the order in which they apply.

The report being circulated that a settlement has been offered to the strikers is incorrect. No offer of settlement and no concession of any kind has been offered to anyone.

T. H. FOSTER

November 12, 1921.

FOUR ALBIANS HURT IN CAR TURN-OVER ON RIGHT-OF-WAY

Albia hunters met with a mishap this morning about 10 o'clock when their car went over the Agency right-of-way. The casualty list includes four and all injured, namely, Thomas Zook, G. F. Scott, W. F. Piltington, Thomas. The car was an Essex and owned by Scott, and WAS is right because it was consumed by flames in the crash.

The men sutained various cuts and bruises but none hurt fatally, it is believed.

No explanation has been advanced for the reason of the turn-over. The party was on their way to Floris on a hunting expedition.

Ottumwa Daily News

UNKNOWN HERO IS LAID TO REST IN ARLINGTON

President and Gen. Pershing and Other High Officials Follow Casket.

WOODROW WILSON IN CORTEGE

Nation's Chief Executive Pins the Medal of Honor and the Distinguished Service Cross on Casket of Dead Warrior.

Washington, Nov. 12.—Laid to rest with all the honors a grateful nation could pay, the unknown hero from France was bivouacked among the gallant dead of Arlington National cemetery.

The highest officers of the army and navy walked beside his coffin; upon but the hands of gallant comrades of the great war were laid upon it. President Harding walked behind his bier to do him homage; former President Wilson made his first appearance in months; General Pershing turned aside an opportunity to ride and trudged beside the body to the last resting place.

Representatives of foreign governments reverently laid their highest military decorations on his casket. With soil from France, where he fell unknown, he was laid away.

Minute guns at Fort Myer boomed their continuous tribute as the funeral procession was passing from the capitol to the great marble amphitheater in Arlington, where the ceremonies were opened with the playing of the Star Spangled Banner by the marine band.

STARTING FURNACES

(New York Herald)

In attacking the problems of the furnace, which will engage a considerable numbe rof our suburban friends today, it is well to discover early in the proceedings whether or not the smokpipe was aken down las spring. If it was not removed, carefully scraped out and stored in a dry place the householder need not expect to get away with his negligence. He should perform the necessary task at once. This is done by snipping the wires which hold the pipe to the caller ceiling and tackling the pipe amidships. Usually it will fall with a lecisive crash, spraying soot generously. It may then be poked, brushed and banged at will unless a summer in a damp and lonesome place has caused rust to eat through its vitals.

OWNED, MORTAGED, RENTED

According to the Department of Commerce, 54.4 per cent of the homes in the United States in 1920 were rented, 28.2 per cent were owned by their occupants and were free from encumbrance, and 17.5 were owned by their occupants but were mortaged. The proportion which the mortaged homes formed of the total number of homes increastd from 14.5 per cent in 1900 to 15 per cent in 1910 and to 17.5 per cent in 1920.

The term "home," as employed by the Census Bureau, signifies the abiding place of a single family, and does ont therefore, necessarily denote an entire dwelling which may house a numger of families, as in the case of an appartment building. Moreover, two or more families may occupy an ordinary dwelling house.

1921

EXTRA! OTTUMWA DAILY NEWS EXTRA!

MARTIAL LAW INVOKED ON OTTUMWA

MACHINE GUNS PUMPING 600 SHOTS A MINUTE TRAINED ON STRIKERS

200 SOLDIERS PATROL STREETS AS RESULT OF SCRIMMAGE TUESDAY; HILLGARDNER SAYS CITY DISGRACED

The packing house avenues are filled with soldiers from the skeleton First battalion, Des Moines, under Colonel Brewer. The 200 men with full complement of arms, including guns, arrived in the city on special train at 4:40 this morning.

At 6:45 when the workers have been accustomed to be entering the gates at the Morrell plant, there were few passing toward the entrance under guard of the soldiers who filled Iowa avenue from Main south two blocks, across the tracks and then into the side streets.

Machine Gun Ready.

The News representative a few minutes before seven o'clock jitneyed to the corner of Iowa avenue and East Main. Three blocks this side on Main scores of strikers and many women moved enbloc in bunches as the uniformed men backed commands with guns.

Quiet and Order.

At 10:30 Colnel Brewer reported "all quiet" and there was little to do except maintain a patrol. The grim, squatty little death dealing machine hat one might pick up and carry, placed in the center of the street at Iowa avenue intersection, was manned by two youngish men, hardly more than youth age, who were lying on a blanket and fingering the mechanism of the rapid fire instrument of murderous mission in event the order came to discharge it, the belt of cartridges shuttled though at an amazing speed. Two machine guns were to be placed a the railroad crossing, another at the entrance to the plant.

There was no disturbance up to noon. The plant had practically suspended business. It was the hush aftr the scenes of yesterday when many were hurt with flying bricks, clubs and stones, women taking a leading part in the scrimmage and only slight personal injuries for the commotion that was staged.

Plenty of Machine Guns.

Colonel Brewer was asked how many machine guns he had and the answer was: "We have plenty." The officer also replied to other questions, saying everything was getting along orderly, that "we have no particular time to remain here, but intend to stay as long as necessary. Yes, there are more soldiers due at noon. Don't know how many total, until they arrive."

Cots and Kitchens.

Bedding is being placed today in the women's dining room for soldiers and kitchen service provided. It is understood they have supplies for 30 days and are stationed under first orders for ten days. Residents in the patrolled streets are making protests to the presence of soldiers in and near their properties.

Martial Law Substituted.

This section of the city designated in the order that made up the injunction program, drawn by county attorney Roberts, et al, was placed under martial law with the signature of Judge D. M. Anderson yesterday, following conference held with Adjutant General Lasher who was first here to report on the situation to Governor Kendall. It was not known until late Tuesday afternoon that the troops had been requested by Lasher. Governor Kendall complied at once with promise of four companies, 200 men. They assumed jurisdiction at 5 this morning and under Colnel Brewer who has his headquarters in the office of the plant superintendent.

Local officers, both city and county, are superseded in the martial law zone, which section will be extended as deemed necessary by th military government. Just outside the zone of artillery and 600-shots a minute machine guns, Commissioner Jones has some men employed from the police department.

Ottumwa Daily News

Deputy Sheriffs Relieved.

At 7 o'clock this morning the 150 deputy sheriffs impressed into patrol duty by Sheriff Giltner were practically all relieved from duty, only a few remaining supplemental and subject to the command of Colonel Brewer. The local citizens who were all wearing stars and guns were happy to get away from the job to which they were assigned under the law. "Don't mention any of our names. We don't want any publicity, none of the boys, because we're here by compultion," stated one of the deoutized.

Wide Uneviable Publicity.

Metropolitan newspapers of the country last evening carried sensational headlines depicting the gravity of a situation that did not exist beyond the scrimmage degree. Hillgardner stated to the News that while there was disorder for about an hour still nobody was really hurt, to his knowledge none in the hospitals of the city. He characterized the order sending soldiers to Ottumwa as unwarranted and pointed to the fact that for four weeks the men have been orderly, lawabiding, as he spoke of the union men.

Here's a sample of the headlining for Ottumwa read by The News publisher yesterday afternoon in Kansas City:

"Fifty injured in street battle—Packinghouse strikers in riot at Ottumwa, Iowa—Fierce fight rages for two hours between police and workers" and then in the text all the injured are expected to recover." What a notoriety!

It was a shock to many away from the home town. And conspicuously first-paged that it might read, as thousands were doing on all sides as elsewhere throughout the whole country where press dispatches reach the public. Ottumwa has no home rule in this state of affairs. Military power supplant local government. In the prescribed zone the colonels and generals and adjutants determine what shall or may be permitted. Their mandates are enforced at the point of bayonet or, if deemed necessary from the military conception that bullets be used, then it is that way.

There are hundreds if not thousands in Ottumwa today who feel that with possible few exceptional instances the strikers have been patient, sincerely loyal to the law, striving after a settlement by committee conference adjustment and that the excitement of yesterday morning was not of such importance as to justify militaristic rule for the people, the whole city if Colonel Brewer decides it necessary.

Then there are those who welcome the soldier here and say it is necessary we have such protection to life and property.

Kendall's Statement.

The governor issued the following statement at 7 o'clock last night:

"The sheriff, county attorney and mayor of Ottumwa wired me tonight that the situation there was altogether beyond control, and asked for troops to save life and property. I have therefore ordered two companies of national guard to report at once. I am not familiar with the questions involved in the dispute between the packing company and its employes and indeed it is not necessary that I should be. Without assuming any attitude whatever toward the labor controversy, I intend to see that law is enforced, and that order is maintained."

WHY?

Why should a municipality, county or state be obliged to pay thousands of dollars as militia expense when the big idea is to get a dispute settled in a local matter and which might easily have been effected by an agreed upon board of arbiters? Is it fair to the public? Haven't they some right to say how these matters are to be handled? Not since the day of Junkin, the murderer, have those state troops been considered, and then we got by without them. Why not now?

—STRIKE SYMPATHIZER.

Editor of The News—As a citizen of Ottumwa I think it my duty to give my views on the situation at the Morrell plant. That corporation is employing people from other towns who are displacing men on strike, who have homes in Ottumwa and pay taxes here. Wives and innocent little children suffer—on account of what?

In the first place, benches that women stood on while cutting meat on tables were taken from them. Then the next cause of irritation was due to hiring girls at so much per day, giving them a good grade of meat, and giving a poor grade to those girls who worked on a piecework basis. When a committee tried to take up these matters and have them settled amicably, they were ignored by foremen and superintendents, I am told.

1921

BURLINGTON GOES ON BUYING TRIP

CHICAGO, Nov. 29.—In anticipation of, and preparatory for, the movement of the tremendous vacation, convention and regular traffic which will move next year, the Burlington Route is placing contracts for 127 passenger cars.

Included in the order are 12 dining cars, 5 chair cars, 54 coaches, 12 baggage, 22 mail and 22 miscellaneous cars. All will be of massive steel construction and will embody all of the latest approved devices and comforts known to the modern car builder. Placed end to end, this equipment would make a train almost a mile and one-half long.

"No Two Good Roads Alike."

"No two good roads are alike. Good and careful a driver as I am, I darn near rolled over out west of Salt Lake City last summer, skidding in the dust—dry, fluffy dust. Why, if I'd been driving 20 miles instead of careful 12 miles an hour, we'd rolled end over applecart, and it was a good road, if you knew how to drive it. Yes, sir. There is not a road in all this United States, not the best, widest, finest, smoothest road, that isn't treacherous if a man's not used to it. I don't mean wild-eyed hummers, but just common folks like me.

"If you don't believe it, you study the road accidents you come upon as you ride across the country. Half the skidding is done where the road type changes, where a man leaves concrete and hits oil surface or where he leaves the waterbound stone for hard pan."

QUARTER SECTION

FOR RENT—Quarter section, six miles north of Albia; good stock and grain farm; good buildings; near school; considerable woven wire. Rented last year for $800 cash; year before, $950. Will take $400 cash in advance if rented in three weeks, as I need cash. Write, phone or call.
Henry Stewart, Route 1, Albia, Iowa.

FORD HAS OFFER TO BUY NAVY

IS UNABLE TO CASH IN AT JUNK VALUE—WHAT THEY'RE WORTH

DETROIT, Nov. 17.—Henry Ford today authorized the ollowing announcement upon his behalf:

"I will buy the navies of the world at junk prices and turn them into agricultural machinery and automobiles if the United States and the other powers will agree to disarm on the sea.

"You may tell those gentlemen in Washingtn that I mean business. They may think that I could not finance such a undertakig, but you may tell them that I can.

"You may assure them that with acetelyn torches and electricity I can cut those warships to pieces and make useful things out of them."

Ottumwa Daily News

THE OTTUMWA DAILY NEWS

OTTUMWA, IOWA, THURSDAY, NOVEMBER 17, 1921

MY GOD, YES, SOON AS POSSIBLE —Sheriff Giltner

We Want to Send the Soldiers Away First Chance --They are Cheaper than Deputy Force However

Cost of Military Here County Expense is Charged to the Taxpayers

Sheriff Giltner, asked at noon today if he was aware that the cost of the soldiers here was charged in part to the taxpayers of Wapello county, replied, "Yes, and we will send them away as soon as possible. My God, yes, as soon as possible."

"The powers of the city and county ceased the moment the soldiers appeared. We have no interest in the strike except that there be no destruction of property nor violence by the people. In the armed militia zone Colonel Brewer is in exclusive command.

Hillgardner on Situation; Statement by Mr. Foster

STATEMENT

As to the situation of the strike at Ottumwa, we are of no change. Our men and women are standing firm. They want to stay out till we get an agreeable settlement. The strikers intend to stay within the bounds of the injunction, as we aim to show the public that we are not outlaws, as some are trying to make out we are. While this injunction forbids the strikers from going from house to house and taking any of our friends who are working at the plant at present, the company is sending out automobiles guarded by deputies to gather up men to take them to work.

What use is hostilities the other day. Had the officers made an effort to cover the trouble it could have been none. It looks to us as though the industries just laid down. We always maintained peace and have done so at all times, and, if the matter had been explained, the governor would not have sent the troops, as it looked like the people are not civilized and have to be guarded by troops.

Last Friday we sent a proposition by a party as a go-between. The company said they would have nothing to do with the proposition. Mr. Manns said Mr. Foster had taken the stand that all men would have to be hired on their own merits. THEY WOULD HIRE WHOM THEY PLEASED, PAY WHAT THEY PLEASED, PUT THE MAN WHERE THEY PLEASED, and right now they have refused some men who have gone back to work and have worked six days. These men have struck again. So you see what we have to expect if we do not stand pat and get a sensible settlement.

Last Friday we sent a proposition by this same party, which is as follows, and we do not think this is unreasonable. The proposition was:

1.—That the company re-instate all former employes in their positions inside of six days.
2.—That the company agree to pay the 40 cent minimum wage per hour for common labor;
3.—That the company agree to see that the women employes receive the proper treatment by their foremen;
4.—That the company will agree to meet a committee of their employes to adjust all differences as they may arise in the future;
5.—That we, the former employes agree if an agreement is reached, to accept the 32-hour guarantee time and also agree to stay at work provided the company will agree to the same guarantee time as that at other packing centers in the future, and if there is any reduction in hour or rating we will accept the same.
6.— That the agreement must be signed by the company and a committee of employes.

ROBERTS DISMISSES CASES VENUED TO JUSTICE CREMER

County Attorney Roberts this morning dismissed all the cases in the court of Justice Cremer that came from alleged disorderly conduct, assault and battery, claimed to have originated in the packinghouse district and in connection with the strike in that section of the city.

"I was advised by Sheriff Giltner that conviction would be difficult to secure in any of the cases, so dismissed them," stated Roberts today noon. These cases were up before Judge Kitto of the police court but on venue sent to Justice Cremer.

HELP WANTED

WANTED—Man who will do hard work, $20 week to start. Phone 2829-W.

1921

THE OTTUMWA DAILY NEWS

HOME PICKETS AND ARBITRATION PLAN

Lewis Offers 5-Men Idea to Settle Differences Between Local Capital and Labor-- Mass Meeting For Tonight at Opera House at 7:30 O'Clock

THE OTTUMWA DAILY NEWS

FOR GOD'S SAKE DO NOT CRAWL BACK
--LEWIS

Stay Away From the Plant, Be Lawabiding; We Have Failed But this Means Prepare For the Fight to Go On-- says Labor Head

"The suggestion led to my putting a proposition in writing, to the effect that the men would agree to a board of arbitrators with the company picking two men, the employes two, and these four to select the fifth member, with both sides agreeing to abide by a decision. I then telephoned Mr. Foster for an interview.

"NOTHING TO ARBITRATE."

"Mr. Foster assented to an interview. I went odwn there at 2 o'colck and, after talking it over, he said, 'There is nothing to arbitrate.' So we argued the points in the case. Mr. Foster asserted, 'WE ARE RIGHT, THE EMPLOYES ARE WRONG.' I told him there might be wrong on both sides and he replied, 'No citizens can come down and run the palnt.'"

"I failed. But I know of no better way than by arbitration. You have been refused that today.

"SINCE THE CHARGE HAS BEEN MADE THAT WOMEN AT MORRELL'S HAVE BEEN MISTREATED AND SUBJECTED TO INSULTING REMARKS, I SAY MORRELL'S SHOULD BE THE FIRST TO DEMAND AND INSTITUTE AN INVESTIGATION.

---

* Why does J. M. Co. say they are *
* paying 40 cents an hour for com- *
* mon labor when they hired myself *
* and others to demolish refrigerator *
* cars at 30 cents an hour? *
*   —HOW COME.   *

Ottumwa Daily News

ELVA GEE TAKEN IN ACCIDENT; WAS INJURED AT WORK

Elva Thomas Gee, who sustained fatal injuries when a bucket used for sand-lifting fell with him at the Shea plant at 11:45 Tuesday morning, succumbed to his injuries last evening at 8:20 at Ottumwa Hospital. His wounds were numerous, those inflicted by the shovel blades, acting as closing jaws, gouging deep holes in his back.

Mr. Gee was born February 19, 1898, the son of Mr. and Mrs. Crate Gee, and resided at 226 Grand avenue. He is survived by a widow, Ruth; one son, James; a daughter, Margaert; two sisters, Mrs. Goldie Jackson and Mrs. Whynema; and his parents.

The body was taken to the Maroney Funeral Home and later to the Gee home. Fuenral services will be held Saturday morning at 10 o'clock, conducted by the Rev. Mr. Fink of the West End Presbyterian Church. Interment at the Isabel Cemetery.

GAVE DYING LINCOLN BED; EATS AS PAUPER

NEW YORK, Nov. 25.—Thomas Proctor, 80, who gave up his bed in his room on Tenth st., Washington, to President Lincoln the night he was shot by Wilks Booth, ate his Thanksgiving dinner in St. Andrew's Brotherhood Home at Gibsonia Pa., after spending the past six years as a ward in the home on Blackwell's Island. Mr. Proctor, with Robert Todd Lincoln, son of the Martyred President, are the only survivors of the small group present when Lincoln died.

KIDNAPERS DEMAND $25,000 RANSOM

ST. LOUIS, Nov. 23.—A demand for $25,000 for the safe return of Dominick Di Franco, 7, son of Constantine Di Franco, "sugar king of Little Italy," has been made by kidanpers of the youth, who was abducted on November 14.

SERUM DISCOVERED TO PREVENT "T B" BY FRENCH MEDIC

PARIS, Nov. 23.—Tuberculosis can be prevented in the same manner as smallpox and typhus, according to what is declared to be the most important medical discovery of the year. The method has just been announced by Professor A. Calmette, assistant director of the Pasteur Institute, one of the most famous French savants.

Before the Academy of Sciences Professor Calmette demonstrated that the Koch bacillus can be rendered sterile by cultivating a preparation of bile, which, injected in the veins of animals, caused an abundant production of "anticorpos," from which in turn the serum is constructed.

The serum, if injected in human veins, especially children of tender years, assures immunity from tuberculosis in any form, it is said.

Professor Calmette emphasized that the serum has no curative powers. Medical circles here hail the discovery as the greatest in the history of the anti-tuberculosis fight.

1921

She Does Not Know Who Called You

Your telephone bell rang. When you answered the operator asked, "Number, please?"

"Why, my bell rang," you replied.

You were answered, "Will you excuse it, please?"

The operator did not know you had been rung. One of several operators could have rung you, but only one answers your line.

Some subscriber had asked for your telephone number, then remembered it was not the number he wanted and hung up. Or you may have been a bit slow in answering and the party tired of waiting.

The Northwestern Bell Telephone Co.

SUNNYSLOPE BIDS ARE REJECTED

All bids on th Sunnyslope sanitarium were rejected this afternoon by the board of directors.

The reason as given for the rejection by Chairman J. B. Sax, is the lateness of the season and the price of materials which at this time are too high to permit building.

The lowest bid received was that of L. T. Crisman company and asks $8,970. J. F. Quinn bid $9,884; Ottumwa Mill and Construction company, $10,489 and Cain Bros., $9,985.

Th directorate of Sunnyslope met in the Board of Supervisors room in the Wapello county courthouse. The board of scpervisors attending the meeting.

Mmbers of the Sunnyslope directorate are J. W. Calhoun, J. B. Sax, Mrs. Edward Emery and J. F. Lewis.

The bids were opened this afternoon. The specifications call for an addition 57 by 50 feet and a bond for $200 is requird as surtey. The addition to the sunnyslope property will be separate from the present building but will be used in the care of tubercular patients.

FAHRNEY TELLS CITIZENS FARE GOES TO 7 CENTS DECEMBER 1

An increased street railway fare effective December 1 was announced by the Ottumwa Railway and light Company today. The fare will be 7 cents cash instead of the present rate of 5 cents. The school children's specil rate of twenty-five rides for 75 cents will not be changed.

"We are announcing the street railway fare increse in a newspaper advertisement today," said Vice President and General Manager C. E. Fahrney. "There is not much that I can add to ths announcement. We do not want to charge more for street railway rides but we have to. The expenses of providing servise have not been reduced in line with lower commodity prices. The cost of operation is vastly more than it was in pre-war years. We simply have no alternative if we are to keep the cars runng. We have gone as long as we can without highr fare and must now join the great majority of American cities, nearly all of which have increased the street railway fares.

"The company realizes that it is under obligation to operate street cars in Ottumwa and will make every effort to provide service. We do not believe that any citizen desires to ride for less tha ncost, but that is precisely the case at present. To maintain service the Company must have more revenue. I feel that our decision will have the support of the public in avoiding a disastrous street railway situation similar to that which has caused so much loss and inconvenience in Des Moinses and other cities."

CORN 32C CHEERING FARMERS

On the heels of official advices from Pocahontas County telling the farmer to burn his corn comes gladdening news to corn growers of Iowa that corn today is selling at 32 cents at many elevators, and right here in Wapello County.

The News is delighted at the opportunity to publish the fact that corn, the great king cereal of the Midwest, has shown a 50-plus per cent advance within one week.

J. B. Sax, interested in all forms of business, says he learned about an upward trend in corn prices while at Osceola Thanksgiving Day, where it was being told that a man in Clarke County wanted to speculate in corn and planned to buy 10,000 bushels. He started out and found the price asked was 30 cents, which was the elevator offering for good corn.

J. F. Webber also stated today that many elevators in this section are paying as high as 32 cents, and named the Neola system, Highland Center and Farson, where 32 cents is the quotation.

Farmers will hail the news that corn at last is coming forward, although hogs at top today show only $6.20 at Morrell's.

1921

TWO STORES ON MAIN FALL PREY TO FLAMES; NELSON CLOAK CO. AND STEVENS

Ottumwa experienced another disastrous fire in the retail merchandising district Saturday night, when flames, discovered at 6:50 o'clock at the top of an elevator shaft on the third story, reached the contents of the Nelson Cloak Company and Roy Stevens stores at 104 and 106 East Main street, but one and two doors west of the site of the big merchandise fire sustained by the N. Friedman firm on January 11, 1916, which probably was the heaviest single store loss in the history of the downtown business district.

WAS CLEAN SWEEP.

The alarm of fire was turned in a few minutes before 7 o'clock, after a colored man, sent by Mr. Wareham of the Nelson Cloak Company store, had reported a blaze in the penthouse, which is the cupola of the elevator shaft, on top of the three-story building.

Chief Sloan officially stated this morning that the fire originated because of the failure of certain parts of the elevator to work properly, the motor whirring away and creating heat from friction. The first intimation of this trouble, it is said, was when the colored lady who had been operating it reported the elevator stuck at the second floor level.

GETTING PEOPLE OUT.

At once the management of the store passed all the people from the building and the firemen went to work. Streams of water were turned loose on the Nelson store, and an investigation was made by Chief Sloan in the basement of the adjoining Stevens store. He found smoke coming through where steam pipes carried heat from the Stevens heating plant to the Nelson rooms. No fire had yet reached the basement. Later, Mr. Stevens advised the chief that fire had passed to the basement of his store.

Then came, with the smoke, an accumulation of gases, generated perhaps by burning paint and varnish, and bringing an explosion that blew out the Stevens store front and wrecked a skylight to the rear. By this time the firemen had the flames in the Nelson store under control.

The Nelson Cloak Company occupied a building owned by the J. T. Hackworth estate. The Stevens building is owned by Stevens. Total loss is estimated at $100,000. Stock losses are given at $50,000 to Mr. Stevens and $25,000 to the costume store.

Both buildings have good walls standing, the Hackworth structure showing interior damage chiefly.

Ottumwa Daily News

THE OTTUMWA DAILY NEWS

WHY NOT PUBLISH THE UNDESIRABLES?

Men on Strike Say "Those Radicals" Were at Morrell's For Years And Never Discharged--Why Now? Why Oppose 99 Pct. of Men He Wants?

THE OTTUMWA DAILY NEWS

SOLDIERS GOING; INJUNCTION STAYS

WOMEN UNDER COURT BAN OFFERED $8.00 FOR 32 HR. WEEK – WHAT CHANCE FOR THE FAMILY? HILLGARDENER

"YOU'RE OWNED BODY AND SOUL IF YOU LOSE THIS FIGHT"

Soldiers who came to Ottumwa 200 strong will be entirely out of the city tonight, and their places as police officials will be occupied by more than a hundred deputies, commissioned by Sheriff Giltner.

"The passing of the militia from our midst will be looked upon as the proper move by many, but now and then some will be found who are fearful, and without cause," stated one of the strike leaders.

Civil rule again prevails in the Ottumwa "war zone" and martial law has vanished.

An estimated 800 men, who regard themselves as locked out of the Morrell plant in the refusal to meet their committee for settlement of grievances, also taking the attitude there is nothing to arbitrate, met in Labor hall at 2 o'clock this afternoon, at the call of Chairman Hillgardner of the strike committee. This the first closed meeting of the men since the strike originated six weks ago.

1921

FOOTBALL BOYS TO PLAY OSKALOOSA

Local football will be foreign to Ottumwa this Thanksgiving Day, the Ottumwa Stars going to Oskaloosa to try out the Quakerites. The expectation is that a considerable number of Ottumwans will make the trip to cheer their talent as they try out the mettle and genius of the enemy. For years the rivalry between Ottumwa and Oskaloosa has been of the same intensity.

Sold in sealed packages only.   Never in bulk

Samuel Mahon Company, Ottumwa, Iowa
Established 1858

STIMULO Coffee
It's minus the chaff

DECEMBER 1921

Dec 1 - Rising prices cause riots in Vienna

Dec 1 - first US helium-filled dirigible makes first flight

Dec 1 -- US Post Office establishes philatelic agency

Dec 4 - Film star Roscoe "Fatty" Arbuckle's trial for murder in the death of starlet Virginia Rappe ends in a hung jury

Dec 4 - Denna Durbin, actress, is born in Winnepeg, Manitoba, Canada

Dec 6 - The Anglo-Irish Treaty establishing the Irish Free State, an independent nation incorporating 26 of Ireland's 32 counties, is signed in London

Dec 13 - In the Four-Power Treaty, Japan, the United States, the United Kingdom and France agree to recognize the status quo in the Pacific

Dec 16 - French composer Camille Saint-Saens dies at age 86

IOWA GAME ON COAST DOUBTFUL

IOWA CITY, Ia., Dec. 1.—University of Iowa officials probably will not request permission of the big ten conference to play in California in the Tournament of Roses game New Year's Day at Pasadena, it became known today. It is understood that Iowa's athletic board is opposed to the project in view of the fact that post-season's battles are contrary to the rules of the Western Conference.

Dr. William Duffield of Los Angeles, who extended an unofficial invitation to the Hawkeyes to play in California, wired the Tournament of Roses committee suggesting the advisability of a direct request from the Big Ten conference which meets tomorrow and Saturday.

DORMITORY PHONE SERVICE COMPLETE

IOWA CITY, Dec. 7.—Telephones in every room at the Quadrangle, dormitory for men at the University of Iowa, soon will be in operation, the system having been installed at a cost of about $30,000. It is the most elaborate system in use in any dormitory in any educational instituton n the country.

All phones are to be handled through the regular exchange, no private switchboard being installed at the Quadrangle. Work on the exchange has been going forward more than two months.

Dr. John H. Slevin, speaking in Detroit, says we are "living in a lie" under prohibition. Even boys spend pocket money for liquor.

This writer believes, and for more than twenty-five years has written, that the drink question would best be solved by getting rid of saloons and whisky, and allowing light wine and beer.

But, give the devil his due, also the angel prohibition.

There is a great deal of whisky drunk, some die of wood alcohol poisoning, but not as many as formerly. There is less drinking than there was; hundreds of thousands of workmen take their pay home instead of spending it in the corner saloon.

Prohibition is not ideal, and a nation on a bootleg basis is not pleasant. But prohibition is better than unlimited whisky with the government as a partner of the whisky makers, sharing their profits.

THE SLACKER CONGRESS
(Chicago Journal)

Congressmen and senators have had time to reach home from their exhausting labors in the extra session. Most of them have not been able to look "around" in their constituencies to any great extent but then not much looking is needed. It should take the average member of house or senate about half an hour to learn that the voters that elected them regard the extra session as a failure.

When the extra session opened, the country was promised three great benefits, namely:

A sweeping reduction of federal taxation.

A definite advantageous economic foreign policy embodied in a new tariff bill

Prompt relief to agriculture

How have these promises been kept? Not at all. Not even a start has been made toward keeping them.

Federal taxation has been reduced little if at all. The excess profit has indeed been repealed; so have "nuisance taxes" which should have been abolished as soon as the war ended, and the sur-tax on extremely large incomes has been lowered. A sop has been thrown in the married taxpayer of moderate income by giving him a slightly larger exemption on his family.

64 WIDOWS OF 1812 GET PENSIONS

WASHINGTON, Dec. 7.—The United States is paying pensions to sixty-four widows of men who served the nation 109 years ago in the war of 1812.

556,000 ON WAR PENSION LIST

WASHINGTON, Dec. 7.—For service in the Mexican war in 1846, pensions are given 109 soldiers and 2,156 widows, for the Spanish war 31,066 soldiers and 8,126 dependents are pensioned.

During the United States year ending June 30, these pensioners received $58,715,000, which was $45,000,000 more than paid out the year before, though 26,137 pensioners died.

The total number receiving pensions is 556,053.

SUNDAY AFTERNOON MEETING AT LABOR HALL AS USUAL

At 2:30 Sunday afternoon is promised another of these usual Sunday meetings. Several speakers from the local citizenship, and some of them not in the strike list, will appear and turn lights on from the various angles. Also information from headquarters just in advance of the Monday 6 a. m. national strike, will be passed to the audience. Chairman Hillgardner said today noon that he hoped to have a woman among the speakers at this meeting, but was not sure he could arrange it on such short notice. There is every promise of a big session. "Not a man from our ranks is missing and the situation is more and more in our favor as the days go by. The order from President Hayes affecting all packing centers has something to do with this increasing interest

"Nothing to Say Today, Mr. Stump."

The News editor called Mr Foster today by phone at 2:30 this afternoon and asked if there was anything for the press today. He replied, "Nothing today, Mr. Stump," in his usual courteous way that has always been appreciated at this office. Asked again if he had any comment to offer in connection with any effects that might be contributed to the Morrell plant by the national strike order due to go into effect Monday morning, Mr. Foster said he had nothing to say on the subject today.

Here's your daily report on the strike.

Last night the usual big crowd at Labor hall, speakers included Secretary Muldoon of the Union, J. Hillgardner, chairman of the strike committe, William Downey, member of the executive committee, Z. Zimmerman and, lastly, with plenty of action, an hour address by John Stark, who admitted he once held a political office in Ottumwa but was not proud of the historic chronicles, saying he would not attempt another service of the kind, as sanitary officer, for $250 a month, and he was free to say the income would appreciated by him

National Strike Impress.

Throughout the meeting there was experienced by all a larger degree of confidence that as the national situation developed with the walkout Monday morning local issues would take on a more encouraging color for the striker in Ottumwa who is now in the seventh week of holding out for a satisfactory settlement with Mr. Foster.

NURSES COMPLAIN IN CITY; SO LITTLE FOR THEM TO DO

Whatever is to become of Ottumwa nurses in a professional way? There is appreciation of the fact that Ottumwa is so healhty nobody can get a call, and hristmas days are near. Said one of these nurses:

"Why, there is hardly anything to do in Ottumwa. I am just released from one case and it seems to be about the only one in the city. Nurses are complaining about a lack of calls—fewer than has been known in Ottumwa for many years at this season of the year.

GRASS FIRES HERE; DECEMBER IS LIKE MONTH OF MAY

Now what do you think of this? Two grass fires, yesterday and today, and the fire department called out to subdue the flames as the vegetation fed the greedy demon.

Grass fires, December 9 and 10, in Ottumwa, Iowa—the first in fourteen years for this late in the season, according to a statement of Chief Sloan! Some weather, is it not so?

There was no damage to property reported after these two alarms, but the men were a bit peeved when called from the shady side of the street to chase after still more heat.

Hurting the coal business like everything, but that's all right with the scant purseholders. The official thermometer, if Ottumwa had one, would be around 80 as an average for the month to date.

JOHN H. MORRELL, LOCAL PACKER DIES SUDDENLY AT HIS HOME

Ottumwa was shocked with the news Sunday morning shortly after 8 o'clock that John H. Morrell, president of the packing company of that name, had been found dead in his bed, at the home, 418 North Market street. He was unattended at the time of demise, although only a few hours previously atention had been given to him and nothing serious appeared in his condition at the time. Mr. Morrell had not been in good health for several months, yet able to be about the city and atended church services only a few hours before the summons came.

Christian nations: The nations that manufactuer the most padlocks.

CLOSED MEETING TUESDAY; RANKS HOLDING FIRMLY

Sunday afternoon the executives and others speaking at the big meeting of packing men had a "no change" report on the local situation. Yet each speaker contributed his opinion to the effect that the outlook is brighter for the men than at any time since the strike started. It is understood that the Big Five men's resistance to a reduction in wage will materially aid and encourage the local men, who now have been one-seven weeks without losing a skilled man from the butchers' ranks, it is claimed.

Chairman Hillgardner spoke of the coming Christmastide and said that probably a number would not have much money with which to do gift shopping. He added that perhaps somebody would be passing out a few gifts anyway, and that on the day after the figures would not loom on the debt side as usual, which might be some compensation for subtraction from the usual blessedness of giving at this season of the year.

The usual incidents were recounted concerning men seeking reinstatement in their old jobs, who re-entered the plant and met disappointment upon being assigned different positions at a lower wage than when they left in mid-October.

CLOSED MEET TUESDAY NIGHT.

Secretary Muldoon announced a closed meeting—for strikers only—Tuesday evening. The official did not indicate the nature of the program to be presented, but it is believed more drastic treatment will be applied, after that date, especially in the matter of considering those who went back to work, walked out again, and then appeared before the relief committee for aid.

It is expected, too, that a number of official advices from the International then will be ready to pass on to the strikers. Along this line it is expected inspiration will be advanced to continue on more determined than ever.

With reports from all packing centers today showing thousands have suspended work because of the packers' announcement of a 10 per cent wage decrease, Ottumwa's state of affairs is regarded as holding out much promise for a conference settlement.

CANNED FRUIT TO HELP FILL BASKETS ASKED BY S. ARMY

Ottumwa's Salvation Army is as busy as ever it was at this season of the year. It is expected that 200 baskets for needy homes will be ready for distribution the day before Christmas. Families having canned fruits, preserve supplies or any item of necessity that can be donated, are requested to telephone headquarters, 990, and an army representative will call.

"We are doing very well in collections deposited in our kettles, three of them, and next week the evening offerings will be received. We hope the jingle of dimes and quarters will be heard every minute in the day," said the captain.

Mrs. W. O. Sayles and Mrs. J. E. Long will be hostesses to the Thursday Club on Thursday evening. A 6:30 o'clock dinner will be served at the home of Mrs. Sayles, 146 Cooper avenue. Dinner will be served at prettily appointed tables. The favors will be poinsettas. The home will be decorated in green and red, and Christmas bells will be used. Carlos Sayles will be Santa Claus. He will come down the chimney, singing "Good Saint Nick" and "Oh! Holy Night" from the fireplace. His majesty, Santa Claus, will present each guest with a Christmas gift. The hospitality of Mrs. Sayles is well known to her numerous friends, who are anticipating a joyous time.

1921

THE OTTUMWA DAILY NEWS

33 YRS. AGO, WEEKLY WAGE, JUST $1.05

John Stiles Was Under 13 When He Stood on a Box and Trimmed Sausage Meat for John Morrell Co.

FOOTBRIDGE TO BE BUILT AT ONCE ON IOWA AVENUE

The city commissioners have received word from the Iowa State Highways Commission that the proposed foot bridge at Iowa avenue will be built at once. The structure will be a convenience to workmen, permitting them to reach the packing plant in the morning without being held up by trains, at the same time avoiding dangers of the crossing. The commission said it is entirely agreeable that work start right away, and the Burlington Railroad, most interested, has engineers now perfecting plans in conjunction with requirements of City Engineer Brady.

The foot bridge will extend over all railway tracks at that point and the cost is estimated at $8,000. The structure will be erected on the east side of the avenue, will extend 304 feet and have a clearance above the tracks of 23 feet.

VETERAN SKILLED WORKER MADE UP TO $25 WEEKLY IN 1921; 18 OF THEM

Says Average Check, 32 Hours Now Figures About $13.00

Read A Real Story.

Here is a little sketch of how one man at the packinghouse has experienced the development of the business and the rise of the workingman to an understanding of his privilege to organize and collectively bargain for a living wage. The News was given this story, briefly, this morning, and nothing was said in bitterness, just a life's narrative, for such it seemed to be.

"I started to work at the Morrell plant when I was 12 and a half years old," said John Stiles, 418 Foster ave. "That was 33 years ago. My first weeks wage amounted to $1.05. My brother Charles was faring better, his income for the six days being $1.15. I was so small that it was necessary to stand on a box to do the work, which was trimming sausage meat. This was before they started to hire girls to do this work.

"How much was my wage the last month before the strike? Well, I received as high as $25 a week. That was the 40-hour week guarantee, then the guarantee was reduced to 32 hours, which basis would of course cut down the income materially. Give me $20. But I was one of the 17 or 18 higher class skilled workmen. The next class was at 60 cets an hour, the 57 1-2. We had no grievance when it was possible to made as much as $20 to $25, but less than 20 of the skilled men could figure on that income with the time cut to 32 hours guaranteed the week, taking chances of getting more than 32 hours.

"How many men were gettnig as high as 50 cents an hour, which would be 16 a wee kon the 32-hour basis? Well, my estimate is that the average wage paid the men would be between 40 and 43 cents an hour, which on a 40-hour week guaranteed, but there were many under 35 cents and hour and under the new hour notice it meant many men would have a weekly paycheck of less than $12.00, which is not a living wage."

Ottumwa Daily News

THE COST OF TROOPS

Ottumwa and Wapello county will be interested in the acount charged to taxpayers by Adjutant General Lasher as he makes demand for reimbursement for services rendered by the Iowa guard at the Morrell plant, Nov. 15 to 29, the soldiers ordered here on request of city and county officials and a citizens' committee following a street brawl in which it is alleged a number of the strikers were involved. Not only was the soldier brought here but two injunctions were issued, 73 of these against citizens as named, the other writ effecting all citizens and warning them against causign any further disturbances through threats of intimidation or by acts of violence.

General Lasher's expense account as follows shows that the total will reach $7,000, and oddly enough comes in the item in favor of the Morrell company for nearly $500 for truck hire and subsistence supplied:

Pay roll	$4,039.79
Railroad transportation	1,432.60
John Morrell & Company	470.66
E. Daggett & Son, Ottumwa, for trucks	161.00
Lowenberg Bakery, Ottumwa, subsistence	123.38
J. G. Hutchinson, Ottumwa, subsistence	101.59
E. H. Emery, Ottumwa, subsistence	96.05
Samuel Mahon Co., Ottumwa, subsistence	62.33
Swift & Co., Ottumwa, subsistence	58.95
Graham & Garretson Co., Ottumwa, subsistence	10.00
Graham Grocery, Ottumwa, subsistence	1.20
J. W. Garner, Ottumwa, quartermaster's supplies	69.50
Hub Clothiers, Ottumwa, quartermaster's supplies	28.00
Haw Hardware Co., Ottumwa, quartermaster's supplies	7.95
Harper & McIntire Co., Ottumwa, quartermaster's supplies	2.70
J. W. Edgerly, Ottumwa, medical supplies	5.40
Charles Wyman, Wapello co. engineer, trucks	28.93
Wells Transfer Company, Des Moines, cartage	8.00
Approximate miscellaneous expenses not yet in	200.00

The above $7,000 state claims is but part of the total expenses when the local charges are duly audited, and the amount is daily being augmented as the deputies keep vigil over the wide-open, vacant, peaceful thouroughfare leading from Iowa ave. two blocks south to the gates of the plant.

HAVE YOU SEEN THEM— NEW 1922 AUTO PLATES?

County Treasurer Walter Young has an auto-plate selling department as a sectional feature of his already heavy business line.

And have you seen the new plates? They contain black figures on an aluminum background, and every number is prefixed with a designating numeral or two. As an illustration, in this county it reads, "92-795," the "92" being the key to where the auto license was procured—in what county. Wapello has 5,000 and a slight plus of motor vehicles, which is the average number for counties in this state.

1921

THE OTTUMWA DAILY NEWS

FREE STATE OF ERIN IS NOW REALIZED

TERMS OF IRISH PEACE GET O. K. OF KING AND CABINET

THE HEART OF HUMANITY IS TOUCHED BY THE GLORIOUS PEACE THAT DAWNS

Ottumwans, Catholic and Protestant alike, rejoice in the sweet peace tidings that come fro mIreland today, as receivers of happiness beyond words, and The News is offering this beautiful thanksgiving from the Reverend Father Foley of the Sacred Heart church as eloquently expressive of the appreciation felt by our great America and all the world besides:

> "All lovers of freedom are indebted to Ireland for the noble fight she made for human liberty.
> "In her eyes might was never right.
> "May heaven that witnessed her sorrow bless her future deeds."
>
> "Father Foley."

LONDON, Dec. 7.—King George cordially approved and the whole cabinet sanctioned the agreement between British and Sinn Fein peace negotiators creating an Irish Free State. No attention was paid today to the plea of Sir James Craig that details be withheld until Ulster should pass on them.

Ulster is given privilege of being a full-fledged province of the new free state or maintaining its present status.

What England Will Do.
Under the agreement England will:
Call all troops from Ireland as soon as possible.
Free interned Sinn Fein prisoners.
Adjust past overtaxation and allow for damage to Irish property in the past three years.
Establish safeguards for Catholics in Ulster if Ulster will stay out.

What Irish Will Do.
The Irish Will
Acclaim allegiance to King George as head of the association of nations forming the British commonwealth.
Recognize the British war debt and responsibility for part of it.
Prohibit interference with education or religious liberties or endowments in north or south.
Permit the use of harbors for British warships.

Rights Given Irish.
In return Ireland is given the right to:
Levy tariffs against all nations, including England and Ulster.
Establish an army in proportion to her population.
Build ships to protect her customs and fisheries.
Should Ireland vote herself out of the association she automatically loses her military and fiscal rights.
The conditions can be revised at the end of ten years if Ireland desires and the terms will be effective twelve months from December 5, 1921, if duly ratified.

OBITUARY

ROBERT SWANSON, JR.

Robert, 7-year-old son of Mr. and Mrs. Robert Swanson, died at Ottumwa Hospital at 1 a. m. this morning. Funeral services will be conducted at the home, 1544 Mable street, at 2 p. m. Friday. Surviving, beside the parents, are two brothers, Albert and Wilbert; three sisters, Elizabeth, Violet and Mary, and other relatives. The Rev. A. A. Heath will have charge of the services.

SCHAFER ICE HOME BURNED TO ASHES

At 2 o'clock this afternoon fire had made a complete ruin of the Schafer ice house, located on Ford street. Ice harvesting tools also were consumed. Insurance to the amount of $7,000 covers the property.

Chief Sloan was out with equipment to combat the flames, but too much headway had been gained to hope even for salvage. The building was located on the north side of the river, not far east of the Shea sand plant.

THE OTTUMWA DAILY NEWS

ALLOW PICKETS AT MORRELL GATES

TAFT DECISION IN FAVOR OF MORE PRIVILEGES; MAY VISIT HOMES AND PARADE

Ruling Is By Anderson

Judge Anderson shortly after noon today, acting under interpretation of the desision from the United States supreme court, read by Chief Justice Taft, authorized a right on the part of the strikers at Morrell's to place one of their men at the gate an dwithout molesting in any manner will be allowed to keep tab on the workers as they enter and leave the plant.

Beside this one man as picket the Anderson permit grants the strikers a privilege of not more than two men to visit homes, if they choose to do so, where they may communicate with those who are working at the plant and in a peaceable way talk with them about the strike trouble. .But in neither instance, at the gate or in the home, may any form of violence or intimidation be exercised.

WOMAN IN ARBUCKLE PANEL SAYS JURY IS NO PLACE FOR WOMAN

SAN FRANCISCO, Cali., Dec. 5.—"There is no place for a woman in the jury."

This is the opinion fo Mrs. Helen M. Hubbard, wife of an attorney, who stood it out to the end for conviction of Roscoe Arbuckle.

"Any woman is a fool to get on one if she can posibly get out of serving. I'd rather die than go through it again.

"The general attitude and language of the men is offensive to a woman.

"Once on a jury, I would vote my own husband guilty, if i really believed him to be that in my heart and nothing could shake me, once that belief was established in my mind."

Germany, telling the allies she can't pay the two hundred and fifty million dollars, gold, due January and February, asks a moratorium. The world will know presently what the allies intend to do. They will declare a moratorium and let Germany pull herself together and make the payments later, or they will carry out another plan, march in, take more territory, mines, factories, etc.

Germany's announcement makes this an important date in after-the-war developments.

1921

THE OTTUMWA DAILY NEWS

MEN FROM MORRELL'S TO SOLICIT AID

BEGIN CANVASS FOR HELP TOMORROW; FAMILIES WANT NECESSITIES FOR FAMILY

Will District City and Present Grievances in Personal Way

Start Town Canvass.

There was a meeting held this afternoon at 2 o'clock, for the purpose of districting the city to be visited by authorized committee from the strikers, soliciting aid and enlisting a favoring sentiment for the cause. This plan will be elaborated soon, to take in the farmer sections as well, according to Hillgardner who says the strikers' fight is one that holds much interest for the farmer as well as the Ottumwan. "We have been receiving much encouragement and from all parts of the country. Our lines are firmly entrenched and we are going right ahead until the fight is won, until we have secured recognition of the right to bargain with our labor product in a collective way, through a committee and not as individuals. It is for this principle for which we contend, demanding the same right of organization and the function of that organization which the employer enjoys and uses to his best interests.

"That the people may know precisely what the strikers are contending for a signed official statement will shortly be issued and setting out the causes leading to the strike and what we are willing to do to effect a settlement, leave the question to arbitration if no shorter way is found to adjust the differences."

We have locked up here 60 per cent of all the gold in the world, our treasury is full of it. It would be worth much to us if, in some wise way, that gold could be put to work, establishing credits that would enable Europe to buy our goods and put our people to work.

N. Y. TO PACIFIC IN 24 HOURS PROMISE

NEW YORK, Dec. 7.—A thirty-passenger Caproni tri plane tried out with success in Italy, and said to be capable of making a twenty-four non-stop flight from New York to San Francisco, will be brought to New York within the next two months. Captain Marlo Cobianchi of the Italian air Service said today upon his arrival fro mItaly. The plane, he said has a speed of 180 miles an hour. It is driven by five 300-horsepower motors.

Dainty Lingerie Washed Without Wear

THE ELECTRIC WASHER MAKES CLOTHES LAST FIVE TIMES AS LONG.

Dainty lingerie and sheerest silks can be entrusted to the gentle washing action of the Electric Washer without fear of harm.

Careful tests have proved that clothes last five times as long when washed in an Electric Washer. Thus, merely as an investment in prolonging the life of your wearables, the Electric Washer will soon pay for itself.

1921

GET DANGEROUS FORGER BY CLEVER WORK; HE SECURED $75 AT OTTUMWA BANK

Sheriff Giltner will leave tonight for Martin's Ferry, Ohio, to bring back, in official custody, A. G. Clark, accused of having forged a check to the amount of $75, which he succeeded in cashing at the Ottumwa National Bank under the name "Burson." He was known to the bank as an inspector at the Morrell plant.

Clark operated on the pretense of being a member of the Knights of Columbus at Norfolk, Va. He came to Ottumwa and was given help by a K. C. man at the packing house, who got him a job and stood good for his board and room. Clark thus secured the confidence he needed to work his scheme.

From the bank he proceeded to the Cruefit store and attempted a check deal there, but, being suspected, he left the store with the remark that he would be back in a few minutes.

Clark made his get-away, but Officer Lightner, finding a torn envelope in the room vacated, took it to Chief Blizzard and, piecing it together, they found it was from Clark's stepmother, a Mrs. Sapp, at Indianapolis. Then things became interesting, a high K. C. official tipped off, and within ten days from the time Clark left Ottumwa he was arrested at Martin's Ferry.

Besides being guilty of alleged check forging, it is said Clark broke into a locker and ransacked a trunk owned by Burson, obtaining a bank book and checks.

No little credit is due all who planned the capture of this man who used the K. C. organization to aid his plans.

MILK PURITY IS FAVORED BY COUNTY DAIRYMEN AT MEETING HELD TODAY

The large courtroom was well filled with the Association membership, also the city commissioners and sanitary officer were present on invitation.

It was stated by one of the officers that the object of this meeting was to induce more attention for pure milk, of the pasteurized quality, keeping the product sold in Ottumwa not only in legal per cent of butterfat, but having it clean and pure and delivered with the utmost care on the part of the dairyman.

Mayor Chilton, interviewed, stated there was no city ordinance governing the sale of milk, either as to quality or as a licensed privilege, as far as the city was concerned. In fact the information was imparted that there is no city license required in the sale of any foodstuffs, either to a few customers or generally distributed by huckstering throughout the city.

WRAP SECURELY ALL XMAS PACKAGES, EARLY, AND INSURE

Packages should be wrapped in heavy paper and securely tied with strong cord or twine, but not sealed, as sealed packages require first-class rate of postage. If the articles you mail are breakable or perishable, advise the clerk, so the words "fragile" or "perishable" may be stamped on the packages.

Insure your packages. The rate of insurance is very low, and if they should get lost the department will refund the value of the article. The insurance fee is 3 cents to cover value up to $5; 5 cents, up to $25; 10 cents, up to $50, and 25 cents, up to $100.

If more convenient for you, you can mail at any one of the postoffice stations which are located as follows:

Station No. 1—Siestrand's grocery store, corner Main street and

Station No. 2—Kidd's drug store, corner Second and McLean streets.

Station No. 5—Mynard's drug store, 631 Church street.

Station No. 6—Sam Redman's, corner Sheridan and Wabash avenues.

Riverview Station—In Riverview.

Christmas Day being on Sunday this year, patrons are especially requested to mail all their packages in ample time to insure delivery at their destination on Saturday. There is no delivery of mail on Sunday, regardless of the holiday, and any mail not reaching our postoffice, or any other postoffice, in time for delivery on Saturday will be held over, and, as Monday will be observed as the holiday, it is possible that such delayed parcels will not be delivered until Tuesday.

Commence at once—buy early and mail early. It will be more satisfactory to every one and easier on the postoffice employees.

CHARLES W. McCARTY,
Postmaster.

LOCAL STRIKE CONTINUES IN SAME DEVOTION TO CAUSE REPORTS UNION OFFICIALS

It was a busy scene this morning at Labor hall headquarters, as the increasing cash and food and clothing offerings were being passed to the many homes where want is making a grim and relentless attack.

Chairman Hillgardner and his executive committee were deeply engrossed in the work of geeting supplies at once to families who are confronted now with a change of weather added other perils to a household of women and children are in need of prompt relief.

Ottumwa has more than 150 families in the strike area today that need care and consideration of the most generous kind. Everything possible is being done to alleviate the distress which is everywhere spreading and lack of fuel making it a dangerous experience in a season pneumonia and kindred diseases.

INCOME IS 75 PCT. LESS NOW

On the top floor of the Federal Building, north suite of rooms, is the internal revenue headquarters for this and several goruped counties.

Present this afternoon when a News man called was Billy McCormick, a real ace in financial matters; Larry Cawley, former county recorder, a genius in digital artistry and 100 per cent accurate in deductions, and, lastly—recently come—our former mayor, Charles A. Warren, going along right from tow and looking the part he is to play as he takes up the political work turned over by T. H. Pickler's high-type administration.

The News asked for an estimate on income tax receipts, compared with 1918, and the assertion was made that receipts are off fully 75 per cent. Quite a confession, of course, but they made it.

(By Walter A. Linton.)

Notice to Corn Growers

COAL vs. CORN

We are going to make you a proposition—We have to buy corn to feed our stock; you have to buy coal to burn, unless you have been foolish enough to burn some of your good corn, as some of the farmers have done, so we will trade you as follows, at our yards on South Wapello street, good clean lump coal for good clean corn—

2,500-lbs. of Iowa Lump, for 2,000 lbs of Corn.
2,000 lbs. of Illinois Coal, for 2,000 lbs. of Corn.

—so you see you cannot afford to burn your corn, for according to the combustion experts at Ames, a ton of Iowa Coal is equal to two and two-sevenths tons of corn in heat value, and a ton of our southern Illinois coal is worth three tons of corn in heat value.

Being in your corn right away for if it comes too strong we may not be able to handle the proposition.

Remember the BEST is always the cheapest-in-the-end coal.

Sold Only By

ROSELAND FUEL CO.

ART MASTERPICES GO AT LOW PRICE

LONDON, Dec. 16.—A Rubens and a Titian were sold at $12 each at the Sothody sale here. A Rembrandt drawing brought only $100. Another Rembrandt, formerly owned by Sir Joshua Reynolds and later by Viscountess Milner, sold for $155. The Titian was the "Baptism of Christ," from the Amherst collection.

1921

READY NEXT OCTOBER.

President Evans of the board informs The News that no penalty is to be exacted if the school building is not completed in a specified time, but under normal conditions it is expected the structure will be ready for occupancy October 1, 1922, or possibly a few weeks earlier, in time for the opening of the September term.

Work has been going forward at high pressure for several months. Concrete was poured for the third floor several weeks ago. There is the most friendly feeling between the board and its contractors as progress is maintained through all kinds of weather.

PATIENT CHEWS UP A DYNAMITE CAP

LOS ANGELES, Dec. 22.—Grieving over an illness, August Snell, 70, a patient at the county hospital, ended his life by chewing a dynamite cap, which blew off his head.

BIRTH CONTROL TO BE ESTABLISHED IN EAST

NEW YORK, Dec. 21.—Establishment here soon of a birth control clinic has been announced by Mrs. Anne Kennedy, secretary of the American Birth Control League, speaking before the Woman's Law Club. Mrs. Kennedy said oral information on birth control could be given legally in eleven states. She asserted the league intends to open clinics in all those states.

WOMEN MAY SMOKE IN NEW YORK CAFES

NEW YORK, Dec. 21.—Smoking by women in cafes has become so prevalent that Alderman McGinnis felt urged to put a stop to it, but the other aldermen would not help him. Amid laughter they tabled his proposed ordinance to fine or imprison proprietors who let women smoke.

SANTA CLAUS WILL VISIT SUNNYSLOPE SATURDAY NIGHT

The News is delighted to note that between 7:30 and 8 o'clock Saturday evening, at Sunnyslope, the six ex-service men receiving hospital treatment there will be regaled with a fine musical porgram which is being arranged by a dozen Ottumwa women interested in the affair. In addition there will be a Christmas tree.

Gifts are being received by Dr. Hammer and Captain Younkin. It is reported Bill Osler will play the role of Santa for the happy occasion.

BERLIN BURNS DIME NOVELS

BERLIN, Dec. 20.—Forty thousand volumes of detective, "Wild West" and Indian stories, put in circulation since the revolution, were burned today by the Association for the Protection of German Youth. The books were turned in by boys who had purchased them.

FARMER SUCCUMBS TO BLOOD LOSS FROM MINOR WOUNDS

Roy Otto Webber, living four miles northwest of Stockport was accidently shot Tuesday morning. The bullet lodged in the right elbow and the victim was immediately brought to the St. Joseph's hospital here. He died at 6 o'clock yesterday evening; from loss of blood.

The body was taken from the hospital to the Mooney Funeral home and held there until 3:30 this afternoon when it was shipped on the Rock Island to Stockport, where funeral services will be held at the home. Interment at Stockport.

HARDING STILL MAY TAKE ALASKAN TRIP

WASHINGTON, Dec. 8.—President Harding indicated today he still had in mind a trip next summer to the Pacific Coast and Alaska. Asked by Harry M. Findell representing the National Association of Newspapers' Executives and the Associated Advertising Clubs of the World, which will hold their annual conventions in Milwaukee beginning June 4, to address the gatherings, the President said he would be present if the time set for the gatherings corresponded with the time for a trip to the far West and Alaska.

FORD PLANT TO BUILD AIR FLIVVERS

DEROIT, Dec. 9.—The "air flivver" will be Henry Ford's next manufacturing effort. Intimation that he intended to builds planes for commercial purposes, which have been in circulation some time, became more positive today, following a meeting at Dearborn yesterday between Ford, Thomas A. Edison and Rear Admiral William S. Sims in the Ford experimental laboratory.

ANNUAL
Christmas Exercises
at the High School Auditorium
TONIGHT, 8 P. M.

Christmas Pageant and
Chirstmas Carols

Admission 25c

U.S. CROPS 5 BILLIONS YEAR 1921

Total is 3 Billion Less Than 1920 and 8 Billion Below 1919.

WASHINGTON, Dec. 29.—The important farm crops of the United States this year are valued today at $5,675,877,000 by the Department of Agriculture in its final estimates of the year. That is almost $3,400,000,000 less than last year's crops were worth and $8,000,000,000 less than the crops of two years ago, when high prices prevailed for farm products. The values are based on prices paid to farmers on December 1, and the crops comprise about 90 per cent of the value of all farm crops.

There were only two billion-dollar crops this year—corn and hay—while last year four crops were valued at a billion dollars or more. Production was below last year for almost every crop, although the acreage of the important crops was slightly larger, except cotton, 1,000,000 ACRES LESS.

The area devoted to important crops this year was 348,736,000 acres, compared with 349,067,000 acres last year.

SOMETHING ELECTRICAL FOR EVERYBODY

—and the Old Nest—

ELECTRIC LIGHT!

Many times you've thought of wiring your home for electricity, and have visioned the comfort and convenience it woudl bring. Do it now! Enjoy the soft glow of an electric lamp in your home this Christmas; light the tree with safe, sensible electric current; make it possible your wife to have a labor-saving electric washer and cleaner in the new year.

Wire Your Home for Christmas!
Time Enough if You Order This Week

Ottumwa Railway & Light Co.
Second and Market Streets

THE OTTUMWA DAILY NEWS

CHAS. (RED) ELLIOTT SUES FOR $50,000

CHILTON, KEEFE, BRYANT NAMED AS DEFENDANTS; CONSPIRACY IS CHARGED

DEPOSED POLICEMAN TAKES STEP LONG CONTEMPLATED

At about 9:15 on the night of June 6, 1921, in the rooming house managed by Ida Bryant, 303 West Main street, Charles A. Elliott, policeman, was confronted by Mayor Chilton and Commissioner Keefe and accused of having of taking a ten-dollar bribe from Mrs. Bryant.

The commissioners had set a trap for Elliott.

What happened when Chilton, Keefe and Chief Blizzard insisted that Elliott give up his star and resign or he would be placed in jail, was recited in The News in particulars. Elliott resigned rather than take the notoriety that would result if the accused was put behind bars pending a hearing or trial of his case.

Dead To Rights.

According to the story related by the city hall men the morning of June 7, Elliott was "caught dead to rights, with the goods on him" and had he not taken off his star on demand at the moment when accused and the money found on his person, probability was immediate imprisonment.

Sues For $50,000

This afternoon Elliott's attorney filed a notice of damages in the amount of $50,000.

Elliott, although acquitted of the charge of having accepted a bribe, when his case was called for trial in the September term of court, where the testimony did not support the charge that he had actually and willingly taken a bribe, still there has been assurance right along of the action to be taken against the city hall officials and charging conspiracy.

When the evidence was submitted to the jury, Mrs. Bryant, the woman who was named as giving the money to Elliott, would not say that on this occasion the money was placed in the outstretched hand of the patrolman, which in a way supported, at least not denying the claim of Elliott that the ten-dollar marked bill was thrown into his lap by Mrs. Bryant who left the room with an excuse that she wanted to visit a sick person a moment in another part of the house.

Money Thrown In Lap.

Elliott testified Mrs. Bryant said to him that she felt she owed him something, that she had been giving money to others, and that he told her that she couldn't give him money and refused to accept any. He told before the jury that his call there that night particularly due to having been requested to do so by Mrs. Bryant who claimed to have a tip where a raid could be made. On the Saturday night just previously, Elliott, on a Bryant tip, accompanied by two officers, did make a raid. He said he thought he could get more information on Monday night and was there for that purpose, although always under orders from the department to occasionally visit the place and inspect the register and see that there

Was A Frame-up.

No one ever said otherwise tahn it was a trap set to catch Elliott "dead to rights" when the officials waited in a side room until money was given by Mrs. Bryant to Elliott, "put in his lap as she left the room,... and the fram-up at the time was believed absolutely successful, but failed to hold in court before a jury. Elliott was released, foud not guilty, just as he was in the case six months before when charged with taking money from Hans Buwoski, 817 East Main street, this trial before the police commission board.

Elliott Had A Record.

Officer Elliott, it was conceded by members of the police department had made more arrests, "twice as many" as any other officer during his three years service. When restored to the department, resuming a "beat" after the first trial, he was transferred to the west end beat and at once the calendar showed up well in Elliott's behalf, his ability as an officer again demonstrated.

But his acquittal in September did not find him again in uniform as a peace officer. Today is the first entry made in a legal way to balance the account Elliott and his attorney, Lloyd L. Duke, maintain lacks a considerable if the former policeman gets his deserts.

THE AIRSHIP ROMA IS CHRISTENED

WASHINGTON, Dec. 17.—The army semi-rigid airship Roma, purchased from Italy, recently assembled at Langley Field, is to be christened with a bottle of liquid air on her arrival here today. The unique christening also will take place in the air. Miss Fenrose Wainwright, daughter of the assistant secretary of war, dropping the bottle from a free balloon on the bow of the craft.

1921

GENE DEBS, NOTED SOCIALIST FREED BY HARDING ORDER FROM PRISON AT ATLNTA

WASHINGTON, Dec. 24.—Eugene V. Debs, America's most noted political prisoner, will be a free man on Christmas Day.

Announcement that Debs' sentence had been commuted, along with sentences of twenty-two other political offenders under the war-time espionage act, was made by president Harding at the White House late yesterday. Five American soldiers serving life sentences were pardoned at the same time.

It has been generally expected that Debs would receive a full pardon, and his friends have stated they would accept nothing less. Under a commutation of sentence his civil rights are not restored, although it was pointed out at the White House that full pardon, carrying restoration of citizenship may be forthcoming in time.

Changes come rapidly. A while ago the wireless telephone was a vague possibility. Now, in and around one city, a hundred thousand private individuals have wireless telephone apparatus and listen every day to concerts and news messages. Recently they listened to the singing of Emma Calve, on her way to this country, 200 miles out at sea.

BASEBALL FOR THIS CITY IS REMOTE POSSIBILITY --FEW PARKS AVAILABLE

Dr Bonham and A. P. Owens returned last night from the baseball conference held at Cedar Rapids yesterday when it was hoped a Central Association might be re-formed, including eight cities that would provide for 1922 league games.

In his report Dr. Bonham says a number of cities were represented, about thirty promoters present, but owing to the considerable without parks, as in Davenport and Waterloo and some of the applications not regarded admissible for best results, it was decided to hold the matter up for another month, a meeting again January 15 when it will be known what the Three-Eye league is goin gto do about Moline and Rockford." I am afraid Ottumwa would not be able to reach the higher class salaries if two Illinois cities were in a newly formed league. We are class D. in our plans and it is a big question whether Ottumwa is to have league ball next year."

COUNTY HOME GETS MODERN LIGHTING AND REAL HEATING

Within two days the county farm residence and other buildings adjacent will be provided with a new lighting system, ready for immediate operation.

It is a Delco, installed at a cost of $1,785, a local firm having been awarded the contract several weeks ago. The "plant" has arrived. It will be installed at once and the 75 patients will be happy once more in having the convenience of modern illumination. For days the home has had to rely upon lamps, lanterns, candles, and there has been considerable danger of fire because of overturned and exposed flame.

HEATING EQUIPMENT WORKS.

In addition to the lighting equipment the supervisors have purchased for $800 a boiler, the original cost of which was $2,900. Expenses of setting it, together with freight charges, make a total of $1,150. Perfect heating now is assured every ward in the big house.

These expenditures were deemed unavoidable if the indigent and helpless are to be properly cared for, and the supervisors state they are well pleased with the outcome of their plans.

Ottumwa Daily News

THE OTTUMWA DAILY NEWS

VOTE 444 TO 12 TO CONTINUE STRIKE

SECRET BALLOT IS TAKEN BY MORRELL STRIKERS; IS "NO SURRENDER" VERDICT

SACRIFICES IN MID-WINTER ARE SEVERE; FUELLESS--FOODLESS MENACE IN MANY HOMES

Last night former employes of the John Morrell Company took two ballots on whether the strike should continue or decide that the executive committee should officially declare it off.

First the sentiment was expressed by lifting of hands, and appeared to be practically unanimous, then Chairman Hillgardner asked that he make it a secret ballot so there would be opportunity for each person present to vote exactly the way he or she felt about it.

The result of the secret ballot stood 444 to keep the strike principle in effect, 12 voted to go back to the plant without terms except those advanced by the company, 2 ballots were blank. The executive committee, which was assumed to be solidly against a return to work, 32 of them, did not participate in the ballot. It was estimated that at least 80 strikers were out of the city last night and a considerable number, owing to the cold night, not attending.

Analyzed by the union officials there was a 40-to-1 "strike on" determination expressed. "The figures that practically everyone who came out as union strikers are still on strike. More than 600 in our list that started the fight October 19 for an agreement are still in line, and others have come into the organization, additions to the striker list, since that first day. Of course some men have gone back to work, a few of these in certain skilled employment, but the big unionized force is still active and we expect to win our cause."

1921

70-Day Morrell Strike Ends; Cost Estimated $700,000

With a majority ballot counting less than 30 last night it was voted to declare the strike officially ended at the John H. Morrell Co. plant. Many of the strikers did not mark their ballot. The executive council which composed also the strike committee, did not register their views in the ballot taken, leaving the matter at disposal of the strikers not in the direction of the strike from its beginning, October 19, 1921.

So the strike that lasted ten weeks less 12 hours, starting morning of October 19, 1921, and ending December 27, 1921, is now history. Those who have been devotedly given to the cause are now in the ranks and awaiting an opportunity to return to their former positions in the big plant.

Foster's First Statement.

Mr. Foster issued his first public statement through the press evening of November 5. He declared at that time "These Union ex-employes now realizing that an unfortunate mistake has been made—as was made in March at the time of last strike—are asking us to make some 'concessions,' that they may return to their work which they left voluntarily without giving notice and without presenting any grievance. They ask us now to give their present predicament consideration they denied us when they walked out of our plant and left our property to perish."

It was made clear in the attitude taken by Mr. Foster that the men would be welcome in returning to their work but they must make it an individual application. He said: "The large majority of our employes are fair minded loyal men and women; this strike was not of their making; they did not desire it. They need employment; we need their services. To all such our gates are open; we urge them to return to their places with the assurance that as rapidly as work can be found they will be reemployed."

Men Ready to Return.

This morning the men were applying for their former places. The Morrell management are reemploying as they can. The strike is over. Ottumwa is delighted at the announcement made. It means the best butchers and meat packers in the world, five hundred of them, are now desirous of resuming work at the best packinghouse in the world. And this is the best city in America, and all the bitterness, and sincerely there was not much of this, is wiped out. The skilled hand, the experienced training, the splendid citizenship that has been endeavoring to secure concessions, agreements, guarantees similar to those claimed for other packing centers, is now taking up where they left off, and this perhaps will prove the better way as costs of living decline with possibility of a full 48-hour week for the majority of the workers, at least for some time to come, owing to the fact that this is a busy season and there is a strong demand for meat, more so since the nationwide strike is effective to a degree in all sections, 50,000 or more men not working.

Cost a Quarter Million.

It was figured at the first that the loss in wages alone would run $30,000 a week. Then as the plant partially resumed this estimate was somewhat less, but a conservative wage loss for the nearly ten weeks is around a quarter million dollars. How much was lost to the plant will not be known, but undoubtedly it was a startling one. Then damage to the market privilege enjoyed by the farmer would total heavily, figured by some at $2.00 loss on every hundred pounds of pork that was made ready for market but losing out on what would have been paid at once for the hogs during the first few weeks of the strike. Then there was a big loss in the retail district, stores losing patronage and many of those working at the plant the later weeks coming from a distance, or from the farms, and taking their pay checks to some other point to use.

Both sides lose. Either faction was bound to lose even though winning, as the term is generally interpreted. This strike that for a time affected 1200 men and women, finally approximately one-half that number, as strikers, and in money costing probably footing in the totals an average of $10,000 a day for the 70 days, $700,000, has been the most expensive labor trouble known to industrial Ottumwa.

The News has been regarded as very favorable to the strike people, and in a degree this is the correct viewpoint, because this paper, in behalf of Ottumwa's interests which were greatly affected by the trouble, and the disputants unable to negotiate, believed the principle of arbitration should be applied in such an important matter. The Morrell company refused the opportunity to arbitrtae, said there was nothing to arbitrate, and therefore the protracted strike until the necessities of life denied the homes there was nothing left, eventually, but surrender, capitulate. This has now been done in a straightforward way and no agreements reached whatever except the understanding that with the possible exception of a few—perhaps a dozen or so—all may expect reinstatement as rapidly as the conditions of the business will permit.

Ottumwa has passed through a strike that has been a heavy money loss, a period of great sacrifices and many deprivations, but Ottumwa has been made aware that the quality of her people is of the kind that makes to bigger and better things for the future. In this revelation as never before disclosed, all have found a precious compensation in the strike experience.

A. J. Stump.

WIFE CLAIMS HER AGE WAS 15 WHEN MARRIED; FILES PAPERS

In the office of the clerk of the District Court this afternoon a petition was filed by a wife in which the complainant makes the unusual statement that she was only 15 at the time of her marriage and that her husband is 48. Annulment of the marriage is sought.

A state law permits a girl of 14 to marry if she has the consent of her parents or legal guardian.

LICENSE NUMBERS CHANGED IN 1923

DES MOINES, Dec. 30.—County numbers on automobile license plates probably will be the same in 1922, with one or two exceptions, according to W. M. Colladay, superintendent of the motor vehicle department.

An 0 before a car number means a nonresident automobile. These numbers are for such concerns as the Standard Oil Company, whose home office is outside the state.

In the case of trucks there will be a complete reassignment of numbers in 1923, Colladay stated. Truck plates are all preceded with the letter T and have no county number. The numbers are progressive, from 1 to 1,000 for nonresident trucks to 41,901 to 42,300 for trucks in Wright County. As a number of counties are likely to outgrow the limited number of numerals assigned to them there must be a shifting all along the line.

OBITUARY

Fred Dale, 24-day-old son of Mr. and Mrs. Fred Swanson, 322 West Williams street, died at 6 o'clock this morning. Funeral services will be held at 1 o'clock Saturday afternoon, the Rev. Mr. Marsh officiating. Interment at Cuba cemetery, southwest of Eddyville.

LIVING IS BETTER AND CHEAPER FOR OTTUMWANS

Just a bit more reassuirng—the problem of getting living necessities in Ottumwa. Improvement is noted in labor circles, supplemented by news that prices are lower for household supplies. All of which is interesting to 100 per cent of our people.

Soon you will be able to buy 18 pounds of sugar for $1. Eggs are selling off more than a dime and are expected to reach a 30-cent level with temperate weather to insure supply. Butter at 40 cents is reasonable indeed.

Potatoes are steady at $1.25 a bushel and it is not anticipated that they will be higher. In the fruit line, oranges are lower than at this time last year, also lemons, and both are due for a decline in two weeks, when heavier shipments will result because of the California crop coming in.

STRAWBERRIES ON THE WAY.

You haven't seen any strawberries in Ottumwa this week, but they have them in the larger cities at an opening price of 75 cents a box, and soon you can order shortcake at the cafes and get a goodly portion at a modest price. Before January is history strawberries will be selling at about 45 cents a box, possibly as low as 40 cents, stated one authority this morning.

Drinks Cheaper Monday; Taxes Will be Lifted

Why not be thankful for a few favors that are to come in less taxation burdens, due to arrive 12:01. midnight, December 31.

The government will collect no tax after that hourly time and date on soft drinks, ice cream, nor as dealers' excise taxes, on silk shirts, silk hosiery, the super-fine and luxurious lines of clothing of any description.

It has been remotely estimated that this will mean at least a hundred dollars a day saved on soda fountain patronage alone..

The popular drinks will be at the old friendly price of 5 cents. Manufacturers and distributors of syrups will be taxed.

What about the movie? If the admission is not more than ten cents next Monday no tax charged, if more than ten cents as usual.

Railroad fare and berth charges taxless beginning Jan. 1st.

Iva Lenore, 16, daughter of Mr. and Mrs. T. O. Hewk, 155 North Davis street, died at 1:30 this morning after a few days' illness. Deceased was a high school student and was one of Ottumwa's most estimable young women. Funeral services will be held at 7:30 Saturday evening at the home, with the Rev. Alpha McClure in charge. Burial at Hopewell cemetery.

DESCRIBES DRINK IN ITS TASTE AND FEEL

NEW YORK, Dec. 13.—"It tastes like hell, but makes you feel like heaven."

That was the description of a home brew concoction George Lehman of Mount Vernon gave Judge Appell in court today. George said it consisted of wood alcohol and wood naphtha.

The judge figured Lehman had had punishment enough and suspended sentence.

OBITUARY

Hattie Freelan Benton, colored, died at the home of her daughter, Mrs. Mate Clark, in Battle Creek, Mich., Sunday. The remains will arrive here on Burlington train No. 9 this evening and will lie in state at the Sullivan & Jay undertaking parlors from 7 until 9 o'clock.

Mrs. Benton had been a lifelong resident of Ottumwa until a year ago, when she went to Battle Creek to make her home with her daughter because of failing health.

1921

THE OTTUMWA DAILY NEWS

OTTUMWA, IOWA, FRIDAY, DECEMBER 16, 1921

MORRELL'S LEAD OFF FOR RECORD YEAR

START 2-GANG OPERATION MONDAY; KILL - CUT WITH DOUBLE PROGRAM METHOD

100 NEW POSITIONS OPENED

Last evening The News reflected hope entertained that this community would be sharing more generously in desired improved trade conditions with the advent of 1922.

Trooping along comes increasing evidence today that this sanguine contemplation of the immediate future is entirely warranted, by circumstances local in character, peculiar to the city's leading influences and prestige.

View of John Morrell Company Main Building.

Morrell's Start Things Monday.

Superintendent Earnest Manns of the John Morrell Company permits the following under a sanction that will bring happiness to hundreds, even thousands of our people.

Starting Monday morning the Morrell company will operate on the double-shift or two-gang plan, at once opening positions for a hundred or more, the payroll correspondingly increased, the production increase from 25 to 50 per cent.

"We have decided on this method of taking care of the Morrell business and begin at once. Killing in the forenoon and cutting in the afternoon has been the program. Monday will see both killing and cutting in both forenoon and afternoon.

"Gee, Dad, some class to the house all lighted up this way!"

The Welcome of a Brightly Lighted Home

is the kind of a welcome we all like. The cheerfulness of the bright interior is reflected in the hospitality of the beaming windows.

WIRE FOR ELECTRICITY

so that your home, too, may bespeak this cordial greeting to family and friends. Wire for Electricity so that the many conveniences of Electric Service may lift from the shoulders of your wife the arduous tasks of household routine.

Now—with the long winter evenings ahead—is the time to have the work done.

Ottumwa Railway & Light Co.

Phone 109.   2nd. & Market St.

Index
major subjects represented in articles

Agriculture 15, 38, 56, 61, 78, 129, 133, 138, 144, 145, 151, 159, 173, 181, 196, 197, 199

Automobiles 23, 24, 25, 62, 63, 68, 69, 86, 96, 100, 102, 103, 104, 130, 131, 132, 133, 154, 165, 172, 173, 191, 206

Aviation 49, 51, 54, 79, 87, 110, 134 , 142, 151, 169, 171, 194, 199, 201

Baseball 34, 46, 54, 118, 122, 202

Basketball 16, 18, 19, 48

Boxing 101, 109

Caruso, Enrico 26, 54, 127

Cigarettes 57, 75, 81, 101, 114, 156, 198

Dempsey, Jack 101, 109

Edstrom, David (sculptor) 129

Education 10, 123, 128, 139, 142, 151

Elliott, Charles A. 18, 140, 155, 201

Fashion 54, 55, 119, 132, 168

Football 184, 185

Grand Opera House 34, 83

Hackworth Trust 135

Harding, Warren G. 44-45, 58, 61, 64, 95, 116, 117, 135, 151, 163, 199, 202

Housing x, x, x, 148, 173

Immigration 17, 36, 71

Iowa State Fair 51

Iowa state flag 57

Ireland civil war, new nation 69, 112, 192

John Morrell & Co. 10, 42, 43, 142, 158, 159, 160, 167, 170, 172, 174-175, 177, 178, 183, 187, 189, 190, 191, 193, 194, 197, 203, 204, 208

Ku Klux Klan 56, 144, 149

Labor issues 11, 24, 42, 43, 158, 159, 160, 167, 170, 172, 174-175, 177, 178, 183, 187, 189, 190, 191, 193, 194, 197, 203, 204

Marriage issues 20, 57, 65, 137, 146, 204

Medical 11, 13, 16, 26, 28, 30, 33, 47, 60, 66-67, 97, 120, 126, 131, 141, 153, 157, 162, 179, 187, 199

Movies 31, 43, 83, 124, 139, 193

Ottumwa High School 10, 22, 81, 199

Ottumwa High School construction 30, 35, 36, 56, 59, 74, 79, 93, 126, 141, 143, 150, 198

Ottumwa Public Library 135

Parks 12, 101, 107, 114, 116

Politics 39, 119, 136, 139, 186

Prohibition 8, 28, 35, 43, 52, 53, 63, 86, 102, 104, 119, 127, 138, 140, 144, 148, 153, 154, 163, 186, 207

Racial issues 56, 80, 90-91, 92, 94, 96, 109, 128, 134, 144, 207
Radium 12, 103
Railroads 7, 9, 76-77, 100, 110, 114, 151, 165, 171, 176
Roosevelt, Franklin Delano 143
Ruth, Babe 34, 65
Scarlet fever 66-67
Smallpox 141
Streetcars 65, 106, 146, 156, 181
Streets and roads 15, 35, 68, 67-77, 79, 85, 97, 98, 102, 104, 110, 113, 118, 123, 140, 141, 151, 154
Sunnyslope 13, 124, 141, 181, 198
Taxes 114, 115, 117, 124, 128, 129, 147, 207
Telephones 43, 64, 120, 152, 180, 186
Tennis 50
Tilden, Bill 50
Tulsa race riots 90-91, 92, 94
Turkey Island 106
Typhus 26
Unemployment 8, 10, 58, 73
Unknown Soldier, Tomb 173
Wage cuts 24, 42, 53, 74, 81, 88, 114, 151, 156, 178, 197
Wapello County Home 148, 202
White Sox scandal 46, 69, 122
Wireless 28, 37, 68, 82, 138, 202
Women 48 as candidates 31 as jurors 7, 83, 193
World War and aftermath 15, 19, 21, 37, 40, 48, 52, 61, 64, 75, 80, 89, 94, 107, 116, 120, 126, 135, 136, 137, 162, 173, 173, 186, 193, 198
Wrestling 41, 52
YMCA 18, 19, 52

About the Editor

Leigh Michaels is the author of more than 100 books, including contemporary and historical romance novels, non-fiction works about writing, and volumes of local history.More than 35 million copies of her books have been published in 27 languages and 120 countries. Six of her books were finalists in the annual RITA competition for best romance novel, sponsored by the Romance Writers of America.

She owns and operates PBL Limited, a publisher of niche-market non-fiction, based in Ottumwa, Iowa. She also teaches romance writing online at Gotham Writers Workshop (www.writingclasses.com)

Sources consulted in creating this book include Bill Bryson's book *One Summer: America 1927* and websites https://www.onthisday.com/events/date/1921 and https://en.wikipedia.org/wiki/1921

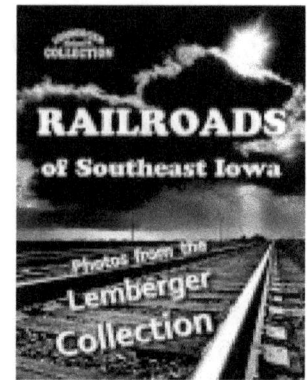

www.pbllimited.com

www.ingramcontent.com/pod-product-compliance
Lightning Source LLC
Chambersburg PA
CBHW080541170426
43195CB00016B/2636